About

Norma Clarke is a writer and literary historian whose publications include *Dr Johnson's Women*, *The Rise and Fall of the Woman of Letters*, *Queen of the Wits*, and *Brothers of the Quill*, as well as five novels for children. She is currently Professor Emeritus in English Literature and Creative Writing at Kingston University. *Not Speaking* is a memoir of her family: of her beautiful and vivacious Greek mother, her working-class father and her five siblings, including the celebrity hairdresser Nicky Clarke.

Not Speaking

Not Speaking

Norma Clarke

unbound

This edition first published in 2019

Unbound
6th Floor Mutual House, 70 Conduit Street, London W1S 2GF
www.unbound.com
All rights reserved

© Norma Clarke, 2019

The right of Norma Clarke to be identified as the author of this work has been asserted in accordance with Section 77 of the Copyright, Designs and Patents Act, 1988. No part of this publication may be copied, reproduced, stored in a retrieval system, or transmitted, in any form or by any means without the prior permission of the publisher, nor be otherwise circulated in any form of binding or cover other than that in which it is published and without a similar condition being imposed on the subsequent purchaser.

ISBN (eBook): 978-1-78965-026-6
ISBN (Paperback): 978-1-78965-025-9

Cover design by Mecob

Printed and bound in Great Britain by Clays Ltd, Elcograf S.p.A.

For Rena and Bill

With grateful thanks to English Literature & Creative Writing at Kingston for helping to make this book happen.

Super Patrons

Sally Alexander
Rebecca Barr
Celia Berridge
Sophie Binks
Eleanor Birne
Tracy Bohan
Jack Bootle
Adrian Borra
Jenny Bourne Taylor
Larry Boyd
Brian Brivati
Linda Broughton
Barbara Caine
Mary Chamberlain
Valerie Champion
Nicky Clarke
Tellisa Clarke
Athena Clarke Sheward
Robert Clouston
Abigail Don
Gillian Dow

Nel Druce
Hilary-Jane Evans
Mary Evans
Phillipa Firth
Regis Gautier-Cochefert
Sian Gledhill
Harriett Goldenberg
James Gray
Catherine Hall
Jenny Hartley
Lise Henderson
Gad Heuman
Kevin James
Sally James
Meg Jensen
Margaretta Jolly
Gwilym Jones
Cora Kaplan
Dan Kieran
Kathy King
Sarah Knott
Janet Lambert
Pete Langman
Thomas Laqueur
Alex Leach
Darian Leader
Elspeth Lee
Mick Lee
Alison Light
Judith Lowe
Keith Lowe
Ian Lush
Daniel Mallory

Mary Manley
Susan Manly
Sonia Massai
Anastasia Mavridou
Charlotte McCarthy
Keith McClelland
Tessa McWatt
Pauline Melville
Mandy Merck
Elizabeth Mitchell Gallagher
Victoria Mitchell
John Mitchinson
David Moed
Janet Montefiore
Susie Nixon
John O'Halloran
Sue O'Sullivan
Johnnie Ormond
Ruth Perry
Jane Phillips
Sally Phillips
Tim Pipe
Caroline Pitt
Derek Pollard
Justin Pollard
Alex Potts
Ed Powell
Jason Powell
Simon Prosser
Matthew Redgrave
Chris Robinson
David Rogers
Antonella Romano

Lyndal Roper
Shannie Ross
Anne Rowe
David Salcedo
Selene Scarsi
Bill Schwarz
Anni Scoot
Silvia Sebastiani
Lynne Segal
Ali and Sarah Smith and Wood
Peter Syme
Barbara Taylor
Jennifer Taylor
Nicole Taylor
Mary Thompson
Henry Tillotson
Jane Torday
Piers Torday
Nick Tosh
Will Tosh
Lisa Tran
Bill Travers
David and Jorge Travers
Susan Travers
Michael Van Clarke
Lisa Vargo
Salley Vickers
Sarah Waters
Kate Weaver
Jenifer Williamson
Lynette Willoughby
Tom Wynn

Sing, Muse, the wrath of Peleus' son, Achilles,
the accursed wrath that brought countless sorrows
to the Greeks...

> Homer, *The Iliad*

What mighty contests rise from trivial things,
I sing...

> Pope, *The Rape of the Lock*

For what we lack
We laugh; for what we have are sorry; still
Are children in some kind.

> Shakespeare, *The Two Noble Kinsmen*

Contents

Preamble *1*

Maida Vale *11*

Southwark *27*

Mayfair *59*

Majorca: the Anchorage *73*

Majorca: Deya *89*

Majorca: Valldemossa *101*

The Devil in the Room *115*

Athens *137*

London *169*

Hastings *225*

Marylebone *235*

St John's Wood *249*

Marylebone *275*

Epilogue *301*

Select Bibliography *307*
Acknowledgements *311*
Patrons *313*

Preamble

My parents married in October 1945 and neither spoke the other one's language. When I tell people this they are surprised and wonder how on earth they managed. Bill, a sergeant major in the British army recently stationed in Athens, did not understand Greek and Rena, a twenty-two-year-old who had picked up a smattering of Italian and German, had no English. The short answer is that at first they depended on the translation skills of Rena's older sister Toni, who had excellent German and some English. The longer answer is that in many respects they never did manage, and the repercussions of their fundamental failure to communicate extended into the next generation, becoming the seedbed for the story that follows.

Our family home in London was crowded and clamorous. At my birth, almost exactly two years after my sister Linda was born, our father despaired of having the son he very much wanted. He blamed our mother: she was one of five daughters and it was clear to him that the pattern would continue. He declared he wanted no more children. Three years later Paul was born. It was good to have a boy at last and for Bill the family was now complete. Paul, fair-haired and pretty, was made much of: he was 'Little Sunshine'. He was our mother's

Not Speaking

pride (none of her sisters had produced a boy to present to their father) and for more than six years he was her prince. Then in 1958 along came Nicky, and two years after him, Michael. There were now two adorable princelings for a mother who loved babies but was less amused by older children who answered back in a language she had only partly mastered. Paul lost his sheen. The princelings pleased their sisters, too. Aged ten and twelve when Nicky arrived, we were ripe for care duties and instruction: drawing, reading, football in the yard. We took our responsibilities seriously, in marked contrast to our attitude towards Paul, the baby brother we had dragged along behind us cramping our style. Nicky was almost eight and Michael almost six when Tina was born. Rena was satisfied. As she liked to say later, 'Your father never wanted any of you. I always wanted six children, three boys and three girls.' She would also sometimes say that if she had her life over again she would have the children but she wouldn't get married.

For a man who 'never wanted children', Bill became the most devoted of fathers. His love was demonstrated through actions, not words; speaking about feelings was foreign to him. He was practical, hard-working, unassuming, unassertive; he liked to be useful and was always busy. When not at work – he was a turbine operator at Bankside power station, now the Tate Modern – he made and fixed things: cupboards, toys, electrical items, shoes. Concentrating on his task, he was available to be chattered to. As each of us grew up, left home, and set up households of our own his availability continued; there was a goodness in this work of his hands that didn't need explaining.

Rena was busy and practical, too. She did alterations for a local dress shop and was contemptuous of English women who couldn't sew their own hems or replace a zip in their husband's trousers. Linda and I often had to return the finished coat or

Preamble

dress and collect the money. I didn't like doing it but I felt a sort of pride walking through the streets holding a well-sewn, well-pressed piece of clothing and knowing that my mother was superior to all the other mothers. It nagged at me when I came across suggestions in novels that dressmakers weren't held in high esteem.

It was Dad who took me to the library. At home I learned early to 'turn a deaf ear' as he put it because it was the only way you could read a book in the small kitchen and scullery where family life went on. I tuned out noise and interruptions ('You're not doing anything, come and dry the dishes') but I was a writer from an early age, listening and observing the things that mattered to me. I always thought I would write about our family.

I had the sense that we were special, or that I was special. 'Family' meant us and my father's brothers and sisters, all five of whom lived nearby: Arthur and his wife Edie, Tom and May, Nellie and Harry, Lou and Reggie, and Vi, a war widow. They were clannish and self-mythologising, glorying in being resourceful, combative, cheery Londoners. Periodically, I took notes of the stories I heard of their early lives in the slums of Blackfriars. My father, born in 1918, was the second-youngest, and it was his childhood that captivated me most. He had no skill in storytelling but Vi, with a fund of lurid, loving memories of hardship, made up for that.

It didn't occur to me that my mother's family was also one to which I belonged. They were far away in Athens and their names distanced them further: Evangelos and Evangelina, Toni and Pericles, Poppy, Spirithoula, Fotini. (Poppy was actually in Lancashire, having married Bill's friend Walter, but she might as well have been in Athens for all that I thought of her as having anything to do with who I was.) The strangeness of this did not strike me until our father died in 2006 and our mother,

Not Speaking

at the age of eighty-two and having lived in England for sixty years, briefly contemplated returning to live in Greece with her one remaining sister, the youngest, Fotini, also a widow, and in need of company.

It was a shock to think she might go back home as if she no longer had any reason to stay. Had she only been passing through (spilling six children on the way)? The resentful about-to-be-abandoned child in me wanted to know if that was allowed. What did family mean if she could leave us so easily? What had she been doing in my life? The question demanded attention although it felt dangerous and wrong to ask. I was warned off by my mother herself who, having heard I planned to write this book, gave me a long look and pointedly remarked, 'Say anything bad about your mother in Greece and nobody respects you.'

There are so many reasons for not writing about family; there is so much, it would seem, that is best left unspoken. And yet it is the primal subject. We know who we are by finding out about our families. *Not Speaking* is the title of this book in acknowledgement of the pressures that exist and the taboos that remain. It also carries the meaning 'not on speaking terms', a state of affairs very common in families. Mostly it signifies 'that which is unspoken', meaning not only secrets and shared but forbidden knowledge, but also a deep level of non-articulation that could be traced back to (or find its excuses in) barriers of language and culture. Literally and metaphorically it often seemed in our closely-bonded and quite talkative family that people did not speak each other's language, the pattern established by our parents.

Dad was eighty-seven when he died but he didn't seem old to us. His loss was immense. I felt my sense of self slip a gear, and I believe something similar happened to my siblings. For all six of us his death altered the internal balance of the family.

Preamble

It took away some restraints and introduced new demands. We all mourned a loved parent but for the youngest, Tina, who had latterly absorbed our father into her domestic life, it was an overwhelming sorrow. She lived in West Sussex, and she wanted him buried near the woods he'd loved on her land. Keeping him close was one way of dealing with the feelings, but there was more to it than that as she, and we, gradually realised.

Tina was haunted by a doubt she hardly dared utter. When she overcame her fears and took steps to establish the truth, she discovered that our father was not her father, a state of affairs also not uncommon in families.

But he *was* her father, the only father she had ever known, and loved, and we were her siblings, the older brothers and sisters in the family to which she belonged. At one level, knowing the truth changed nothing, or so Tina said, and we said. Except that at another level, where deeply buried lies and secrecy had governed her life, the truth changed everything.

'I can't believe none of you knew about this,' she said. 'I can't believe none of you told me.'

It was a difficult and painful period. Little was said. Not speaking was designed to shrink the problem. Instead, it compounded it.

And then, in 2014, a great quarrel erupted among the siblings. It was apparent that sentiments about belonging, assumptions about what might be demanded by one of another, the unspoken expectations that had seemed to knit us together, no longer held. Choosing not to be connected, not meeting, not keeping a part of the self ready for a sister or a brother's call, was alien to our family myth as I understood it, and would have had no traction had our father been alive. The spirit of discord – Eris, in Greek myth – rampaged amongst us and I found myself asking more dangerous questions. What did

Not Speaking

I mean by 'our family myth' and what was it for? Who did it serve? I wanted to be a peacemaker but what was I trying to save? I thought about the different languages of knowledge and feeling. I wondered about truth and love.

As the months went by and family life came to resemble a Greek drama and people behaved in mystifying ways, I turned deliberately to literature. I was the academic in the family; books were my business. The *Iliad* wasn't an obvious guide to life but its opening sentences arrested me. 'Declare, O Muse! In what ill-fated hour / Sprung the fierce strife...' is how Homer launches the story of the Trojan war, in Alexander Pope's translation. The first word, in the original Greek, is 'menin', variously translated as wrath, rage or anger. In Greek myths wrath in men is often caused by wounded pride; in the *Iliad*, Achilles sulks in his tent. The Muse begins with the anger of Achilles, rendered in a modern translation as 'the accursed wrath that brought countless sorrows / to the Greeks...'

Our war was very like the Trojan war, I thought – in one respect at least, and give or take a detail or two. Like the Greeks assembling in support of Menelaus, whose beautiful wife Helen had run off with Paris and who then quarrelled amongst themselves about the best way to achieve their ends, we too were failing to find a solution to a difficulty concerning a woman: our own Helen, our ninety-year-old mother. Or (depending how you looked at it and in what ill-fated hour you thought it all began) we were refusing to collaborate in what had previously been a shared project. She had not run off; she resided in an apartment owned by Nicky in Maida Vale. By 2014, for reasons that were political and personal (the Greek financial crisis, Fotini's death, the birth in London of twin sons to Michael and his new wife, Gaby) it was clear that our mother had no intention of living anywhere but in

Preamble

England. Exactly where she lived, and under what terms, had become the issue because change was afoot.

Many factors fed the wrath that followed a decision made by Nicky, which is not the same as saying he started it. Nicky saw the matter as a refusal of cooperation: he had worked hard and found a solution to the little local difficulty of where Mum should live and who should pay for it; others didn't see it that way. He felt misunderstood, misrepresented, shamefully exploited, let down and unappreciated. 'I hoped for a little cooperation, that's all,' he said, sometimes in sorrow, sometimes in anger. Meeting resistance, encountering stubborn opposition, he withdrew to his 'tent' in St John's Wood, barred the door and declared his perfect willingness never to speak to his brothers and sisters again 'for two hundred years'.

The stalemate that ensued, the directionlessness of the quarrel, was as unfathomable as most of the goings-on in large families and at the same time predictable, a series of variations on familiar themes. Like the Greeks encamped for ten years outside the walls of Troy, we alternately mounted offensives and ignored the war, and were by turns serious and frivolous, tragic and comic. Along with heat and passion and grievances, there was a degree of levity, a flippancy, that was surprising to outsiders but reassuring to me. When we stopped making bad jokes and laughing at each other there would be real cause for alarm. A year went by. Another year began.

I opened *The Rape of the Lock*, Alexander Pope's mock-epic in mock homage to the *Iliad*. *The Rape of the Lock* offered laughter as the antidote to anger when 'mighty contests' arose from 'trivial things'. Since the trivial thing in the poem was a quarrel that started with the cutting of a lock of hair in a country house, I thought Pope might be able to help me out. Hair and houses were my theme. Pope wrote *The Rape of the*

Lock to make 'a jest' of a quarrel between two families in his circle. He hoped the poem would 'laugh them together again'. Nobody should get exercised about a lock of hair, even if, as Pope wrote of the moment the curl was cut, 'Fate urged the shears.'

In our family fate urged the shears and locks were cut in Nicky's salon in Mayfair and in Michael's salon in Marylebone. They were both prize-winning hairdressers, leading theorists and exponents of methods and styles, renowned throughout the industry and beyond.

Nicky's celebrity, his 'glamorous lifestyle', had coloured all our lives. Paradoxically, inside the family it had been a sort of secret, resolutely unspoken. There was some rivalry between the salons, and there had been episodes of not speaking, but the mighty contest that began in 2014 went on for longer, showed no sign of being resolved, and involved everybody else.

As older sisters still imbued with quasi-maternal impulses, Linda and I wanted not to take sides. Linda, a qualified pattern-cutter and seamstress with a fine art degree, was often called on to undertake sewing tasks: Roman blinds, gowns for the salons, jeans that needed altering. She was careful to make sure she obliged each brother equally. We both recognised that we knew nothing of the strains and stresses of running a business. Paul, who for years had driven a London black cab, an occupation he hated, had moved to Hastings and played no part in the quarrel except to complain now and then that nobody ever told him what was going on. I took to the quiet of the library to think about the forces shaping the quarrel. Books told me there was nothing new under the sun: men and women had trodden these routes already and left their signs. Books reassured and comforted.

Pope said of Homer – who gets the credit for beginning it all: story, myth, Western civilisation – that he 'created a

Preamble

world for himself in the invention of fable', he 'opened a new and boundless walk for his imagination.' When we write and read, tell and listen to stories, we create worlds. Our mother used the word 'stories' to mean 'lies'. 'Stories,' she would say, and sniff, not believing someone's version of events. 'It's all stories. Take no notice.' She loved to dwell on her own stories, telling them with great vivacity in her accented, idiosyncratic English. Frequently the telling would end with a rhetorical flourish. 'Was I right or wrong?' she would demand. 'Right or wrong?' There was only ever one answer, just as when she said something especially harsh about a person or an occasion and you protested she would say, 'Why shouldn't I say it? It's the truth.'

The Greek word for story is 'mythos'. It is translated as story, report, tale, and legend, and anything delivered by word of mouth. 'Mythos' gives us 'myth', 'mythic' and 'mythological'. In her widowhood, our mother's vitality and youthfulness acquired mythological status in the family. She was a survivor, fiercely individual and self-willed. Although family was her universe and she did everything she could to bring peace and harmony, the seeds were sown and the fates were at their business. She believed in fate. Like Homer she belonged to an oral rather than a written tradition, but she would say that everything was written in a book, God's book, and whatever happened had been preordained.

When I was a child I wanted to write about our family because I thought that there was something quite extraordinary about the life I lived. Shakespeare reminds us that we remain children 'in some kind', and this is perhaps especially true in all that concerns us as siblings. He also suggests that we need to grow up, learn to take seriously what's missing and value what we have: 'For what we lack / We laugh; for what we have are sorry; still / Are children in some kind.' King Theseus of Athens

Not Speaking

speaks these lines at the end of *The Two Noble Kinsmen*. The noble kinsmen of the title are cousins whose shared values and equal merits have created an intense bond. They passionately adore each other (each perhaps seeing an idealised version of himself) and just as passionately fall out. Jealousy is the poison. One character, Emilia, says, 'Men are mad things.' Shakespeare shows that what they share is stronger throughout than what divides them: what they have, what they want, and what they have to lose are the same.

Everybody has a story and all stories are special to the people they concern. No two stories are the same; no two versions of the same story are the same. Once put into a story, the person named – Achilles, Theseus, Nicky, Michael, Tina, Rena, Bill – becomes instantly a creature of fable. That's the trick that Homer started.

Maida Vale

The not speaking began in the run-up to Christmas, 2014. It was born in a flurry of emails. Offence was given and taken.

On a Sunday afternoon in December our mother, who was speaking to everyone about everything, was upset. When she was upset it made her angry. She was angry at Nicky, who had dropped her off at her door and driven away, and possibly angry at me who had just arrived.

We were sitting in her first floor mansion flat in Cropthorne Court, Maida Vale, and she was in the final stages of moving out. Her ankles were swollen and she had her feet up on the footstool. The curtains and nets had been taken down the day before. The pictures that had covered the walls were gone – huge blown-up old black and white photographs of herself and her sisters as young women in Athens in the 1940s, framed magazine articles about Nicky, photographs of Nicky and Michael receiving awards, pictures of family, pictures of Jesus. They had been packed into boxes. Most of the boxes, along with the heavy furniture, had been transferred to the new apartment in Hall Road, round the corner in St John's Wood. What remained to be done included removing perhaps two hundred icons from the walls of her spacious bedroom. I'd come over for a couple of hours thinking we might do some of that but she insisted she would do it herself, later.

Right now she wanted to talk and tell me how angry Nicky was. 'He's so angry,' she said angrily. 'What's the matter with him? He was shouting and shouting, oh my god, waving his arms around, hitting the roof of the car, shouting. He swears he's not going to talk to Tina for two hundred years. And he says Michael's got to apologise to him. And you, and Linda too – what's Linda done to make him so mad? Everybody. He was like a madman! What have you said to him?'

She hadn't seen the emails (she barely knew what an email was) and hated being out of the loop, especially when – as now – she belonged at the centre. But any attempt to explain would make her angrier still; and whatever I said would become distorted when she retold it, as she certainly would, to someone else, Nicky for example.

I was hoping it would all blow over.

'Did he take you to church this morning?' I asked in a neutral voice, as if I didn't know the answer. Nicky was in the habit of picking her up and driving her to the Greek Orthodox church of her choice every Sunday morning and then driving her home afterwards, as I knew he had done that day.

'Of course.'

'Which one did you go to?'

'St Andrew's, Wood Green. It was full up, so many people. Full up.' This cheered her. 'Men as well, not just women.' She liked to make this point, as if the presence of men was an argument in itself against unbelievers like her children. 'But I don't need him to take me, I can go on the bus. I tell him every Sunday.'

She was very upset.

'Is that your special way of saying thank you?'

No answer.

Maida Vale

'Did he wait for you outside?'

'Yes, he waited, of course. And Kelly, messing with her phone in the front seat. Why does she want to come?'

Why indeed, I thought, not for the first time. I regarded it as a remarkable instance of decent behaviour on both their parts to give up their Sunday mornings in this way.

'And are you going to dinner?' Nicky would also habitually pick her up and drive her to his house for dinner on a Sunday evening. Kelly Simpkin, Nicky's girlfriend, would be there and if my mother needed anything done – tickets booked, arrangements of any kind made – Kelly (messing with her phone) would be the one to do it.

'He said I had to be ready by seven. Has he invited you?'

She knew the answer. No. My brother had not invited me. His familiar Sunday morning text, appearing perhaps one Sunday in every three – 'dinner at mine 7:30 tell me' – had for a little while ceased to arrive.

'Come anyway, it doesn't matter.'

'No.'

'He's so stupid,' she said, spitting out the word 'stupid'.

'Why don't we start on the icons?'

'I've done some already.'

'What, in your bedroom?'

'No, the others, the ones in the spare bedroom.'

The icons had been carefully piled into her shopping trolley and she had taken them, one load at a time, down the lift, along the front of Cropthorne Court, up Hall Road, across Hamilton Terrace, up the three steps into the new apartment block, into the lift, along the long third floor corridor, and to her new home.

'Why didn't you wait for me? I could have helped you. We could have put them all in the car.'

There were so many icons.

Not Speaking

'What's the point of waiting? I wanted to get it done. It's worn me out.'

It was rare for her to admit to any weakness. She was feeling the strain.

'Whose fault is that?' I chastised. It made me sad to see her this way. I meant only to banter, to divert us both from the anger and the upset, but the word 'fault' hung in the air. Whose fault was it? Who was to blame? Was anybody at fault? Why had such a storm erupted over this issue: an old woman, a luxury apartment?

'I'll start on the icons in your bedroom. I won't manage them all but I can pack some. We've still got plenty of boxes.'

Tina had provided the boxes. Tina had done most of the packing, driving up from Billingshurst in West Sussex armed with bubble-wrap and Nurofen. It was while we were wrapping china that Tina made us laugh by asking, 'Are we not speaking to Nicky or is Nicky not speaking to us? Just so I know when I get his next ranting email.'

The icons daunted me, so I was glad when Mum said no, she would do them later. Nevertheless, I made a show of insisting. 'I'll just make a start.'

'No.' She was annoyed. 'I'll do it myself, later.'

I sat down again. Her annoyance was familiar and I understood it. If she agreed to let me do as I suggested she would have to get up and follow me so that she could watch my every move; and her legs were really hurting her. All the packing had been done under her eagle eye. She didn't trust any of us to treat her possessions with respect. It wasn't only the icons. 'Junk?' we would say flippantly, holding up the stuffed dogs and lions and sheep that were crowded on the sofas along with dolls and cushions so that there was never space to sit down. Everything she had was at risk. When I say I understood it I mean only that I had ceased to argue about it, or be annoyed in return, or lecture her about the need to downsize, and that I had begun to get the measure of her compulsions.

Our mother loved to shop, she loved things, and she never threw anything away. The large apartment had been crammed with furniture: cupboards and tallboys, wardrobes and cabinets, in every room and along the long passage, and they in turn were crammed with a lifetime's accumulation of linens and cottons, crockery and glassware, kitchen utensils, shoes, handbags, coats and clothes, rugs, cleaning products, tins of fish, bottles of olive oil, sacks of rice and pasta, flour and sugar, herbs and spices, bags and bags of plastic and paper bags and used wrapping paper. Some of the perishables were many years past their sell-by date. Suggesting they might be binned infuriated her. She was on her guard. We joked, whenever we came upon a broken part of a long lost utensil, 'Can we put this on the Oxfam pile?' and she very graciously nodded, after giving it and us a good look.

'We' were Linda, Tina and me, the three 'girls'. The laborious packing, it appeared, was a female task. It had been spread over several weeks. 'What did I tell you?' Tina asked rhetorically. 'Do you see any sign of Nicky?' Tina, the youngest by far, 'the runt of the litter' as she often described herself, was in charge. Linda, the eldest, and I, the second eldest, came along to help when we could, and only on the days that Tina drove up. It was quickly established that I was useless, and Linda already carried a reputation for having no idea how to wrap anything: on the previous move eight years earlier, of which more later, she was blamed for all breakages in transit.

We were reluctant recruits. The move, first mooted as a necessity by Nicky in 2009, had been repeatedly delayed. Or rather, the request had been ignored. Nobody wanted to face the upheaval. Mum was settled in the three-bedroom apartment even if it was, self-evidently, too big for her and, in Nicky's view, simply encouraged her to get more and more stuff. (He particularly hated the brightly coloured cheap mats she put everywhere on top of the fitted carpets, blocking all doorways.)

'It was never meant to be a one-person flat,' Nicky had said.

'We didn't know Dad was going to die.'

'She can't cope with it. She's in her eighties. It's too big for her. She spends all her days cleaning.'

'That's because she spends her days cleaning. Cleaning is what she does.'

And shopping. And cooking. Now, she was over ninety and nothing had changed. The two large fridge freezers in the kitchen were always full. ('If you would leave a little space in the freezer,' Nicky would say patiently every time, 'we'd be able to chill the retsina that you didn't have space for in the fridge.') She shopped and cooked in quantity, as if she was still feeding a family of six children. She boiled a chicken for stock and made egg and lemon soup; she soaked haricot beans or split peas overnight and next day made soup; she put pork chops in the oven and slow roasted them in a tomato sauce; she roasted legs of lamb; she boiled rice with leeks; she made spinach with black-eyed beans; steamed mussels; grilled fish and served them cold with wedges of lemon; stuffed courgettes and peppers and tomatoes; fried meatballs; simmered mince with onions and garlic and celery in a thick tomato paste for spaghetti; boiled and roasted potatoes; curried cauliflower; stewed aubergines; made the moussaka. Above all, she made the moussaka. She cooked. And then she picked up the phone.

'What are you doing tonight?'

'Er…'

'I've got a lovely moussaka. One of the best.'

Someone was needed to eat it.

Maida Vale

If you said, 'I can't. I'm doing something tonight,' her disappointment was expressed in a note of surprise that verged on astonishment.

'What are you doing?' ('What could you possibly be doing that's better than eating my moussaka?')

'I'm out tonight.'

'Where out?' ('Why are you telling me lies?')

'We're going over to some friends.' I always avoided using the word 'dinner'.

'What friends?'

'You don't know them.'

'You're going out to someone's house for dinner?' ('You'd rather eat what your friends have cooked?')

'It was arranged ages ago.'

'Hmmph. It's a lovely moussaka. It's a shame to let it go to waste.'

It wouldn't go to waste. On the rare, very rare, occasions when nobody was free to eat, the moussaka would be cut into generous portions and transported next day in plastic pots to Nicky's salon for his lunch and to Michael's salon for his lunch. In the old days this was known as 'meals on heels'. Latterly, with her swollen ankles, she wore only flats.

More often you would arrive to find that eight or ten people had responded to the call. Within easy range of Maida Vale there was family in quantity, plus partners, exes, grandchildren with *their* partners, and a few honorary family or employees such as personal assistants and nannies. And although you didn't necessarily want to eat quite so much food as you invariably did – beginning with the table-load of appetisers and ending with crispy semolina cake dusted in caster sugar – you were always glad you went. All my life this had been a constant: pots bubbling on the stove, Mum controlling operations from the kitchen and sending a stream of dishes out to the crowd of noisy, laughing, lively familiars who made room for them on the table. Mum, in the ugly old nightdress she always wore at home, guests or no guests, possibly even in her curlers if she hadn't had time to get down to Nicky's or Michael's, keeping up a patter of gossip and commentary behind the scenes that was so unexpurgated, so bilious at times, it could shock the most seasoned listener.

How was that going to happen now? It had not been her choice to move, though she had agreed to go. To think of her in a smaller apartment, without the big dining table (she couldn't fit it into the window bay, there would have to be a new, smaller, round one) and a smaller kitchen without the kind of storage space she was used to, getting older and frailer as her family warred and split, was a melancholy prospect.

I looked over at the dining alcove. The glass cabinets where she displayed her china and glassware were empty. The table had been dismantled.

Sadly, I said, 'It's a shame about the table.'

'What do you mean?'

'It's a shame you can't take it.'

'What do you mean?'

'It's a shame it doesn't fit. Nicky's going to get you a round one instead.'

'Don't be ridiculous,' she said. 'Of course I'm taking the table.'

Silly me. 'I thought there wasn't room for the table, and the glass cabinets, and the five foot television, and the two huge leather sofas, and the three armchairs and – how many plush-covered dining chairs is it? Twelve? Fifteen?'

'Are you trying to be funny?'

'Just asking.'

She glared at me. 'Take no notice of what Nicky says,' she said. 'He's stupid.'

Maida Vale

We were all stupid when we didn't do exactly what she wanted us to do, but Nicky was especially stupid because he had done the most for her.

Or had he? That was the question, and people's different answers to it, or the fact that the question could be posed at all, was part of the problem.

The mansion flat in Maida Vale that our mother was moving out of belonged to Nicky and his ex, Lesley, who was still his business partner and joint director of the Nicky Clarke brand. It had been offered as a gift to our parents in 2006.

The gesture was characteristically lavish. Nicky customarily spent large sums on those he loved.

Lesley had helped make Nicky, as the *Daily Mail* put it, 'as famous as the celebrity clientele of his Mayfair salon.' She took pride in being the business brain behind what had become a highly successful company. She was a remarkable woman. If Nicky's 'colourful' life had been lived 'in the public eye' so too had Lesley's, for that reason. Lesley and Nicky continued to share property including their separate houses in St John's Wood, and an apartment on the Anchorage Club complex just outside Palma in Majorca, as well as the Maida Vale apartment in which our mother lived, purchased in 2005. They continued to holiday together and always had a family Christmas with their two children, the grandparents on both sides and sundry friends and relations. Lesley harboured a belief in family that led her to insist that no new partners should join with them on these occasions. 'When we're on holiday as a family, we're a family,' she told the *Daily Mail*. She and Nicky still loved and respected each other. They continued to share a bank account. 'I pay half of his household bills and he pays half of mine. It

Not Speaking

may seem like an extraordinary situation to some people, but that's what we have done for ten years now.'

It was an extraordinary situation and some might think it extraordinary to invite a journalist into your home to confide such details. The situation became a problem when the sharing ended and the dividing of the spoils commenced. What should have been a private matter between Nicky and Lesley about how they separated their finances and stopped paying half of each other's bills had repercussions that drew in the wider family. Nicky, passionately loyal to Lesley, was saying nothing. Or rather, he was saying a great deal about how generous Lesley had been for so many years and how it was now time for his siblings to step up to the plate.

On the face of it, what he asked was reasonable. He had found suitable, in some ways better, accommodation for our mother nearby. It was a two-bedroomed, two-bathroomed apartment in a luxury block with 24-hour porterage. There was a catch, of course. The apartment was not for sale. It was a rental property. The rent was steep, though he had managed to negotiate it down for the first year at least. And, he argued, we were many and mostly solvent, and if we shared the load it would not be too burdensome. It wasn't fair, Nicky protested, that he alone should be supporting our mother in the style to which she had become accustomed in her widowhood. He didn't expect there to be any difficulty. He was appealing for cooperation in a tight situation and looking for practical assistance from a family that had always, as he believed, subscribed to an ethic of sibling-service.

Everybody knows siblings quarrel and brothers and sisters fall out. They often quarrel about money, and often people say it's not really about money. But this was about money. It was really about money, although if we ask what the money was about we ask a deeper question.

Maida Vale

Michael and Tina said no.

Nicky pressed ahead regardless.

Happy or unhappy, the family is a cauldron. (According to Tolstoy in the opening line of *Anna Karenina*, happy families are alike, unhappy families are unhappy in different ways.) Secrets and misrepresentations, wounds and feuds are the stuff of family life, as are love and belonging. The vehemence and wrath unleashed in 2014, the refusals to cooperate – or be coerced, it depended how you viewed the matter – were less surprising than the prevailing tone of mockery. Nicky's request elicited a degree of levity from others towards him that he found intolerable in spite of all his experience.

For me, as I tried to make sense of what was happening, some of which concerned me, some of which didn't, our father's death was key. And, by extension, that meant his life also, and the great undoing that began when he died and Tina summoned the courage to look her past in the eye. As my siblings argued in person and increasingly by email through the autumn of 2014 over what it was appropriate to do about our widowed mother ('She's ninety-one and you're evicting her!' 'She's moving into a luxury apartment!') I thought more and more about our parents' sixty years of marriage, the rules of family by which we had lived and the truths that were spoken and not spoken.

Sitting across from my mother as the afternoon wore on in Maida Vale and she dozed in her chair with her feet up and I messed with my phone as we all did, checking Twitter, checking Facebook, idly Googling (here's Kelly, here's Nicky, here's Lesley, here's everybody else) I felt an immense tenderness. I had grown closer to her in recent years, a development partly facilitated by Nicky when he sought his sisters' help in keeping up our mother's routine of annual summer holidays with him in Majorca. My mother and I had

Not Speaking

not been friends when I was a child and young woman but we were friends now and I was proud of that – proud of her and proud of us both. I knew her story. I had lived some of it and heard more. On our many journeys to and from Majorca, over late breakfasts on the terrace, on the beach, at waterside cafés – her impulsive, 'Let's stop and have a coffee', always meant an hour or two out of the day – she had talked freely to me and I talked freely with my sisters, pooling what we were told, what we remembered and discovered. Dad's death loosened a self-protective layer inside us; a need not to know came undone, and as that happened something better emerged in its place.

The 'boys' were not included in these conversations; it was emphatically 'women's talk'. They had their own spheres of knowledge and intimacy, but the phrase 'Don't tell your father' had become, by a very easy transition for our mother, 'Don't tell Nicky', a sign that in her reordering of her sense of family, he was now head.

Who at any time was 'number one' in the family was one of our standard jokes. It had its beginnings in a ratings competition: which words did one hear uttered most often by our mother on any one visit, was it 'my Michael' or 'my Nicky'? But as Sigmund Freud observed, jokes are serious business.

Freud was fascinated by sibling rivalry. He saw it as arising from the competition for parental love and attention. He took it for granted that the elder child would ill-treat the younger and that the younger would envy and fear the elder. Cain, after all, kills Abel. The 'family romance', Freud declared, was full of hostility, rage, jealousy and murderous violence. In the Oedipus myth, Oedipus kills his father. Every child, according to Freud (who by 'child' tended to mean 'boy') was a mini-Oedipus whose first sexual impulse was towards his mother.

The mini-Oedipuses in South London had more than one

Maida Vale

sexual rival, for it was soon after Michael was born that Mum – but I will call her by her name, Rena – began the long-lasting affair that was to have such an effect on all our lives. The brothers' Oedipal drives to be number one by symbolically killing their father, Bill, was complicated by Bill's prior displacement and symbolic castration by a man he would have described as a flash boy if he'd ever spoken of it, which he didn't. The flash boy, Louki, had a wallet full of money. Louki's largesse predated and laid the pattern for the celebrity abundance that was to follow. But as every benefit that had flowed from him was a loss to the father, the sons' Oedipal rage was twined around an impulse to protect. Their father had to be shielded; his silences respected. Meanwhile, destined to be flash boys themselves, they imbibed with their mother's milk the mandates of masculine success.

Daily existence in our cauldron was a richly creative, silent collaboration. While our father lived, we were conditioned to be the guardians of our parents' togetherness against the odds. Once he died that job came to an end, although we didn't understand this at the time.

The main thing we were instructed not to tell Nicky had to do with money, our mother's money. In widowhood it pleased her to have absolute control of it, with no more interference from our father. And it was probably because she broke her own injunction and started speaking to Nicky at length, repeatedly, with undimming animation, about her savings, and how they were growing, and what she wanted done with them after her death, that the not speaking started. Because the accumulation of money that gave her such pleasure was largely made possible, so Nicky thought and with some reason, by means of his generosity.

'He made a rod for his own back,' Tina said.

Ill feeling followed and the tragicomedy or comi-tragedy

Not Speaking

unfolded. The move out of Cropthorne Court had become non-negotiable; now it was almost completed. A new era was beginning. I, for one, was not *not* speaking to Nicky although I couldn't be sure if he was or wasn't, at that moment, speaking to me. Judging by my mother's report the answer was negative. But I also knew she was right when she interpreted his anger as distress: 'I'm so worried about Nicky. He misses all of you.' Achilles in his tent would be missing the camaraderie and laughter. He would be feeling alone (not least in his dealings with our mother). Two hundred years was really too long to hold out. He had to start seeing the funny side.

I put away my phone and went home. I had a lecture to revise on *The Rape of the Lock*. Pope's poem was one of the texts on the eighteenth-century literature course I taught, but a difficult one for undergraduates lacking the background in the classics that educated eighteenth-century readers took for granted. I was far from being a specialist in the ancient Greeks myself. My re-reading of the *Iliad* had begun as a duty – to remind myself of its connection with Pope's poem – and evolved into a fascination. Pope's version gave the opening line as, 'Achilles' wrath, to Greece the direful spring / Of woes unnumber'd, heavenly goddess, sing!', which I liked less well than the translation by Jenny March in her *Dictionary of Classical Mythology*: 'Sing, Muse, the wrath of Peleus' son, Achilles, / the accursed wrath that brought countless sorrows / to the Greeks...'

The anger of Achilles, his sense of being dishonoured (or disrespected, we might say now) reverberates through the *Iliad*. When at last it collapses into grief and pity it is because Achilles, mourning his beloved Patroclus, is moved by the sorrow of King Priam mourning the loss of his great son Hector, killed and dishonoured by Achilles. Priam implores

Achilles to think of his own father: 'See him in me, as helpless and as old'. Achilles is 'touch'd with the dear remembrance of his sire'. They weep together, the father for his son, the son – Achilles, torn by conflicting emotions – for both his father and Patroclus, and implicitly for Hector, the mirror image of himself.

Homer offers no judgment about right or wrong. The *Iliad* addresses consequences, the sorrows that resulted from the quarrel. But it also represents complex feeling. The scene between Achilles and Priam is intensely moving. We may read it and feel there is nothing to be done but weep, and yet it also tells us there is healing power in the memory of a loved father.

Southwark

In 2006 our parents lived on the Heygate Estate at the Elephant and Castle in Southwark. Nicky and Michael spent their teenage years there. The Heygate was a model council estate, and Bill and Rena, with their four youngest children, had been among the first tenants to move in when it was built in the early 1970s. They rented a four-bedroom maisonette at 3 Cuddington, a low-rise block facing the rose garden. Upstairs they had three bedrooms and a bathroom, and downstairs a decent-sized sitting room and a kitchen big enough for a table that could seat eight at a squash. There was also a box bedroom and a lavatory. At the back was a tiny garden that gave onto a small grassy slope.

The estate was pleasantly landscaped with numerous trees. The architect had had the idea that residents would prefer to make their way along walkways above ground rather than on pavements; hence, there was a lot of going up and down steps and walking between concrete barriers, and a general air of the estate not quite belonging to its surroundings. Our parents hadn't minded this. They were excited by the newness of the maisonette and the space it offered. They liked the convenience of the situation. Dad could easily cycle to

Not Speaking

Bankside on the south bank of the river Thames at Blackfriars. Paul was a trainee manager at Fine Fare supermarket in Clapham. (He was given the box room as his own bedroom, near the front door.) Nicky and Michael were at Archbishop Tenison's school in Kennington, a bus ride away. (They shared an upstairs bedroom.) For Tina, still at Surrey Square Junior school, there were two secondary schools nearby on New Kent Road: Trinity and St Olave's. (She was given the small upstairs bedroom to herself, though it was crammed with Mum's tallboy and wardrobe.) But above all, what everybody liked was the novelty of living in a house with a bathroom.

Before the Heygate, for almost thirty years, there had been Madron Street, off Old Kent Road. The entire length of Madron Street (apart from a small bomb site in the middle) was a terrace of paired houses with basements below and narrow bay windows above. The front doors stood rather grandly atop a railed flight of stairs. Each house was rented out as three units – and all were rented, none owned by the occupiers: one family in the basement, one in the middle and another upstairs, middle and upstairs sharing the front door and passage. Each unit was the same: there were two small rooms off a passage that led into a little kitchen and scullery extension, and then an outside lavatory. There were no bathrooms, no running hot water, and nobody had heard of central heating. (A coal fire in the kitchen was the only heating in winter.) All six children were born to our parents during their long occupancy of the middle flat at 35 Madron Street, most of us being home births as was usual and thus entering life in the unheated front bedroom, the midwife helped by willing aunts. Housing, the problem of overcrowding, the need to persuade the council to offer our family a council house, and our father's lamentable failure himself to provide a big enough house for his growing family, was a defining theme of the Madron Street years.

Southwark

Nicky, born at Madron Street in June 1958, went out into the world from the Heygate Estate. He got a job in hairdressing directly on leaving school at sixteen. It wasn't a future Nicky's father had ever envisaged for him and it required persuasion; Nicky was urged to think about taking up an apprenticeship at Bankside. In the 1960s, hair was an issue that divided the generations: teachers and parents wanted it short, while for the young long hair was a sign of rebellion. As for cutting other people's hair, that was surely effeminate. Nicky, having seen Warren Beatty in *Shampoo*, knew that a hairdresser could be heterosexual and sexy. Linda and her friends laughed, 'You'll be doing blue rinses! Won't the old ladies love you!' But it was one of Linda's friends who advised Nicky to apply to Leonard of Mayfair. Leonard took him on. After a bitter probationary period of fetching and carrying, watching and learning, Nicky became John Frieda's junior and life began in earnest. When John Frieda left Leonard and opened his own salon, Nicky, who had begun to develop his own style, went with him. John encouraged him to do magazine shoots where he mingled with other working-class talent. Hairdressing was part of the new, young vibe – music and photography, fashion and design – where a cockney accent was an asset. He travelled. He met stars and celebrities. He attracted attention.

Michael, born at Madron Street in July 1960, also went out into the world from the Heygate, but his original plan was to stay at school to do A levels in science and maths and perhaps go to university. As a big sister, I had set a precedent for the university route, although nobody in the family thought the results impressive: in my mother's eyes university had made me an atheist, and everybody else noticed I hadn't become money-rich. Michael had an aptitude for schoolwork and an intellectual grasp of the finer details of money-making. He was artistic, too. He became passionate about photography

Not Speaking

and bought a small video camera and an editing machine and taught himself to cut and splice film and set a soundtrack. In the summer holidays after Michael's first year in sixth form, Nicky asked him to film an event at the Royal Albert Hall. Spending long days alongside Nicky, introduced into the world of *Vogue* photo shoots and fashionable glamour, Michael was soon hooked. He abandoned the idea of university. John Frieda took him on as a senior-junior. Our father wasn't happy.

Our father's own future was uncertain at this time. In the late 1970s it had become clear that Bankside power station was being run down and would shortly close. Bill had worked there for almost its entire operating life. He was a fit and active sixty-year-old, not ready for retirement and very aware that he still had a child at school (Tina, born in 1966). He hung on as long as he could, but when the station closed and the remaining men were being bussed downriver to Medway, he called it quits. There was a generous pay-off and a decent pension, which didn't stop him worrying about money; worrying how he was going to fill his days was worse.

There wasn't much to worry about, however, because Michael had seen the future. Working hard as a junior stylist at John Frieda, Michael was making a good income. Servicing the wealthy, he understood the value of ownership. By the early 1980s the housing market was starting to heat up. To his father's horror, Michael took out a bank loan and bought a large ground floor dilapidated flat in Belsize Park. It cost £42,000, a colossal sum it seemed at the time. (To put this in perspective: in 1978, just a few years earlier, my then-husband and I bought a four-bedroom terraced house in Harringay, North London, for £18,500. Admittedly, the Harringay Ladder, as the area was known, had none of the cachet of Belsize Park.) Owing such an amount of money to a bank was almost criminal in Dad's eyes, or at least lunacy. He had to do whatever he could to protect Michael from his youthful impetuosity, and thus it was that the problem of retirement was solved. Bill, with a background in plumbing, painting and decorating, and carpentry, joined forces with Michael. Michael had no intention of living at the flat for long. The plan was to tear out the interior, modernise it to a high standard, and sell at a profit. Michael was working the usual long hours at John Frieda but he went every evening and at weekends and joined Dad who went to the site every day. It was a two-year building project that they later looked back on with tremendous fondness. They did all the work themselves except plastering, which Dad could also have done but when it came to it he advised bringing in specialists. (This was a new departure and he surprised himself. Forever after he always mentioned how he brought in the specialist firm of plasterers when they were doing the job on Michael's Belsize Park flat, 'because you always wanted to be sure about the plastering', as if it still needed explanation.)

The flat sold for £185,000 and in 1988 Michael put the profits into a new purchase. He had decided it was time to strike out alone and open his own business. Again he took out a bank loan and again Dad wanted to protect him from his folly – with more reason by now for the housing bubble had collapsed and the mortgage interest rate was rising. Number 1 Beaumont Street, near Marylebone High Street, was a once-beautiful Victorian pharmacy. It wasn't a particularly fancy address then but it seemed fated to be Michael's because the mews behind was called Clarke's Mews, and one of the first named lease-holders, in 1782, was a William Clarke, who paid £20 per year in rent.

The property at Beaumont Street was double-fronted and on a corner, with windows on three sides giving good light. Fitting it out as a salon had to be done at speed and a building

Not Speaking

crew was employed, but Dad still worked on-site. Michael was also able to buy the two floors of living accommodation above. Dad, the all-purpose handyman, loved working there. Upstairs he built wardrobes and cupboards, plumbed in fancy showers and tubs, helped install the kitchen. Downstairs in the salon, following Michael's designs, they were producing an original look, far away from the steel chrome and black that seemed de rigueur in the salons of the 1970s. Bill made himself useful. Michael wanted to convey the impression of an English country house, using natural materials and creating a homely – as in, aristocratic home, not Heygate home – feel. Leather armchairs were grouped around a fireplace and heavy art books lay on the coffee table. When Michael decided to dig out the basement, Bill supervised proceedings. Soon Tina had joined the company as a partner, managing the reception desk and shop floor.

There was muttering among the siblings that Michael had claimed Dad for his own. Nicky had been used to having his father on the job when needed at his Tufnell Park house. Dad moved between Nicky at Dalmeny Road and Michael at Beaumont Street. Under protest, he had agreed that Michael could buy him a car, the first he owned, its boot filled with heavy tools. We older ones had had our share of Dad's help and we looked on at these developments a little disdainfully. In our houses rooms had been knocked through, chimney stacks knocked out, sash windows repaired, ill-fitting doors planed, shelves put up, garden fences erected, mice and rats eliminated, electrical faults rectified, washing machines plumbed in, no end of walls and woodwork painted in colours that ranged from magnolia to purple, long before these young ones were even done with school. Dad did everything. No task seemed to daunt him, and as long as he'd had a good breakfast (he was religious about having a good breakfast) he could work

Southwark

all day. When we were children our cousin Robert called him Commander Energy.

Nicky, meanwhile, stayed at John Frieda expecting to become a partner. John had promised him a share in the flourishing business. Lesley, however, was urging Nicky to move forward, to think about his own potential and follow Michael's example. Relations between John and Nicky became strained, and in the summer of 1990, instead of giving his protégé a share of the business, John Frieda sacked him. For Nicky it was catastrophic, like being thrown out of the family. John Frieda had been his mentor and guide for over fifteen years. Devastated, hurt, Nicky took John to court for breach of promise. John settled out of court. Lesley put together a business plan and raised a bank loan. She would later say to journalists who were writing pieces on Nicky that she 'nagged him' to open his own salon. Nicky soon realised that the break with John Frieda was an opportunity rather than a catastrophe; with Lesley's help, it galvanised him to do as his younger brother had done.

But he had no premises. In order to keep his clients Nicky needed a place to work. Michael, with some hesitation but pressured by his mother ('You can't leave your brother on the street! He's your brother!') agreed that Nicky could temporarily share the premises at Beaumont Street. Nicky felt he was doing Michael a favour; he wasn't planning to stay, and could easily have gone elsewhere.

The arrangement did not last for long and it left a bitter residue. Each blamed the other for hostile behaviour of various kinds, and Lesley and Tina clashed.

Nicky took a lease on a three-storey property on the corner of Mount Street and Berkeley Square in 1991. At that time there were no other salons in the neighbourhood. Like Michael, he devised an original aesthetic. Nicky's answer to

Not Speaking

clean lines and clinical vistas was antique statuary, gilt mirrors, pictures and more pictures on the walls. He hung great swags of sweeping curtains in the bow windows. He, too, had a vision based on the imagined or actual homes of his high class clients. Nicky was already doing the hair of royalty. He was a regular at Buckingham Palace, often going several times a week when Sarah Ferguson the Duchess of York needed him, through the big front gates in full view of the tourists, in through the Privy Purse entrance, down huge corridors where footmen milled about and up to the duchess's apartments. He wanted to capture some of this grandeur in his salon. (Evidently he succeeded: he was himself 'very like royalty' according to Deborah Ross in the *Independent*.) He wanted to convey the idea of a flamboyant, eclectic collector in a grand, private house. Louis Vuitton trunks, picked up for small sums, served this purpose along with other glitzy bits and pieces. The big items, the antique furniture, the statue of Neptune, the massive mirrors, belonged to a friend, dealer and designer Christopher Hodsoll, who was running out of showroom space. Occasionally Christopher would bring a client to look at an item *in situ*, and if the client liked it and wanted to buy, it would have to go, but another item would come in its place. Nicky enjoyed refreshing the décor and it was a cheap way to look expensive.

In May they had an unofficial opening. The night before, Nicky was still in the downstairs salon at midnight, rearranging the furniture, when Gianni Versace walked in. The statue of Neptune had caught his eye. Versace was in town for the seventy-fifth birthday party of *Vogue*, due to take place along the street that same evening. They chatted. It seemed an omen. 'Come to our party,' Nicky said. 'I'll be wearing one of your jackets, bright green, you won't miss me.'

In December, with the classic 'look' established, came the

Southwark

grand official opening. This proved to be a newsworthy event. Invitations went out and the caterers were told to expect about 300 guests. That day Nicky's booking sheet was full as always with clients, including Sarah Ferguson. In the late afternoon he dashed over to Buckingham Palace, and while cutting the duchess's hair he told her about the opening and she asked if there was anything she could do to help.

'You could turn up,' Nicky said.

Returning to Mount Street he found the pavements crowded and thought it was a party at the advertising agency next door. Going into the salon by the back door he found the place crammed. Over seven hundred people had turned up. Friends, clients, celebrities, other hairdressers were out on the pavements and couldn't get in. And then the duchess appeared.

Nobody had given any thought to having a ritual to mark the event. Someone said they should cut a ribbon. The cry went up: the duchess could cut a ribbon. Put a ribbon across the door! A ribbon was found, but who had a pair of scissors? Where were the scissors? They couldn't find any. In the mayhem it was impossible to get through the crush to open a drawer. One of the duchess's bodyguards produced a penknife. Would this do? It would. They cut the ribbon.

'The press loved it,' Nicky recalled. Of course they did. It was the perfect mock-heroic moment. The idea that a hairdressing salon should have a royal opening was not only novel, it allowed for many kinds and degrees of laughter. Whatever your perspective, high or low, pro or anti, solemn or scurrilous, there was mileage in the common pursuit of a good coiffure and in the notion that the commoners who provided it were being treated like royalty even by royalty.

The press loved Nicky. A front page article in the *Sunday Times* complaining about how outrageously expensive top-end hairdressers had become instanced Nicky's charges. To have

Not Speaking

your hair cut by Nicky Clarke in 1991 cost £60. (The article, in mock-heroic spirit, compared this price with the cost of a dog-coiffeur: £5.) Women journalists wanted to know what you got that made it worth £60 and persuaded their editors to send them along to find out. They described Nicky's black leather trousers, his long hair. They loved the way his hands flew, how he held his scissors, how he handled the dryer. Getting your hair done wasn't a chore any more, it was an experience, it was rock 'n' roll.

The framed photographs of Nicky that lined the passage at the Heygate were mostly publicity shots from this period. Here he is in a suit, his hair tied back fetchingly in a pony-tail, striding through urban grime; here in the luxury of home, with Lesley, under the crystal chandelier; here with baby Harrison; here sporting a beard; here with Michael on the cover of the *Evening Standard* magazine; here again with Michael in the *Observer*; here in the *Tatler*. I've read the press cuttings, and I know that these were the days before everybody had a PR company issuing press releases, but the coverage about Nicky and Lesley and their exciting new salon with its stunningly original look is so gushing you'd think they'd written it themselves. And it went on that way. The great Lynn Barber wrote in the *Observer* in May 2006 about how 'absolutely thrilled' she was after a first visit to Nicky's salon and how she went out 'smiling at the world'.

Awards and prizes came thick and fast. Twice Sessions Hairdresser of the Year; three times London Hairdresser of the Year; Fellowship Image of the Year, twice; World Master Award for Art and Fashion Group USA; the Golden Scissors Award; British Hairdresser of the Year, and so on. He was the first hairdresser to be listed in *Who's Who* and *Debrett's*, and one of the first to be given an OBE. He appeared in television soaps and comedies as himself, most famously with Joanna Lumley and Jennifer Saunders in *Absolutely Fabulous*.

How did it happen? Was he just so much better than everybody else?

'Why me?' Nicky would say, giving a practised answer to a familiar question. 'I was still young enough, photogenic enough. It was like the 1960s and the way it happened with David Bailey. At that time it was photography. Suddenly photography seemed to capture the spirit of the age. I came along when it was time for hairdressing to be in the foreground. And we had the vehicle in the media – what other country had ten national newspapers, and now all the channels and 24-hour TV? It's a lot to fill.'

He played up to the media. He was doing so much magazine work and he had a list of high-profile clients – royalty, actresses like Liz Hurley, supermodels like Naomi Campbell. 'I became part of the story because it gave journalists something extra to talk about when they wanted to write about Naomi Campbell or Sarah Ferguson.'

There were other stories Nicky preferred not to play up to. I remember what it was like in those early days when Mum and Dad were learning from the newspapers things no parent had any need to know, and how painfully embarrassed Dad was. Even Mum was taken aback at first to find that the newspapers could print such things, though she was frankly, voyeuristically, excited. 'Do you think he really did that?' she would say, laughing, having enjoyed what was read to her from the *Daily Mail* or the *News of the World*. I also remember how they both quickly adjusted to the fictionality of it all. Mum collected the articles and photographs indiscriminately, whether they were about the salon and hairdressing awards or Nicky's sexual adventures, carried them in her handbag and showed them proudly to her friends. The words mattered less

Not Speaking

than the thing, these scraps of printed paper; and the Nicky who walked through her front door and sat down at the table with her wasn't the Nicky in those articles. Or rather, he was and he wasn't. Being of interest to the papers was a sign of celebrity, but celebrity itself dwindled in the process. If the papers were all about Nicky, then the papers weren't anything special after all. And anyway, as she frequently observed, her father had been just the same sort of character.

Michael won prizes too, but he took a different route. He focussed on developing his team, teaching new techniques to his stylists, and encouraging juniors to be professional and ambitious. While Nicky won hairdresser of the year Michael won salon of the year in the British Hairdressing Business Awards, among other prizes.

They were both successful and they liked displaying the trappings of wealth. Michael bought a Porsche. On their wrists were Rolex watches. They took expensive holidays and wore expensive clothes to eat in expensive restaurants. And they competed to provide luxurious gifts for our parents. There were cruises for Mum and Dad to Miami and Alaska; the Bahamas; Barbados; a trip on the Orient Express; and every summer, three weeks or a month in Majorca. First class cabins required first class clothes. These were provided. Dad had his dinner jacket, Mum her silk dress. Certain kinds of behaviour went with the look and Michael and Nicky did their best to explain. Michael made up little envelopes with money inside to be given as tips to cabin staff. It was like staging theatricals. 'And Dad, when you're at dinner on board ship,' Michael laughed, 'and people ask what you do, just say you're in power. You're "in power", that's all you have to say.'

Everybody joined in the fun. Mum took it as her due and Dad let himself be pampered but, increasingly, he resisted. He would rather paint Nicky's VIP room than go on a cruise.

Southwark

It troubled him to be grumpy about such matters and he struggled to be properly grateful. But he had no ambivalence when it came to another matter: the store cards.

Nicky gave our mother a Marks & Spencer charge card and a Tesco charge card with the airy instruction that she should use them as much as she wanted. She should go shopping and pile her trolley high and then present the card. No money need be taken from her purse for the goods she purchased. She experienced it as a kind of magic, a spell cast by Nicky's name. She took out the card, explained that she was Nicky's mum, and the cashier smiled her through. Occasionally the magic failed, as when the card expired and Nicky forgot to renew it, or the computer systems in the store were down, and that lent an edge of anxiety to the affair, but each time she sailed from the store with her trolley loaded it restored her belief. She was entranced. Her life was as it should be, except that Bill persisted in objecting to the arrangement. Her use of the cards made him angry. 'Your father is so stupid.' Paul was a spoiler too. When she offered to buy him his groceries he refused; he was being 'difficult'. Linda was being difficult as well and so was I. My mother didn't care. 'Meet me at Marks & Spencer's in Oxford Street,' she would say. 'We'll have a coffee and we'll do some shopping. I'll pay. I've got my card.'

As our mother tried to distribute Nicky's largesse, she convinced herself she was doing him a favour. He was far too fond of giving money away, spending it extravagantly on his friends, wasting his substance. She, by contrast, spent wisely, and by making use of his money she was able to save her own. In this way she kept it in the family. 'Don't worry, he'll get his share back after I'm gone. I'm looking after it for him.'

This logic satisfied her. Dad threatened to cut the cards up.

When Lesley was explaining to the *Daily Mail* that it was her dedication that had built the £50 million group of companies under the Nicky Clarke brand (the journalist noted the 'Tiffany diamond at her neck and, on her wrist, a Cartier watch that glitters as she pours the champagne for lunch' in her £10 million house) she revealed one secret of her success: her vigilant attention to detail. 'Every piece of paper goes by me.'

As a general principle, Lesley shared Nicky's view that money in a family should flow up to the parents as well as down to the children. Some of the cruises our parents enjoyed were holidays with Lesley's parents. They all had medical insurance. They all had the right clothes. Properties were bought.

It was anomalous, under the circumstances, that our parents still lived in a rented council property. They liked where they were; they had no desire to move. Dad, born and raised in Blackfriars, belonged in that patch of South London; and, transport links from Elephant and Castle being excellent, Mum valued its advantages. She could take a bus or train 'from her doorstep' to Nicky's salon and Michael's salon and to any of the Greek churches in Bayswater, Camden Town, Kentish Town, Camberwell, Wood Green, Holloway. They had no desire to move, but like it or not, they were going to have to.

In 1977 Horace Cutler became leader of a Conservative-led Greater London Council (GLC) and in 1979 Margaret Thatcher (Lesley's 'idol' as she told the *Daily Mail*) led the Conservative party to victory at the general election. The Conservatives were keen on selling council houses, especially in the south east and especially in London. According to Michael Heseltine, there was a 'deeply ingrained desire for home ownership' in this country. The scheme that came to be known as 'Right to Buy' was enacted in legislation in the 1980 Housing Act. (It had in fact first been proposed by the

Southwark

Labour party in its 1959 election manifesto.) It was an attractive deal for tenants with access to a little capital. The price of the property was set at market value but there was a hefty discount based on length of occupation and rents already paid. By the end of the 1980s some one in three of all council houses had been bought by their tenants. This had the immediate effect of bringing money into councils' coffers, not only through the lump sums paid but also in maintenance charges and taxes that the new property owners were now obliged to meet. On the other hand, it reduced the council housing stock. The number of homeless families had trebled by the end of the decade.

'If you don't want to move,' Nicky said, and Michael said, and Lesley advised, 'at least buy your house from the council. Stop wasting money in rent.'

Michael was particularly exercised about the idiocy of renting. It was worse than throwing money down the drain in his opinion. He was passionately in favour of buying.

But our parents had no desire for home ownership. Michael Heseltine was wrong: they had the motivation to modernise and improve their home and all the attitudes of independence and self-reliance that he considered the bedrock of a free society, while paying rent for socially owned property. They both thought that a government that looked after people was a good idea.

They took a lot of persuading and, like everything to do with money between our parents, it caused grief, but eventually they bought 3 Cuddington on the Heygate estate. They paid £18,000 for it. Mum put in £12,000 and Dad £6,000. Mum paid the £500 solicitors' fee.

Southwark Council, however, wanted to knock the Heygate down. Quite why they wanted to do so is open to debate, but clearly our parents were not the only people to appreciate the convenience of its situation. Property developers had their

Not Speaking

eyes on the land. In the late 1990s it began to be said that the model estate had been a mistake. The Heygate and the Aylesbury estate next door had been 'instant slums', it was said, from the moment they had been put up. People living in the tower blocks complained about lifts that did not work and the presence of junkies on the stairwells. The walkways supposedly encouraged crime. Residents were apparently too terrified to leave their homes. Other points of view got little airing at the time. In February 2004 Southwark Council passed the plans that enabled them to 'decant' the people and demolish the buildings.

Our parents had to sell their home and find a new one. Neither of them, it seemed to us when we huddled in the kitchen exchanging views, registered the urgency of the situation. They had to be made to see sense. They had to understand that it was time to move on. They had to do so quickly because soon the flat they owned would be worth nothing at all.

Together and separately, Nicky and Michael set about searching for a suitable property where our parents could contentedly live out their last years. If they found somewhere they would buy it at once; they wouldn't wait for the Heygate flat to be sold. North of the river seemed to be indicated since Michael was in Marylebone and Nicky in St John's Wood, I lived in Tottenham and Linda in Winchmore Hill, but it was hard to imagine Mum and Dad agreeing to that. And everything was complicated by the fact that Dad had started to be ill.

In the spring of 2004, aged 85, he had a bad dose of flu. He stayed home for weeks, fending off our concerns. He was furious when Nicky sent a private ambulance after Mum said he wasn't eating or drinking, and insisted he get in it and allow himself to be taken to the Wellington Hospital. Nicky, due to

Southwark

make a celebrity appearance that day at Bluewater shopping centre in Kent, had phoned me and I was there. I travelled with Dad in the ambulance, in which he sat upright as if it was a taxi, his little old-fashioned suitcase by his feet, and all the way from Elephant and Castle to St John's Wood he protested at the waste of time and money. They wheeled him in and shortly afterwards his heart stopped. He had been massively dehydrated. It was fortunate that he was in the hospital and they brought him back quickly but the damage had been done. He recovered, and over the next two years gave a passable imitation of his former self. He swam, he walked, he visited his sister Vi who had moved into an old people's home in Peckham, he flew to Majorca with Mum for their annual summer holiday with Nicky, he built a chicken hut for Tina and helped clear the woods around their house where they kept the pigs, he babysat Tina's dogs and bottle-fed Tina's new lambs. He was still 'wonderful' for his age and that was another reason it seemed sensible to plan for the future.

'You both need somewhere without stairs.'

'Mum, listen. If we find a place in Marylebone, or St John's Wood, or Maida Vale, you will still be able to get to your churches. They do have buses in North London, you know.'

'You'll be nearer to us.'

In fact, Dad had started spending longer and longer periods of time down at Tina's house in Sussex where his life was more peaceful. Tina took care of him. His main concern, if he had to move, was to be near Waterloo station for Billingshurst and within easy travelling distance of Vi at Peckham. With his own room at Tina's and a series of small tasks, he was happy and felt he was being useful. He profoundly disliked the idea that his sons would be providing him with a home. To him it felt like failure even though, as was repeatedly pointed out, he had for the past quarter of a century, all through his seventies and into his eighties, provided them with skilled labour and practical support in their homes and salons, virtually on a full-time unpaid basis.

Mum seemed to have agreed in principle to the move but could not be satisfied with any of the suggested properties. There was always a reason why it wasn't worth pursuing whatever was being proposed although she enjoyed being told the details.

'But you haven't seen it,' Nicky would say when she multiplied objections. ('A white carpet? I can't have a white carpet.')

'I don't need to see it. I don't like it.'

It was perhaps for this reason that when they found 32 Cropthorne Court Nicky and Michael didn't take either of our parents to view it. Everybody had lost patience, and that was understandable. What was less understandable, and became one of the problems that led to the not speaking, was the fact that when it came to the point, Nicky and Lesley bought the flat as a part of their property portfolio. Michael did not contribute; he was not included in the purchase. Recollections differ about why this happened. The effect is not in doubt. Michael was aggrieved and backed off. Thirty-two Cropthorne and all that went on inside it would be Nicky's responsibility.

Lesley supervised the renovations, choosing colours and fittings, playing safe by keeping to neutral tones throughout (no white carpet). She made sure to install all the usual units in the kitchen including a roll-out cupboard like the one Tina had and which Mum coveted. She assured her there was a dedicated wall in the bedroom where icons could be mounted, and there would be a shelf for the holy candle.

Mum was uneasy about the whole business and Dad increasingly unhappy. Both did their best to ignore it.

Southwark

'If I have to go there,' Mum said, 'I'm changing the locks as soon as I go in.'

It wasn't that she thought Nicky's goodness towards her would ever fail. Open-handedness was an article of faith with him. By nature he was one of life's givers not takers, good-natured, easy-going, accepting, living in the moment, spontaneous, abundant, willing – all of which she approved of in a man, so long as she was the woman towards whom his generosity was directed. She trusted Nicky to want to look after her; she didn't trust him to look after himself or his finances.

It was complicated when there was another woman in the case. And Lesley – beautiful, clever, successful – was a rival, even if she was no longer Nicky's sexual partner. Rena and Lesley were intimates who enjoyed each other's company enormously. When they were together they talked at and over each other in the way Rena and her Greek friends always did, shouting louder when necessary, loving to gossip, adoring a bit of malice, giving voice to daily experience. 'Your mum and I are like sisters,' Lesley would say. Or, 'I'm the number one daughter.'

Linda and I agreed that Lesley was much more like our mother than we were.

Mum said, 'Nicky won't hear a word against her.'

Once the renovations to Cropthorne had been accomplished, a date was set for stage one of the move out of Heygate: Saturday, 11 February 2006.

Nobody suggested hiring a removals company. The move was to be a family affair. Tina's husband, Lee Sheward, a stuntman and stunt coordinator in the film industry, who not only fell from high buildings and crashed cars and dangled from air balloons but lifted and shifted props with professional efficiency, would provide the truck and muscle and leadership.

Not Speaking

Lee was used to starting work early. He was already there when I arrived at 7:30 a.m. Boxes marked 'Ornaments' and 'Fragile' and 'Photographs' were being loaded into a cavernous truck. Dad was helping: wrapped up warmly in a coat, scarf and hat, he was sitting on the tailboard keeping guard over the goods, just in case any Heygate ruffians were up and about and interested in Mum's ornaments. Tina said to me, 'Keep an eye on him.' He was thinner than when I'd last seen him, faded, dusty somehow. He'd had a fall outside Tesco, but he wouldn't talk about it. He insisted it was nothing. Nor did he want to talk about the move. For years the moment had threatened and been held off and now it was here and he just wanted to get the job done. After half an hour he told me he had to go indoors.

My task then was to keep Mum out of the way. She was in a fury and berating Dad. He had failed to turn the gas ring off when he made his breakfast; they had run out of newspaper for wrapping and it was his fault. 'For once I listened to your father. Normally, I would never listen to him, he's so stupid. For once I listened to your father and I threw away the newspaper.'

While the boys were still loading I said, 'Mum, we'll go on ahead to Maida Vale in the car. Let's go see where you're going to live. Lesley will be there, she'll let us in.'

I was glad to get away. I also blamed Dad – in much the same terms as he blamed himself. It was painful to see him so depleted, too painful to tolerate.

We piled some special things into the car: holy water, icons, and a number of bags filled with empty bags. Mum's shoulder was hurting her and she was treating it with cotton-wool dabbed in holy water. For most of the journey she fulminated against Tina who had arrived that morning with a heat pad.

'Why did she bring me that?'

'Because you said you had a sore shoulder.'

Southwark

'I told her I didn't need anything.'
'She was only trying to be helpful.'
'I told her to take it back.'
'I expect she will.'
'Why did she bring it?'

This went on for some time. It wasn't until we were driving alongside Regent's Park that I understood her reasoning. She couldn't use the heat pad because if she did it would mean she was showing no faith in God's medicine. The fact that Tina had brought it in the first place was an attack on God. Mum believed in prayer, penance and Providence, and the holy water that she kept in the fridge.

'I've got my cotton-wool,' she said resentfully. The cotton-wool, damp with holy water, was lodged inside her bra. Now and then she took it out and rubbed her shoulder.

I let her talk to me about the saints. On her lap was the very large leather bag she always carried that contained elastic-bound packets of religious leaflets which she would read intently in spare moments. She was also carrying her passport, bank-books, some jewels, and a massive wad of fifty and twenty pound notes – her secret savings. Holding these things excited her.

Before we went into the flat I mentioned that Nicky and Lesley were anxious that she might not like it. She looked at me suspiciously. 'Why won't I like it? What's wrong with it?'

'Nothing as far as I know. I haven't seen it yet. We're still standing on the doorstep.'

'What makes you think I won't like it?'

'Nothing. I'm just asking you to think about their feelings and try not to say something horrible the minute you walk in.'

'Do you know something about it they haven't told me?'

'No.'

Lesley was wearing flat shoes. She'd had both knees operated on and was in pain. She showed us round less like a plutocrat dispensing large gifts than a petitioner hoping to please. She spoke fast, descriptions and explanations tumbling out. Here was the dedicated wall for icons, here would be a shelf for the holy candle – 'The carpenter's coming on Monday.' The wardrobes had no handles, 'I don't know what happened, we lost them, but they'll be fixed on Monday.' The spare room had no curtain, 'But we'll have it up by Monday.' 'Nicky thought you'd like this room,' – a large room with a wall of wardrobes – 'and Bill could have this one, and we'll put his telly up here,' slightly smaller, but no less attractive. There were two luxury bathrooms and a guest room with built-in cupboards for towels and linens.

Mum admired the apartment, though without taking a great deal of interest in it as it seemed to me, and then we went with Lesley to Carluccio's in St John's Wood High Street for a long and lively lunch.

Mum ordered swordfish, I had a grilled steak, Lesley chicken breast. We had a large glass of wine each. There was plenty to talk about, beginning with a piece in the *Sunday Times* the previous weekend. Mum pretended innocence and asked Lesley why Nicky was so upset about what had been said in the newspaper. Since Nicky's being upset had taken place under her own eyes, and since she had raised the subject with him several times in the course of the morning and he had explained at great length that Octavia, his then girlfriend, was upset at something Harrison was reported as saying, and Harrison upset by being told off by Octavia, and Octavia upset by being rung up by Lesley ('Do what you like with Nicky but upset my children and I'll come and throw a brick through your window and follow it!'), I had to assume she only asked Lesley the question in order to keep the pot boiling. Nicky had told her not to believe everything she read in the press. Lesley amplified this advice, explaining that the PR company had been remiss in leaving Harrison alone with 'a hack journalist'. He was, after all, a tender youth, a mere nineteen. What did he know? The fact that nothing Harrison said was untrue, or even, to my eyes, particularly startling, was neither here nor there. The offence lay in some words that denigrated hairdressing. 'That's not an attitude you want to have going out into the world.' There was hard, financial logic beneath the histrionics. Nicky's personal life was an aspect of his profile as a brand leader in the industry. Ranged behind Nicky and Lesley were many people and organisations whose incomes stood to be affected if things were not carefully managed.

In the car afterwards Mum reflected on a happy outing and the prospect of a new home. She said to me accusingly, 'Why did you think I might not like it? It's lovely. What made you think I wouldn't like it? Are you trying to cause trouble?'

I dropped her off at her friend Lucy's in Elephant and Castle so that she could watch Greek television and drove into the Heygate. At the house I found Dad sitting in the kitchen, ashen-faced. He had fallen again, this time hitting the back of his head.

He was alone. We had made no provision for him even though he had fallen two days before, was noticeably weaker than he had been, had a nasty cough and – the most devastating thing – was obviously utterly miserable.

He had been cooking himself a bacon sandwich. I got him to take the pills he hadn't yet taken. I told him about our lunch. When Lee came back the two of them went to look at his old bench and tools in the little back garden – Lee thought they could be put to use in one of his barns. But when the cold air hit him Dad had another funny turn. I came into the living room to find him in the armchair looking as if he'd been punched.

Not Speaking

Enraged, he got up and staggered upstairs telling me to leave him alone. He wanted to lie down and then he'd be OK. I went up with him. We sat for a bit. We chatted. Furious at being old and weak, he couldn't bear to be so useless. Watching Lee, whom he loved and admired, stamping back and forth – strong, efficient, good-humoured and exceptionally hard-working, a man who deserved a day off when a rare one came round – was agony to him. He desperately wanted Lee to be able to finish the job so that he could set off home. He kept saying, 'And even after he's done it, he's got to drive sixty miles. It'll be midnight before he's home.'

He reproached himself for the physical frailties of old age, and used his misery to heap on more. As he saw it, none of this would have been happening, none of it would have been needed if he had bought a good-sized home of their own earlier, when he was young and fit enough. The ugly boxes and bin bags piled in the living room had been a sort of indecent exposure. It had been a day of pain and humiliation. A mistake.

More mistakes followed. I should have called an ambulance then and there. Nicky was expected, Paul was due, Mum would return. I went home, fed up with the whole thing.

It was on Valentine's Day evening three days later that the message went round. Dad had collapsed and was in hospital. He must have been having small strokes and now he'd had a larger one. We all converged on the bedside.

For the next two weeks he lay in a room in the Wellington Hospital, Tina watching him round the clock, the rest of us doing shifts in different combinations. Nicky said of Tina, 'That girl deserves a medal.'

Mostly Dad slept. Sometimes he came round and tried to say things. His ankles hurt. He wanted all the tubes out. 'Cut them all off,' he would say. 'Scissors. Give me scissors.' He couldn't

Southwark

swallow, and his left side was limp, but with his right hand he managed to pull out the nasal-gastric tube and the catheter. He would have ripped out the stomach tube and pacemaker if he could. Tina moistened his lips.

He was gruff, sullen, fearful. Whenever he'd been in hospital before he always got on well with nurses, being obedient and courteous, liking being looked after and scared of whatever treatment or diagnosis was in store. He was the classic model patient. At the end he was a 'bad' patient in the way stroke patients often are, and a bad father failing to appreciate all the effort being made on his behalf.

As the days passed his condition steadily worsened. He seemed to be stiffening, turning into a corpse in front of our eyes. To me, the feeling that he was gone was the most palpable feeling in the room every time I entered, but Tina continued to talk of him as a patient who would get better. This was the line everybody took. Nobody talked about death.

Mum came by and scrutinised him. She said, 'I feel so sorry for him. Look how skinny he's getting.'

'They're feeding him through the tube.'

'I want to see him with a fork and knife in his hands.'

She didn't stay long.

I wanted to see him with a cup of tea, and to hear him say as he bustled into the house, 'Put the kettle on.'

The doctors understood that Tina was the person to whom they should direct their remarks, even though there might be seven or eight people in the room.

'It's for your own good, Dad,' she would explain when the doctors advised another uncomfortable, futile procedure.

We would stand over him, smiling tightly, upset and angry. What did he think he was doing lying there leaving us? We pretended to try to hear what he was saying when he gestured impatiently that he wanted all the tubes out, out, wanted scissors to cut away whatever it was they were putting in his veins to keep him alive. He was done with it all, finished, over. But we weren't done with him.

I'm glad I found the courage once, when we were alone, to show I understood what he meant. 'Do you want it all out, Dad? Have you had enough?'

He said, 'I've gone far enough. Take it out.'

I imagined holding a pillow over his face and ending the misery.

To the consultant who asked him what he wanted, Dad said, 'I want to shoot my daughters.' It was a joke. We laughed. They were the last coherent words I heard him say.

Tina had always been physically affectionate towards Dad, hugging him and kissing him and sitting on his lap. But when he left for good on the first day of March he just left and there wasn't any hugging or kissing goodbye.

There were two things our father used to say: 'I hope I drop dead at a bus stop,' and 'I don't care what you do with me after I'm dead.'

He was not a believer in any kind of God or afterlife. The closest he came to religion was in his feeling for family. He left no instructions because death was never going to happen. For the same reason, nobody asked him if he preferred to be buried or cremated.

Tina wanted to bury him on her land in the field on the edge of the woods. The spot she had in mind was an old vegetable patch, just visible from the kitchen window, where Dad had liked to potter. It could be landscaped and made pretty. Fenced off and with a gate, shrubs, paths and benches it would be somewhere all the family could congregate, a place to sit and remember. She had already researched the matter. There was no law against it, although there were constraints with regard to the water table, and you had to pay the council a fee. The local vicar would officiate.

Gentry landowners built their own chapels. The aristocracy kept their ancestors close. Tina thought Dad would see the funny side and enjoy being treated like an aristocrat. There was some squeamishness among the siblings but the combination of grief and gratitude that Tina was organising everything kept it muted.

Only our mother expressed dissent. She was glad he was being buried: as a practising Greek Orthodox who anticipated the resurrection as a bodily affair she passionately objected to cremation. But she was upset that he wasn't in holy ground. She said it was like burying a cat or a dog.

After the funeral, we still had to complete the move and our mother still had to be settled in Maida Vale.

For weeks Mum had camped at the Heygate flat, alone, most of her possessions in boxes in the new apartment. All kitchen equipment except a kettle had gone. But her bed and a few other things including the fridge freezer weren't being moved and they were still there. She insisted that she preferred sleeping at the Elephant. Any enthusiasm for 'that other place' where nothing was properly sorted had vanished. She couldn't stand the strangeness. She had lost her husband. 'I've lost my husband,' she would say. She spent the evenings at Rita's or Lucy's, both of whom had Greek television, and then, often after midnight, she would go to the emptied out flat. One bitterly cold night the key broke in the lock. She went back to Rita's and Rita's son called a locksmith.

'What will happen to me if something like that happens at

that other place?' she said next day. 'I've got good neighbours here.'

A light bulb went out in the passage and fused the lights. Dad wasn't there to fix it. She became uncharacteristically tearful.

Bit by bit, going in the daytime, she worked on the boxes at Maida Vale. She didn't know what to do with Bill's things but she wasn't upset about that in the way she became upset about the contents of the old fridge freezer at the Elephant which she was trying to transfer, a few lumps at a time, wrapped in newspaper and packed in her trolley. The new fridge freezer at Maida Vale was full.

'I have to have another fridge freezer.'

'Where are you going to put it?'

'I don't care. I have to have one.'

'Are you sure you should bring all that frozen stuff on the underground?'

'There's nothing wrong with it.'

'Why don't you just chuck it? It's probably been in the freezer too long anyway.'

'I told you. There's nothing wrong with it.'

The day she decided to sleep the night at Maida Vale Tina drove up to help make progress with the unpacking. Boxes were still stacked to the ceilings. But Mum had other plans. She had to have the second fridge freezer. She showed Tina why: the fridge freezer (standard size) provided in the fitted kitchen was risibly small. Tina protested there was no space to put another one. As she stood in the kitchen, the sheer volume of material objects waiting to be processed nauseated her. Why did Mum want to add to the difficulty? Couldn't she just buy a bit less food for a while?

'Don't be stupid.'

Southwark

An extra freezer would not add to the difficulty. It was a solution.

'Why didn't you make an effort and just defrost and cook all that stuff before you moved?' No answer. 'That would have been a help, you know.'

They went down to the car, drove to John Lewis in Oxford Street, and bought a fridge freezer.

On the way back Mum said, 'You're right. I should have done what you said. *Now* I understand that. But it's too late now.'

She moved in. She changed the locks. She had moments of panic, trouble with the appliances, problems with the boiler, and couldn't work out the radiators. We all tried to help. None of our help was satisfactory. We agreed she was coping much less well than we expected. She was slow to adapt to her changed circumstances.

It distressed her when the workmen left some tools in the passage. Dad would never have done that. A bucket with a random assortment of dust-and-plaster-covered tools made her furious. The workmen's drills released powder from the walls. Dad's drills didn't do that sort of thing.

She wanted to take everything out of the cupboards and wash everything down. We had always thought she was a typical Greek in her attitude to cleaning, but this was a revelation. The drill and the bucket signified contamination.

'I'll take them away,' I said, meaning the tools. But the harm had already been done. 'I'll help you clear it up.'

'No.'

She needed to take everything out, clean and put it back, getting on a step-ladder to reach the high shelves. The job had to be done by her own hand.

When she unpacked and put away her clothes it too had a ritual quality. Everything had to be carefully ironed before it

Not Speaking

was folded or hung. Linda sat patiently for hours, not allowed to do any but the simplest of tasks such as folding a pile of nice clean cashmere sweaters that had been taken out of one drawer to be put in another. Linda said, 'It doesn't matter if we don't do anything. It's fine just to sit and chat.'

And then the thing our mother feared did happen. She had put three locks on the door of 32 Cropthorne, some turning one way, some another. It was confusing. She came home from church, desperate for the bathroom, and couldn't open the door. She stood there crying. A man who lived upstairs helped her.

She said, 'I didn't cry all through the funeral and I'm crying now.'

I said (we were speaking on the phone), 'You're under a lot of stress. Try to take it easy.'

'How can I take it easy when this place is upside down? I've been crying all morning. I feel like throwing myself under a train.'

This was so unlike her it was shocking.

She had imagined that living in North London closer to Nicky and Michael would mean that she saw them more frequently, which in her mind meant more or less every day. 'They said they would visit me,' she complained.

'You had dinner with Michael yesterday.'

'And now he's gone away to America for a week.'

'He's running a business.'

'They don't come here like they used to.'

It was true that Michael didn't like going to the new apartment.

'It would be different if your father was still alive. Then they would come like they used to. It's horrible being a widow.' The boiler was playing up. 'I rang Nicky. He said he would come. He hasn't come. He hasn't sent anybody.' She was tragic,

Southwark

angry. 'I should never have left the Elephant and Castle. Why did you let them do it? Why didn't you say something? You could have stopped them.'

I wished my father was still alive too, and I wished she had stayed at the Elephant and Castle and that everything was as it had been. I wanted to cry, instead of which I lost my temper and shouted.

'No, I couldn't. And anyway, you had to move. Southwark Council wanted to knock the estate down. In any case, you've done it now, and it's nice, and you like Maida Vale, it's clean, and posh, and you like saying you live in Maida Vale, and even if you don't see Nicky every day you do see quite a lot of him, and of Michael, and Tina rings you every morning, and sometimes in the afternoon, and before you go to bed at night, and Linda comes round, and so do I, and if Paul wasn't too busy drinking himself to death in Hastings he'd be here too, so honestly, Mum,' I started to calm down, 'I don't see what you're complaining about.'

I really didn't see. With hindsight I made allowance for the traumatic weeks and months she had endured, the calamity that was bound up with the move to Maida Vale. But I still thought she should have tried a bit harder to help us in our sorrow and bewildered grief.

One day she opened the door and spoke to me in Greek as if I was one of her friends from the church, and continued speaking in Greek as I took off my coat and went to make a cup of tea and brought the tray into the living room. It made me feel like a foreigner. I was foreign. She had been married for over sixty years to a foreigner who had taken her to a foreign land and had now departed leaving her with her foreign children who had grown up and had lives of their own, English lives.

Mayfair

Several months have gone by. The receptionist at Nicky's salon directs me down the ('gold balustraded', 'Hollywood-style') spiral staircase to the basement. There I find Lesley, having a treatment. She lies with her head resting on a pillow on a washbasin and with a towel over her eyes. Also in the salon, getting her nails and hair done in preparation for the flight to Majorca next day, is Lesley and Nicky's daughter, Tellisa. And sitting in a chair next to Tilly, gowned and shampooed, talking and waiting, is my mother. At her feet rest an assortment of battered bags which she courteously declines to have removed from her and put elsewhere.

It is a surprise to see so many family members, but it's not uncharacteristic. Nor is the fact that Nicky isn't here yet. 'He'll be here soon,' Tilly says loyally.

Lesley waves a hand but keeps the towel over her eyes. Mum welcomes me warmly, mistress of her surroundings. She breaks off from cross-questioning Tilly about her boyfriend to interrogate me about my sons, checking off possible catastrophes – disease, injury, unemployment – and romances: beginnings, ends and progress of. She absorbs the gist of an answer, never the detail unless it hides the larger story, but

Not Speaking

in any case I tell her almost nothing. Fine, we are all fine, everything is fine. The boys are working? We are all working. (For men to be out of work would mean being 'stupid' or 'lazy' in her lexicon. As for the women, that's more complicated.) Then she asks me if I've seen Linda lately, when did I last see Michael, have I spoken to Paul? She herself speaks to Tina every day so she doesn't ask about Tina.

Since Dad died, her fierce self-assurance has become muted. She hates living alone, and says so, but hates even more the thought that she might be forced to live under someone else's roof, even that of one of her children. Occasionally she conveys pathos, a mood none of us knows how to deal with.

The fact is, having moved to Maida Vale and into an apartment owned by Nicky and Lesley, she feels herself to be dependent and vulnerable. She has nightmares about being thrown out onto the streets. She doesn't tell Nicky this, but she tells me, and Linda, and Michael and Tina. We tell her such fears are nonsense.

Still, Michael has asked Nicky, twice, to sign a one-page document giving Mum secure tenure for life, but on neither occasion was it convenient for Nicky to sign it. Nicky is offended at the thought that anybody could think he might ever evict his mother.

Mum depends on Michael to manage her finances. All the paperwork that comes through her door goes to him: leaflets for takeaway pizza, special offers, letters telling her she's won half a million in a faraway lottery ('Are you sure it's rubbish?'), along with bills and bank statements. It goes into a plastic bag and is deposited with Michael every few days. Taking the papers to Michael gives her a sense of order in the way that walking to pay utility bills over the counter at the electricity showroom, the gas company and the post office used to do.

Mayfair

'We have to get direct debits set up,' Michael says, but she won't agree to this invisible removing of her money.

She takes comfort in her savings, boosted by the sale of Cuddington (£236,000). There had been some anxiety that the flat would never find a purchaser but in the event it proved worth somebody's while to pay the money and put a number of tenants in for the duration. Michael handles that side of things. It is time-consuming ('I don't know why he's taking so long to sell the house') and troublesome. Later, he will help to put the money away in bonds and securities, distributing it into different accounts. Mum has a widow's pension from Dad's old job, and a state pension. Most importantly, she has her store charge cards; and with Dad gone, there is no-one to stop her doing all her shopping on Nicky's cards. This paperwork goes directly to Nicky Clarke.

She shops now at Waitrose (pronounced 'Whatross') on Edgware Road. Nicky has set up an account for her with a taxi company so she doesn't have to haul her over-filled trolley onto the bus. But she likes the fact that the bus stop is outside the apartment, as if it was specially put there for her convenience. There are several buses that go from Maida Vale to Oxford Street and her favourite store, Marks & Spencer. From there it is an easy walk south down Davies Street to Nicky's salon, or north up Marylebone High Street to Michael's. Or it would be easy if she wasn't carrying heavy bags: shopping, holy water, icons, and the vast amounts of money she doesn't like leaving behind the triple-locked door of her apartment. Also weighing her down is the religious literature she takes everywhere. In the bags at her feet I see the dog-eared pamphlets from Greek Orthodox churches and monasteries. They contain exhortations, stories of miracles and the lives of the saints, and reproductions of icons. At intervals she gets them out and half-reads, half-prays, kissing the pictures and making the sign of the cross.

Nicky arrives wearing white jeans, pointy leather ankle boots, a leather belt, and a white shirt tucked in. The shirt is open to the midriff and a number of dangly things, including a large gold cross, drape his chest. He's not particularly tall and certainly not fat but there's nothing *slight* about him – he exudes strength and physical presence. His forearms are massive, his hands square, large.

He greets everybody, grabs a chair on wheels and sits astride it. He's at the centre of the circle and here we are, ranged round him: wife, daughter, mother, sister. Nobody finds it odd that at the end of a long day he's still doing hair. And anyway, tomorrow we fly out. Cheerfully he sets to work, organising assistants, rustling up some food, asking for orange juice.

Nicky loves hair. I suppose all hairdressers must love hair, as writers must love words, and his is an evident passion. He loves to handle it, to make it do this and that, to feel its silkiness and bounce, its sensuousness. He enjoys the drama, the sociability. Writing, I reflect, is a solitary and largely invisible activity. Only writers know how much labour goes into a book, how many hours of grinding work it can take to make a page read sweetly. When Gustave Flaubert was searching for *le mot juste* and writing *Madame Bovary* he was probably not very good company. Nicky is great company when he's doing hair.

Patterns establish themselves in families. Nicky isn't consciously imitating Dad but, like Dad, he likes to be busy and he gets pleasure from pleasing people. Even his notorious lateness has something to do with that: often he's late because he's pleasing someone else. The key is to not be the person three miles away and waiting but to be the person in his line of vision, here, now, sitting in the chair, receiving the ministration of his flying hands.

Mayfair

Covertly, I look at my watch. It's even later than I had thought. No matter. I am the person sitting in the chair.

And his hands do fly. He's concentrating and there are a lot of us to get through and Mum is talking. She's asking Nicky about 'that woman with the much younger boyfriend', and at first Nicky doesn't know, or pretends not to know, who she's talking about. 'Your friends. We went out to the restaurant, last summer in Spain.'

'You'll have to give me more clues than that. We always go out to a restaurant.'

'The woman with the much younger boyfriend.'

Nicky registers who she means and launches into an amusing story.

'He's much younger than her,' Mum says, having waited till he stopped. 'How old is she?'

There's a burst of laughter. Among the moral absolutes about being female in our house, never telling your age was pre-eminent. (It vied with, 'Never open your purse when you're out with a man.') We've been lied to all our lives about our mother's age. Nicky, as a boy, believed her when she said she was twenty-seven. I believed her when she explained she married at fifteen and had to get a special licence from the priest. My son believed her when she told him she was thirty-two, though he was puzzled because, as he explained, his own mother was thirty-six.

'Our friend doesn't care who knows her age,' Lesley says. 'She's proud of it.'

'She's good-looking,' Mum says, as if her question might have been misunderstood and she wants to correct a misperception. 'I'm not saying there's anything wrong.'

'Would it be wrong if she wasn't good-looking?' I ask automatically.

I'm preoccupied with my own thoughts and don't register

the significance of this interest in the woman with the much younger boyfriend. Rena lets the subject drop. My question wasn't the right one, and my notion of what might or might not have been wrong, irrelevant. Rena was recalling her own past with satisfaction: she had indisputably been a looker.

In our family being good-looking – and its concomitant, retaining a youthful appearance as you aged – were also moral absolutes. Beauty was truth, with a vengeance.

Linda was the pretty one, I was the clever one. The inferior status gave me a certain freedom. And even as a child I could see that Linda's negotiations around our mother's interest in her good looks were complicated.

For Lesley, who came on the scene later, there was instant acceptance. Lesley was always a beauty and now had 'an elegant glamour that belies her years' (*Daily Mail*). In a nutshell, she met my mother's standards. When Lesley says, 'I'm the number one daughter, really,' I think to myself: she's right. To see them together is to see two women who share fundamental values.

Does women's pursuit of beauty dumb them down? Is beauty a form of coercion, as Naomi Wolf argues in *The Beauty Myth*? Trying hard not to catch sight of my own image in the mirror, I consider beauty and the social construction of femininity which, having read the books, I know is a masquerade – a word I like. Simone de Beauvoir famously wrote that one is not born but becomes a woman. In other words, it isn't anatomy that makes the difference, but culture. Women were *The Second Sex*, as in the title of de Beauvoir's 1949 book, because men must always be first. Women become women by servicing men: as sexual partners exchanged between men; and as walking wombs for the reproduction of the species, men's children.

Mayfair

In the *Iliad*, women are the prizes of war. All through the *Iliad* women are handed back and forth along with goods and cattle as warriors flourish or fail. The anger of Achilles is first provoked when Agamemnon, his commander, demands and takes from him his 'spear-captive' Briseis, a woman won as a war-prize but loved as a wife. Briseis has no say in the matter: unless they are goddesses like Athene or Thetis, Achilles' mother, women have few speaking parts in the *Iliad*.

I try to think of exceptions to the rule of mostly mute women. Muteness isn't natural; it doesn't even reflect the stereotype. And surely no human being truly wants to come second. In Euripides' *Trojan Women*, a play set in Troy in the aftermath of defeat, all the main characters are women and they, necessarily, speak: Andromache, Hector's wife; Hecuba, his mother; Helen, whose fate is not yet decided; and Cassandra, who is to be taken off as spear-captive to Agamemnon (and who can foresee Agamemnon's death on his return from Troy – serve him right). What they speak are the laments of the losers, and their intelligence and reasoning are compelling, but none has power over her own destiny. What happens to them will be decided by men.

The classic essay on womanliness as a masquerade is by Joan Riviere and it describes female intellectuals as 'women who wish for masculinity'. That formulation was characteristic of the 1920s when the essay was written, in the aftermath of the Victorian era when arguments for women's rights were posed in terms of women's similarities to men rather than (as the Victorians had insisted) their difference. In the early 1900s masculinity was the ideal. Girls' schools were modelled on boys' schools, women aped men's clothing – wearing not only the newly-invented bloomers to ride bikes, but also ties and shirts. They cut their hair short. They gave each other boys'

Not Speaking

names. My ex-husband's mother, born in 1903 and christened Rosamond, was always known as Rob, and among her girlfriends were Mike and Billy. Women wanted what men had – the rewards of masculinity.

Riviere saw what she called the 'mask of womanliness' as a strategy. It was something women adopted to fend off male retribution for stepping on their turf. 'Women who wish for masculinity,' she wrote, 'may put on a mask of womanliness to avert anxiety and the retribution feared from men.'

I don't know how far Riviere's analysis takes me as I sit getting my hair done in the heart of the beauty industry, and it is a long time since I felt the need for any mask of womanliness. None of my essential comforts depend on pleasing, placating or appeasing men. My sons are grown and I am in a civil partnership with a woman of my own age, both of us professors in English universities. My wish for masculinity, if that is what it is, doesn't have to be veiled.

Riviere uses 'masculinity' to mean power. Patriarchy confers power on men. But on the ground, in the family, the reality is often laughably far from the patriarchal ideal. Beauty is power too. And not only beauty. I grew up surrounded by strong women and yielding men.

In Greek families, the son is a little demi-god and he loves his mother. The word 'patriarchy', like 'democracy', is Greek. Some of my mother's disappointment in her marriage, which began early and became corrosive, was because my father wasn't patriarchal enough. Her Greek father was patriarchal; her husband was 'soft'. He didn't stand on his natural authority, he didn't assume his rights. He was too easy to deceive. He was too decent, too English.

I want to ask Nicky what he thinks about this but can hardly do so now, and anyway I don't know how to frame what will inevitably be a delicate question. And what would Paul say?

Mayfair

And Michael? Barbara, my wife, one of the Clarke daughters-in-law, surprised me when she said, 'It's possible the girls in your family survived their upbringing better than the boys.'

It is unacceptable to Rena as a rule of life that what happens to women should be decided by men, but as a fact of life it guarantees a degree of male attention. My apparent willingness to give up male attention and leave a husband of some twenty years, a man she liked, a very decent Englishman, to live with a woman, made no sense to her. You could always have women friends. And any man who tried to impose his will – which men, if they were real men, must do – could be managed by a proper woman.

None of the girls has slipped out of the family orbit in the way Paul, the eldest son, began to slip away after his marriage ended and his drinking increased. From the age of six, when his position in the family began to be undermined, Paul had to struggle for favour. The princelings out-shone the prince. In recent years he had taken himself off to Hastings; and yet there had been a time, when he married and settled in Bermondsey, when he was the one who lived closest to our parents and whose way of life most resembled what Bill probably imagined for his children. That was no accident: Paul modelled himself on Dad. He took pride in being a good handyman. He loved to see a crowd gathered around his table (he became a keen cook). He bought a caravan and enjoyed spending weekends fishing and cycling with his two sons. He recalled his pleasure in a couple of walking holidays he had taken with Dad when he was still single, just the two of them, in the Lake District and in Jersey. But happy interludes of intimacy like that were rare. Mostly Mum's presence dominated and bit by bit Paul was to be seen less often at Sunday dinner at the Heygate.

Paul's identification with Dad was fertile ground for his ambivalent but developing hostility to Rena. Some of his masculine assertion was almost parodic in its Bermondsey-boy cockney swagger, as if showing his father what was needed. At the same time Greek patriarchy appealed to him too and he was learning Greek, declaring that the Greek way of life suited him and he would like to go and live on a Greek island.

His absence at the Heygate wasn't remarked, but when he showed up his whisky consumption was noted and reproved, loudly and insistently, by his mother. It was a sufficient deterrent. He would also have to hear about or witness the wealth of his younger brothers.

Becoming a celebrity early, Nicky loved to shower the blessings of stardom on his parents. It wasn't only the Rolex watch and smart Savile Row suits, the designer dresses and jewelled gold cross, the restaurants, the cruises. It was also gala events – he liked them to be there at awards ceremonies. He enjoyed taking Dad to football matches, once flying him up to Manchester to mingle in the executive lounge at Man United as a guest of one of their suppliers. In 2007, the year after Dad died, when Nicky heard he was getting an OBE in the Queen's next birthday honours, his delight was tinged with grief. It was good news and bad news, he told me. 'It's bad because Dad's not here, Dad won't know about it.' I understood at once what he meant. The OBE was recognition inside English traditions that Dad respected. And it would have offered them a chance to play together. When the time came Nicky would deck himself out in a morning suit for Buckingham Palace, relishing the pomp and circumstance, but for him some of the meaning would be gone because he couldn't dress his father up and take him too.

The press were interested in another question. What was the correct etiquette, the *Evening Standard* asked: 'Does one take one's wife or one's girlfriend to one's OBE ceremony at Buckingham Palace?'

The family twisted the knife further. What about one's mother?

'He should be taking you, Mum,' Michael insisted. 'Don't you think it's about time you met the queen? After all, you always said Prince Philip is Greek.'

'Prince Philip *is* Greek. His father was Prince Andrew of Greece.'

'I thought the royal family were all Germans.'

'German and Greek,' she explained patiently. 'Philip's mother was Princess Alice of Battenberg. That's German. His grandmother was Queen Olga of Greece. He was born in Corfu. He took his name in this country from his mother's side, his uncle Louis of Battenberg, who called himself Mountbatten.'

'Louis Mountbatten who was blown up by the IRA?'

She isn't sure. Not that one, she thinks, an earlier one, or perhaps that one, but yes, Mountbatten. 'His mother's family. They were German and English. But Philip's father was a Greek prince. And his mother, Princess Alice, she was a very good woman. She became a Greek Orthodox.'

'Really?'

'Yes. She was very religious. She was a nun. And she lived in Athens all through the war. The others went to South Africa – the Greeks kicked them out anyway, they weren't really Greek – but Princess Alice wanted to help the Greek people. She wanted to do good.'

'Nicky really should be taking you, Mum. It is time he introduced you to the royal family.'

She insisted she didn't want to go. 'Your father was all for that sort of thing, kings and queens. I'm not interested. Anyway, I've told you, he hasn't invited me.'

Not Speaking

'And by the way,' Tina reminded Nicky, 'you do know, don't you, that Dad got the equivalent of the OBE at the end of the war. It was called the BEM, the British Empire Medal.'

None of us had known this until after he died. It was not something he ever spoke about.

Nicky's girlfriend at the time was interior designer Kelly Hoppen. They had met at a party at Elton John's house. The *Evening Standard* explained that on the day of the investiture of the OBE Lesley would accompany Britain's leading hairdresser (a haircut now cost £450) to the ceremony, along with Tilly and Harrison, while Kelly was in charge of the post-Palace party at Nicky's house.

The invitation Kelly had sent out amusingly depicted the 'significant people' in Nicky's life: Kelly, his mother and father, sisters and brothers, children, and a few close friends. Lesley did not feature. She wasn't invited to the party that followed the investiture. The *Evening Standard* reminded readers that she lived only five doors away.

Nicky did invite his mother to the ceremony, however. She's in the photographs ('everybody else so tall and me so short') and she can also be seen in the DVD that the Palace helpfully produces for sale on these occasions, each one tailored to the individual recipient. 'There's you,' Nicky said, pointing, 'in the audience, look, that's you, fast asleep.'

Human life in the *Iliad* is a never-ending battle driven by anger and ruled by the gods. Achilles displays various types of anger: his fury at Agamemnon's military incompetence is distinct from the insult he feels when Agamemnon demands Briseis, and different again from the rage that rises when his beloved Patroclus is killed by Hector. Achilles is a warrior and has been fighting for almost a decade in the Greek siege of

Troy. But to tell the story Homer doesn't begin with the siege, nor show Achilles in his armour until the very end. Homer gives us a trivial quarrel that erupts in the ninth year of the war, a sequence of events lasting less than two months, and a man whose emotions are hot and unpredictable.

The gods stir up rage in men but they also quarrel amongst themselves, like men. They're all-powerful, and yet full of fear. A recurring motif in Greek myth is the fear of parricide. Kronos attacks his father Uranus and slices off his genitals. (The Furies grow from the drops of blood that fall on the earth.) Kronos subsequently fears that his children will murder him, and so he swallows them at birth – all except Zeus who is saved by his grandmother. (The others, Poseidon and Hades, are regurgitated.) Zeus will not marry Thetis because of a prophecy that she will give birth to a man greater than his father: she weds Peleus, a mortal, and gives birth to Achilles. Priam takes against his newborn son Paris and exposes him on the mountain because of a prophecy that he will bring disaster to Troy. Shepherds rescue Paris and he grows up tending flocks until his princely lineaments are recognised and he is restored to the palace, ready to fall in love with Helen and set in train the eventual destruction of Troy.

In the *Iliad* Zeus is the eldest son who, in the sharing out of the inheritance, was given the skies as his special domain, while Poseidon was given the seas, and Hades the murky darkness of the underworld. The earth was common to all three, hence the squabbles about territories and privileges. Poseidon resents Zeus's assumption of superiority; he has no intention of obeying him. Poseidon wants Troy destroyed and will whip up a storm to help the Greeks if he chooses. Zeus is supporting the Trojans. (But the gods are capricious and will shift their allegiance on a whim.) Iris, the messenger, urges Poseidon to be more yielding: she doesn't want to take his fierce answer

Not Speaking

back to Zeus. She reminds the younger brother that elder brothers have 'guardian fiends' and must not be insulted. Poseidon furiously plunges into the sea.

These guardian fiends are the Furies. They are goddesses of retribution who punish serious crimes. Hesiod gives the story in his *Theogony*. Aeschylus, coming along later in the sixth century BCE, put the Furies in his trilogy of plays, the *Oresteia*, which tells of Agamemnon's return home from Troy. Troy fell, but any love Agamemnon's wife Clytemnestra felt for him had turned to hatred early in his absence because of the decision he took to sacrifice their daughter, Iphigenia. Clytemnestra, with her lover Aegisthus, kills Agamemnon. Some years later Orestes, their son, comes to avenge his father's death. His sister, Electra, recognises the lock of hair he has placed on his father's tomb: it is like her own. Orestes kills his mother and her lover. The Furies pursue Orestes. They want to drink his blood.

The Greeks invented tragedy and they located it in the family. They understood the extreme feelings of mothers, fathers, sons, daughters, sisters, brothers, and the conflicts that might arise. The stories were mythological and therefore remote, but the loves and hatreds, fears and hopes, were immediately human. Nothing, it seems, was off-limits to the Greek imagination.

Of course, the Greeks also invented comedy. The Greek god of comedy is Gelos, the word for laughter. Even in the tragedies there are light moments – generally in scenes given to lower-class characters. Aristophanes wrote racy comedies with lots of sexual innuendo and scatological jokes. Aristotle in his *Poetics* describes comedy as a kind of farce, where the audience laughs at ugly or foolish people blundering about and getting things wrong.

Majorca: the Anchorage

Arrangements for Majorca in the summer after the OBE were complicated. Lesley was having a hip operation and wanted to spend some time convalescing at the Anchorage, their usual holiday destination west of Palma, but didn't know exactly when she would feel strong enough to travel. Nicky and Kelly Hoppen planned a fortnight in Ibiza. Nicky booked an apartment for Rena at the Anchorage but, worried about leaving her alone, offered to take her to Ibiza for part of their stay. 'We've got a huge villa,' he urged, because she wasn't keen. 'There's plenty of room. There'll be lots of other people. Sienna and Savannah are coming for some of the time.' Sienna and Savannah were Kelly Hoppen's stepdaughters. Mum had never met them but Nicky thought they would be good company. He could arrange for Mum to fly to Majorca from Ibiza. Tilly could fly with her. Nicky might want to stay on Ibiza longer. Depending.

'Depending on what?'

'Just depending,' he said. 'See if Linda, or Norma, or Tina can go to Majorca and keep you company.'

'Depending on what?'

'Well, depending a bit on what Lesley does.'

Not Speaking

'Is Lesley going to Majorca?'

'At some point, yes.'

'Are you going?'

'Yes.'

She gave him a scornful look. 'If Lesley lets you.'

'It's not about if "Lesley lets me." It's about sharing.'

The terms of Nicky's sharing meant that Kelly was not welcome in the neighbourhood of the Anchorage whether Lesley was likely to be there or not.

Rena agreed to go to Ibiza with Nicky and Kelly Hoppen and 'lots of other people' for a week. I agreed to go to Majorca for the week following. Linda agreed to take over from me, stay a week at the Anchorage, and travel back with Mum at the end. We were 'taking the strain off Nicky'.

Anticipating the strain on myself having already done this once before, I resolved to make it a project. I would use the opportunity to quiz my mother on her early years. I was the self-designated family historian, I scolded myself, and yet I still knew remarkably little about my mother's childhood and growing up in Greece. I needed to systematically record her memories. True, this was the resolution I made the first time and it hadn't worked out, daily life having kept us fully occupied. In between cooking, swimming and keeping a check on Nicky and charting how much we saw of him, and complaining about deficiencies in housekeeping (light bulbs, electric sockets that didn't work, water supply), Rena had had much to narrate about the more immediate history of her summers in Majorca. Arm in arm we'd walked the Anchorage grounds while she pointed out the different (better) apartments she'd stayed at, and where other members of the family had stayed at different times. Each location had its story or stories, grooved by repeated telling. Most I'd already heard, and I'd seen the countless photos that recorded the years of Majorcan

Majorca: the Anchorage

holidays: tanned smiling faces, swimsuits, dark glasses, restaurant tables, the prow of someone's boat, a beach, the pool. 'This one,' she stopped in an archway, indicating the nearest of two doors, 'is where Michael stayed the summer that Linda spent a week with them, helping to look after the little girls.' Michael and his ex, Frances, had four girls. We joked that Michael had been trying to rival his Greek grandfather in the number of daughters. Beyond the archway, down a staircase and past a clump of pines was the apartment Tina and Lee once rented when their children were small – 'this was the swimming pool they liked'. There were many apartments Nicky had taken over the years. I was specially shown the big one they'd all once shared, Mum and Dad in one bedroom, Nicky and Lesley in another, the children in a third. (I was impressed by that – wow – full marks to everyone.) For Nicky's children the Anchorage had been a second home: every summer they ran with a gang of English children who in term-time were at schools like St Paul's, Highgate, Harrow, Eton.

It was easy to understand why Nicky came back year after year, and why he and Lesley were in the process of buying an apartment that they could take turns to occupy and which would give the children a base to return to. The setting was beautiful. Climbing above a rocky bay, carefully landscaped, the buildings were all of a piece: soft orange and pink stucco, with Spanish colonial decoration and green or blue wooden shutters. Bougainvillea draped from balconies. Out on the water, pretty boats clinked and blinked. Along the paths and walkways, around the pools, gardeners discreetly manicured all day long, and at night guards no less discreetly patrolled.

Nor was it hard to understand why Mum wanted to keep on with the annual routine now Dad wasn't here. Under the Mediterranean sun and with a simple rhythm of days, with

Not Speaking

nights out at lively restaurants where they were known and the staff welcomed her, she could easily have been in Greece, although why she wasn't in Greece – or rather, why Nicky had chosen to make Spain and not Greece his regular holiday destination, and if that was a conscious choice, I didn't know.

Our slow walks were like a royal progress. We stopped to talk to a variety of individuals, none of them named: they were 'darling' or 'dear'; I was 'this is my daughter'. To some she explained, 'I lost my husband,' and received condolences. All were addressed in Rena's version of English that sometimes bemused. Afterwards, as we walked away, she filled me in with biographical details and accompanying commentary.

Her memory, she proudly believed, was excellent and comprehended everything. When I frowned blankly at some story she would say, 'What do you mean you don't remember? What's wrong with you?' Her interpretation of events was invariably shrewd, as it had always been, and lacking in empathy – and that, too, was as it had always been: the notion that you might see something from the other person's point of view was not only 'stupid' but somehow suspect.

I liked it when she said, pointing out a pretty path alongside the tennis court, 'Your father and I went this way down to the beach', or, 'Your father always liked to buy the paper and we would walk and have a coffee', and it gratified me to be able to say, 'I like to buy the paper, too, we can walk down to the village and have a coffee', for it made me feel like a dutiful daughter sharing memories with her sweet, old, widowed mum.

Our circumnavigation generally brought us to Nicky's apartment and I generally saw it as my task to prevent her knocking on his door.

'Don't you want to say hello?'

'No. We'll see him later.'

Majorca: the Anchorage

'We don't know what we're doing later.'

'We never know what we're doing later, but we will know, later.'

Sometimes she would agree and walk peaceably away from temptation. She made it clear she was only doing so for me: it was her version of being well-behaved as a mother in accordance with what I insisted on in my role as well-behaved daughter. Other times she felt she needed to set me a better example. 'What are you afraid of?' she would say, knocking boldly. He was her son. If she wanted to knock on his door she would knock on his door.

I hadn't rented a car the first time. Some of the strain that ensued had been about groceries – her need to pile the supermarket trolley high, our difficulty in getting it home. We took taxis, but she was adamant that no taxi driver was to be allowed a tip and watched vehemently to enforce her rule. Mostly I ignored her, and the bad temper that followed. Or we waited indoors for Nicky to drive us to the shopping centre at Porto Pi at an agreed hour, a mistake if ever there was one. I knew better second time around. With our own car we would be able to organise our time freely and, as my mother put it, 'see something of the island'. She was critical of what she considered Nicky's unadventurous spirit. 'He's been coming here for years and he knows nothing except restaurants and clubs.' Before leaving London I read up on Robert Graves at Deya in the 1930s and about French novelist George Sand and Frederic Chopin in the 1830s at the monastery at Valldemossa. A monastery seemed a good bet for a day out.

It pleased me, picking up the car at the airport and stowing bags that were heavy with books, to drive along the coast road knowing roughly what I was heading into. Nicky had not arrived yet – he was in Ibiza until the end of the week. Lesley was in residence, along with Tilly. There would be an

Not Speaking

assortment of young people to chat to at the café by the water's edge, under the shade of the umbrellas and in the intervals between swimming and working.

The apartment that year was one we would stay in for several succeeding summers and I became fond of it, but our stay did not begin auspiciously. My mother opened the door to me and from her lips issued a stream of complaint. Everything was 'rubbish'. The water supply was erratic, most of the plugs didn't work and, 'You can't see the sea when you sit on the terrace.'

But what was really rubbish, I intuited, was that she had been put on a plane and dumped in Majorca when Nicky was still in Ibiza, with another woman.

She had arrived from Ibiza the day before. She didn't have much good to say about it. Yes, Sienna Miller was there. It was, 'Parties, nothing but parties.' But I could tell she had enjoyed herself. Nicky's friend Adrian and Adrian's Italian mother were among the company; they had been her gang, and although she was doing her best to hide it she was still glowing from Adrian's attentiveness and what I guessed was full-on deference from everybody else. She was polite at first about Kelly. 'I don't dislike her.' 'If Nicky's happy.' But a little quiet reflection confirmed that Nicky was stupid after all. There had been a dinner at a restaurant for a great crowd of people, 'and none of them put their hands in their pockets. Kelly said, "Nicky will pay!" Nicky paid. Stupid.'

We sat at the table on the terrace. The apartment was set a little way back and there were trees between us and the sea, but you could catch glimpses of the water and hear it softly susurrating. She had made an egg and lemon soup and a dish of meatballs, and she put out cheese, Serrano ham, olives and salad and bread, apologising that she hadn't made a proper meal. The litany of complaint continued.

Majorca: the Anchorage

'Mum, is there any white wine in the fridge?'

There was white wine but not in the fridge. I put a bottle of *Vina Sol* in the freezer.

'Your uncle Pericles did that once and forgot about it,' she said disapprovingly. 'Pouf! It went everywhere.'

'But I don't intend to forget about it.'

The apartment was spacious and comfortably furnished. Everything was white: sofa, armchairs, table cloths, paintwork, television stand, chest of drawers, bust of Greek god, giant china fruit bowls and vast china plant holders and the pillars upon which they stood. The table lamps were white, as were the candles in the chandeliers (three chandeliers in the sitting room). On the terrace were two large white china dogs. What couldn't be white was glass – the crystal in the chandeliers, mirrors (quite a few), drinks table – or blue: vases and decorative plates. I found these Greek colours pleasing, but I was concerned about the electrics since I needed to charge up my laptop and phone. 'Are you sure the plugs don't work?'

'Rubbish. It's all rubbish.'

I went round testing. Most of the sockets were fine.

There were two bedrooms and two bathrooms. In my bedroom I cleared the dressing table and set up my laptop and books. I was glad I'd brought the books.

I had researched Princess Alice of Greece and discovered there was a biography by Hugo Vickers. This I displayed prominently. The standard historical work on Greece under the Nazis is *Inside Hitler's Greece: The Experience of Occupation, 1941-44*, by Mark Mazower. I had the paperback with a photograph of Nazi soldiers in front of the Acropolis on its cover and I put it next to Princess Alice. These I expected my mother to pick up and ask me about, but she never did. I'd read a biography of the travel writer Patrick Leigh Fermor by Artemis Cooper and brought one of Leigh Fermor's books,

Roumeli, along with an old favourite I planned to re-read, Edward Trelawny's *Records of Shelley, Byron and the Author*. Trelawny was a nineteenth-century, gun-loving adventurer about whom scholars of Shelley and Byron are invariably sniffy. (Can we trust what an action man says about poets?) Trelawny was in Italy when Shelley drowned off the coast at Leghorn and helped burn the poet's body on the beach, and he travelled with Byron to Missolonghi where Byron died of fever. Patrick Leigh Fermor tells a story about finding Byron's slippers in a remote Greek village and I hoped Trelawny might shed light on that. (He doesn't.) I also had a book about the British army in Greece, *Scobie, Hero of Greece: The British Campaign, 1944-45* by Henry Maule. My father was in the Royal Army Ordnance Corps under Scobie's command in Athens when he met and married my mother. These were my essentials. In addition I had George Sand's *A Winter in Majorca* and Robert Graves' *The White Goddess*, along with William Graves' *Wild Olives, Life in Majorca with Robert Graves*; and on my laptop and Kindle: Pope's *Iliad* and *The Rape of the Lock*; Henry Miller's *The Colossus of Maroussi* (another old favourite I didn't get round to re-reading); *The Slap* by Christos Tsiolkas, a Greek-Australian novelist, which I did read, marvelling at how exactly he captured the cadences of a Greek mother's speech; *Eleni* by Nicholas Gage, about tracing the fate of his Greek mother, killed by the Nazis; the works of Euripides, including *Medea* and *The Trojan Women*; and the complete works of Shakespeare, Dickens, Tolstoy, George Eliot and – especially – Jane Austen in case things got desperate.

Rena had a matching dressing table in her bedroom across from mine at the end of a small passage. She set up her icons

Majorca: the Anchorage

and holy candle and incense burner. Like me, she piled her reading material: saints' lives, prayers, miracles.

My resolution to make notes about her childhood, family and young womanhood in Greece was again confounded. There was too much still to be said about Ibiza. I wrote some of that instead.

In Ibiza Rena had found herself a privileged witness to her son's sex life, and it had been a mixture of unexpected bonus and poisoned chalice. In the mornings, as we drank our coffee on the terrace after she'd finished praying, she launched into a full review. Bit by bit she divested herself, but it took time. 'Nicky's still in touch with Octavia,' she might begin, as if she hadn't told me this the day before and as if it was something I urgently needed to know. Octavia now lived on Ibiza. Nicky had taken over some hair products for her. 'And Octavia phoned him, when Kelly wasn't there, and he went to see her. He had sex with her you can be sure. *And* he's got someone in Palma. I asked him. He was going to try to come over to Majorca for a few days. He said he had to talk to Lesley. Do you think Kelly will let him do that? I don't think so. Why does he want to speak to Lesley? He can speak to her in London. I tell you, he's got a woman in Palma. I said to him, Nicky, have you got somebody in Palma? Yes Mum, he said. But don't tell anybody.' (There was no 'woman in Palma'.)

In the pause, as I had nothing to contribute, she dipped her bread into her coffee and ruminated. 'Nicky's mind was always on girls. When we were in Greece one summer there was a young woman who was interested in Paul. Paul was eighteen. The woman wanted Paul to go to her house but he was shy. Nicky, twelve years old, said, 'I'll go,' and I had to tell him he wouldn't do.'

My mother, knowing nothing about Freud, wasn't a bit embarrassed to say, 'I had such a funny dream. I dreamed Nicky

Not Speaking

was my boyfriend. Octavia was in the dream somewhere. And I was trying to make Michael jealous. What was that about?'

A few steps from our front door was a semi-circular swimming pool, the largest and nicest of the five pools distributed over the Anchorage enclosure. A beautiful trio of tall palms rose above the arched wooden bridge separating the paddling basin from the main swimming area. In the morning it was fresh and in the evening the sun lit the trunks of the low growing palms and glinted among the oleanders, the pines towered and the firs made a lovely dark backdrop. The bougainvillea, starting to brown, still flashed purple.

We first saw Lesley in the pool, doing her exercises and being helped by a friend. The crutch was lying alongside. She hobbled out and we admired her neat scar and discussed the operation on her left hip. 'The doctors swore I'd be leaping about after six weeks,' she told us glumly.

'All lies,' Mum said. 'It'll be a year at least.'

Lesley came by after dinner and we had late night drinks on the terrace. She was wearing a beautiful low cut orange evening gown, clipped at the cleavage with a massive silver knot of a brooch. Her bracelets were heavy silver and diamonds and there was a silver choker round her neck. She was a vision of glamour and loveliness, albeit on a crutch, a wonder to behold, especially considering she had merely gone to the local restaurant for dinner and had come to call on us and sit on our terrace. Her presence lit up a dull evening for my mother. Of course Lesley wanted to hear all about Nicky and Kelly in Ibiza, and there had been only half the enjoyment in bitching to me about it. Lesley was accomplished in following our mother's narratives. She knew that someone scathingly dismissed as 'that woman with the funny mouth' or 'that man who didn't put his hand in his pocket' was probably an uber-celebrity or multimillionaire. She could fill in the gaps, just as

Majorca: the Anchorage

the rest of the family did. By the time the *Vina Sol* was drunk Lesley's virtuous beauty had put everything into perspective and the two of them were laughing uproariously as they agreed it was a mystery how Nicky could even bear to look at her (they leaned their heads towards each other, collusively) let alone anything else.

The morning being the best time, I would get up early, make tea and take my laptop out to the terrace. I could usually be sure of three or four hours before my mother appeared and started talking. On the subject of Nicky and Lesley or Nicky and Kelly she was inexhaustible. She needed no prompts, the monologue was ever her natural form; she was a one-woman Greek chorus. Of other subjects, the two that predominated were money and miracles. She wanted to rewrite her will when she returned to London. Her bank-books had always been among her treasures but now, annoyingly, the bank tellers no longer wrote down how much money she had. She liked contemplating the figures – if it were gold sovereigns she would have piled them up in front of her – and so she had taken to calling in at the different banks to ask them to update her books. She wanted to be sure we would be able to find her money 'if anything happened'. The sums were substantial, and growing.

'You know where we go for coffee in Marks & Spencer?'

I do.

'Well just round the corner from there... not far. It's a little building.'

'Do you happen to know the name?'

'And in another place, across the road.'

'Where exactly?'

She could give neither directions nor a name.

'And of course there's that bank near Michael.'

Michael had chosen these accounts for her, so I was relaxed

Not Speaking

about the details. Her money was for her children. It was to be divided equally between all six of us, although she wasn't sure if it was a good idea to give it to Paul (the most financially needy) because he was an alcoholic, and Nicky and Michael had both told her at different times they didn't expect her to leave them anything. 'I hope I live a long time but you never know, and when you die is up to God,' she would say contentedly every time she returned to the subject, which was often. Meanwhile, Lesley had been encouraging her to spend the proceeds from the sale of the Heygate house. 'Go on another holiday,' Lesley said. 'Don't worry about leaving it to us, you enjoy it while you've got it.'

Mum says darkly, 'She wants to get rid of me.'

I think that Lesley, quite reasonably, is telling her to spend her own money. But Lesley must know by now that Mum's pleasure is in banking her money and spending Nicky's.

I say, 'Does Tina know where these accounts are?'

'Not yet, but I'll tell her.'

I'm sure Michael has already discussed it all with Tina.

'So long as Tina and Michael have the details,' I say, 'there won't be any problems locating the money.'

'Yes,' she says dubiously and then laughs. 'But don't tell Nicky.'

The phrase 'don't tell Nicky' that still trips so easily off her tongue comes with the same frisson of pleasurable guilt as the now redundant 'don't tell your father'.

We go to the beach at midday, putting on our costumes and wraps and making our way slowly down between villas and apartments beside well-kept borders and neat lawns. She doesn't swim so she can't go into the deep water by the ladder on the rocks, and the Anchorage beach is pebbly, so we walk over to the bay alongside, a route that involves awkward footwork over broken concrete. 'Your father always helped me

Majorca: the Anchorage

over this bit,' she says, holding out her hand to me. 'When I come down here it reminds me of him.'

We pad over the hot sand and find a place to put our things. She can't sit down easily and here there are no loungers. We walk into the sea. She goes in up to her armpits. She loves the sea.

'Why didn't you learn to swim?'

'My mother would stand on the beach and when the water went over our ankles she started crying, "Poppy, Irrenoula, come back, don't go in so deep." No wonder I never learned to swim. Your father tried to teach me.'

Swimming was one of Dad's great pleasures. He knew all the public pools within reach of Old Kent Road and Elephant and Castle. He taught each of us to swim, taking us regularly to Walworth Road baths, Grange Road baths, or the open-air pool in Southwark Park. These expeditions were walking expeditions, never by bus, but on the return journey we got a bun or pastry from the bakery. Swimming made you properly hungry, and that accounted for his unusual deviation from the rule of not spending money if it could be avoided.

I swim far out to the boats, showing off, loving the movement, feeling grateful to be strong and fit and confident in the water. My mother watches me, then she talks to the people around her and joins in whatever fun is going, laughing as the children jump off their fathers' shoulders, flicking back the odd beach ball, smiling at the lovers. Her zest for life in her mid-eighties is undiminished. I'm surprised she couldn't learn to swim. Then I reflect that learning to swim, like swimming itself, involves trust.

Don't tell your father.

I think Nicky achieved something remarkable when he began inviting our parents to join him on holiday. I think they were happy in Majorca as a couple. Mum's tone whenever she recalls their daily routine is full of affection. And credit, too, to Lesley and the children. It was a family effort. It can't always have been easy.

I make a wide loop and swim round to the far side of a sleek anchored boat flying a German flag. On deck are a middle-aged couple, seated at a small table. It occurs to me that the same was probably true of the cruises that Nicky and Michael competed to provide. The subtext was an enforced coupledom. It would be hard to live separate lives on board ship, and out at sea our parents were a couple.

'Your father used to say to me,' Rena said with a shy expression as we left the beach, 'that it was nice, sometimes, when we were alone, to be alone, without any children to worry about.'

Lesley goes back to London. Nicky arrives from Ibiza. In the evenings we put on bling and go to a restaurant. Or Nicky cooks. Or we cook. We are family. It seems we do everything en masse. Wherever we go he is recognised. People ask for autographs and to take photos. They are polite and pleasant, apologising for disturbing him. He is obliging. We wait.

'When they come up to tell me they hate me,' he explains, when I ask if he minds, 'then I expect I'll feel differently. But while they're being nice why shouldn't I be nice back?'

We are part of the entourage. I enjoy this, it feels like a holiday from myself. What I don't enjoy is being absorbed into the cost. Nicky pays. Nicky pays for everything.

I go back to London. Linda and her partner Geoff arrive for a week. Linda and I establish a pattern that continues for many years. Barbara joins in; she comes, too, and we both stay with Rena in the white apartment. Tina helps out with planning but becomes increasingly unenthusiastic about taking

Majorca: the Anchorage

a shift; she will agree to do half a week if Lee, who is filming in Poland, or Hungary, or Morocco, can get away for a few days and meet her there but she would rather book a holiday with Mum somewhere else. Michael, maintaining a little distance, stays at a hotel near Pollensa and drives down for dinner some evenings. One year Mum persuades Nicky to fly Paul over; it will do him good. Nicky arranges it.

Kelly Hoppen is replaced by Kelly Simpkin ('young Kelly', younger than Kelly Hoppen and a lot younger than Nicky). It is confusing at first but everybody likes her, and when I write 'Nicky arranges it' the truth is that most of the arranging is done by Kelly. Even our mother agrees that Kelly is good for Nicky. She tells me confidently that she is sure he has given up 'that woman in Palma'. She thinks he may settle down.

As the years go by we see less of Lesley. Young Kelly becomes a fixture. Young Kelly becomes family, and what is most surprising to me is that my mother shows no inclination to gossip maliciously about her.

Majorca: Deya

Deya is a mountain hamlet between Valldemossa and Soller, north-west of Palma. Nicky knows about it because Richard Branson once owned La Residencia, the luxury hotel where Diana, Princess of Wales retreated after the breakdown of her marriage to Prince Charles. Nicky has partied with Branson and knows other rich people who have bought villas in or near Deya. But he doesn't know quite where Deya is, nor how long it will take us to drive there.

I know about Deya because it was where Robert Graves, poet, author of *The White Goddess* and of one of the best First World War memoirs, *Goodbye to All That*, as well as of many historical fictions set in ancient Greece or Rome, such as *The Anger of Achilles*, *Homer's Daughter*, *I, Claudius* and *Claudius the God*, and much much else, settled in the 1930s. In its remote fastness he built a house and established a little English colony – wives, children, girlfriends ('muses'), admirers, hangers-on.

Nicky is surprised it is so near. 'Everybody told me it was an hour and twenty minutes' drive away! What was all that about?'

'Twenty-five kilometres, it says in the guide book.'

It is to be a brief outing as we've started late and need to be

Not Speaking

back by four but it amuses Nicky to take me to Magaluf on the way (it's not on the way) and point out PJ's Bar and Fred's Fish and Chips which he thinks I'll be snobby about. Mum sits contentedly in the front seat; she's next to Nicky, she has his attention. We wait in the car while he collects his dry cleaning and then goes into the supermarket alongside. He comes out with bottles of water and an armful of newspapers including the *Guardian*, handing this to me muttering, 'You leftie types.'

Nicky is not a 'leftie type'. Among the subjects we (or at least I) avoid discussing are Ken Livingstone, Labour leader of the Greater London Council (GLC) in the 1980s and Mayor of London from 2000 to 2008, in particular Livingstone's introduction of congestion charges, and indeed anything to do with traffic laws that stop people parking where they like when they like for as long as they like.

'Robert Graves used to have *The Times* airmailed in from London and read it at the same café every day at Deyá,' I say, pleased to have the *Guardian*, pleased to be in the back seat of Nicky's car, looking forward to seeing the landscape and thinking my own thoughts.

For over forty years Robert Graves, a tall and commanding figure – 'like an ancient Greek God' according to one of his numerous progeny – lorded it up at Deyá. He was 'Don Roberto', the *senyor* to some of the locals and a mad foreigner to others. In more or less constant residence amongst the Catholic villagers, many of whom looked askance at the goings-on, he never integrated. His house (the 'cottage'), with Aga installed in the kitchen, his orchard and garden and terraced field under the hillside with a Greek-style amphitheatre complete with proscenium arch for annual amateur dramatics, was an English bohemian fiefdom. The profits from *I, Claudius* and other books on ancient history and myths as well as some lucrative film deals paid for it. Graves worked tirelessly. He published over fifty separate volumes of poetry along with the prose works that were his bread and butter. But however much money he earned, he never had enough, according to his biographer Miranda Seymour. Graves had a 'weakness', she writes, 'the generous and proud one of wanting to play the role of general provider. The friends who visited Deya were told to put all their local purchases on his account and were offered daily hospitality… If he went out for a meal in Palma with friends, it was always he who paid the bill.' He liked to lead 'an open-handed way of life'.

I say this last out loud. Nicky doesn't hear me.

Graves had a gift for the popular. His writing was lively and immediate, never pompous. He leavened the scholar's voice with a personal note now and then, and always aimed for clarity. He had a singular view about the *Iliad*, arguing that it was a satire rather than a solemn tragedy. Homer, he explained in an interview with Kenneth Allsop, was an iconoclast with a deep sense of irony whose satirical purposes had been 'consistently misunderstood'. Graves regarded Hector as the hero and saw in Achilles 'the real villain of the piece'. His prose translation, *The Anger of Achilles: The Iliad*, was judged by one reviewer to be 'the most charming translation' since that of Pope, which may not have pleased Graves since he loathed Pope, as he loathed all eighteenth-century English poets. (They were too 'rational' in his view, their poetry had no 'magic'.) His novel, *Homer's Daughter*, posited that a Sicilian princess, Nausicaa, was in fact the author of the *Odyssey*. This was in keeping with the high valuation Graves accorded women and his conviction that Western society had taken a wrong turn in ancient times when the patriarchal system became institutionalised.

Not Speaking

Classicists can be sniffy about Graves; Graves seems to have enjoyed upsetting them. He ranted against literary scholars in universities and mocked poets he considered barely poets at all. Invited to give the Clark Lectures in Cambridge in 1954, he attacked everybody: Milton, Pope, Dryden ('How university professors hate me!'), and his own contemporaries: Yeats, Pound, Eliot, Dylan Thomas. He delighted in being contrary, mischievous, outrageous. He was called a philistine, which was nonsense, and vain and boastful, which probably wasn't.

Deya gave Graves what he wanted as a writer. It met his requirements: 'sun, sea, mountains, spring water, shady trees, no politics and a few civilised luxuries such as electric light and a bus service to Palma.' The island had little industry; it was still ruled by the old agricultural cycle. Graves thought of himself as a guest, the perfect guest, using his influence to keep mass tourism at bay (tourism had already presented itself as a threat by the 1950s) and protect his precious tranquillity. While some locals would have welcomed development, Graves was reassured that Majorca had few exploitable attractions. There was nothing to hang an advertisement on. Bad roads and difficult access to the sea helped. It was a sign of desperation, in his opinion, that George Sand's association with Valldemossa was being touted in tourist literature.

Robert Graves produced a little book about the island, *Majorca Observed*, but the book is rare and the English bookshop in Palma didn't have a copy. What I had instead, and had read in preparation for our visit, was *The White Goddess*, Graves' profound and detailed study of ancient myths which he wrote after he returned to Majorca at the end of the Second World War; and the remarkable memoir, *Wild Olives: Life in*

Majorca: Deya

Majorca with Robert Graves, by Graves' son, William, the first of four children by his second wife, Beryl.

The White Goddess knits up broken strands of myth, legend and fragmentary scraps of prehistory – movements of peoples, transporting of stories – to argue that before Christianity with its emphasis on God the Father, even before the Greek philosophers of sixth century BCE Athens, in Minoan times and earlier, the language of poetic myth in the Mediterranean and Northern Europe was a magical language bound up with popular religious ceremonies in honour of the Moon-Goddess, or Muse. This was the language of true poetry, and it had been lost when patrilineal institutions squeezed out the matrilineal and then – here is where Graves is so much fun to read – falsified the myths to fit the new story. Ancient Greek philosophers were opposed to magical poetry and lent their weight to a rational poetic language devoted to understanding the social world and the self. Plato wanted no poets in his ideal republic. Poets were fantasists; and myths, so far as Plato and Socrates were concerned, were 'absurdities'. Robert Graves, by contrast, insisted that myths were records of religious customs and events lost in deep time.

Graves believed that true poets got their inspiration from the female principle. Male logic and reason produced clever witty verses like those of Pope, but true poets served the goddess. Faithful to his calling as a poet, Graves found his matriarchal Moon-goddess muse in a sequence of young women whose presence in his life and bed he deemed essential. The American poet Laura Riding was the first and most significant of these. Absolute subjection to the goddess was the rule, poetry the reward.

Beryl apparently accepted that she would share her husband in the cause of the greater good: his genius and true poetry.

Not Speaking

Biographers describe Beryl as 'wonderful', a clever, kind, calm and stable presence.

William Graves writes about coming to Deya in 1946, a small boy in an English household growing up 'in the shadow' of the great writer. To begin with he went to the local school and learned about himself and the world alongside children from the village. This included what the village thought about his father. It can't have been easy. There were many stories about the *senyor* and his girls. Of his mother, William commented after her death that while she had been affectionate she was 'so very private I could never get through to her on any but a superficial level.' Affection didn't extend to intimacy. His father was affectionate too, but dominating, powerful, very controlling, selfish, and obsessed with his muses.

At puberty or thereabouts young William was sent away to public school in England, even though Robert Graves had written critically of his own public school experiences in *Goodbye to All That*. England wasn't home to William. Majorca couldn't give him a living. It was a dilemma. He became a petroleum engineer and travelled the world. But he liked Majorcan life. He came back; he bought a hotel. By the 1980s development had proceeded apace. Roads were built, villas multiplied, tourists flocked. In 2006 William opened up the house his father had built, Canellun – 'the faraway home' – to the public as a museum, complete with original furnishings, some manuscripts, and the narrow single bed where the poet had slept with his wife and girlfriends.

Like others, some of whom have read the books, some not (there is now a small library of Graves family memoirs and Graves-themed books, as well as a Robert Graves Society and a scholarly journal, *Gravesiana*), we drive into the mountains to see a certain kind of Englishness on display. Nicky tells us he first came to Majorca when he was John Frieda's junior, his imagination saturated in glamour and fame. John was with Lulu and Nicky was going out with Lulu's sister Edwina. His talk recalling those days – 'I was only seventeen!' – is full of excitement: days on the water, nights in clubs, shops, clothes, rich men's boats, and little restaurants in hidden coves. Majorca was the apotheosis of play. It was what money bought you when you had enough of it.

'When you were first with Edwina, you lived in Norwood,' I say, but what I'm thinking about is how different Nicky's Majorca was to Robert Graves', or perhaps how alike.

'Not for long.'

'You had a garden party and you were trying to cut the grass with your scissors because you didn't have a lawn mower.'

'Really?'

'You must remember.'

Nicky doesn't remember doing anything as daft as that.

Mostly what I recall is the screaming rows with Mum because he had wanted to leave home and she thought he was too young. She did everything she could to stop him going, except allow his girlfriend to stay the night.

She would never allow girlfriends to stay the night, ever.

We admire the landscape with its tints of olive and pine and rosemary, the citrus groves, the oak trees, and marvel at the vistas of sea and rock that open before us. Deya, the tranquil backwater that had 'hardly changed for hundreds of years', now attracts ever-renewing streams of visitors. Tour buses, tapas bars, souvenir shops abound. Robert Graves' favourite café, where he read *The Times*, is long gone. It has been too much for William Graves and his wife. 'It's like living in *Hello* magazine,' they told the *Telegraph* in December 2007. They found themselves somewhere else, a remote village on the mainland of Spain, north of Madrid.

A literary tourist in a house I have paid to enter, I think about

Not Speaking

privacy and parents, selfishness and its many justifications, secrecy and exposure – whose secrets? Whose exposure? Was William Graves right to write so honestly and well about his parents? (He does write wonderfully well about the difficulties of life as their son.) What were the ethics here? Whose experience mattered? Did death change the values? Robert Graves died in 1985, after many years of senility and sickness, and Beryl in 2003. Their eldest son's voyage of self-discovery was published ten years after his father's death but while Beryl was still alive. What did Beryl think about it? Did Beryl's sense of privacy come naturally or was it conditioned by marriage to a self-mythologising and much-mythologised public man? What would she have thought about the display of her life in the house three years after her death? Was that a question worth asking? What did the siblings think about each other's writing, each other's versions of events? To whom did the material belong? How was possession established, boundaries drawn? What wars were fought, what peace found?

When I prompt my mother to tell me more about her life, to retell episodes she has already told me, as I listen for the small details that accumulate and sometimes change the entire meaning or logic of an event by altering the focus, as I mentally shape the story, am I doing her a service or stealing from her?

I believe that by bringing to her life a quality of attention hitherto reserved for my studies I have come to know her better and respect her more. But perhaps, like Robert Graves with his 'muses', I have just made her up to suit my selfish desires; or like William Graves and others found a way to take possession of experiences I didn't own. What happens when you listen hard and invite someone to remember intensely? Whose story unfolds?

I notice that when Nicky reminisces about Majorca in the 1980s with Lulu and John and Edwina, he tells us nothing

Majorca: Deya

he wouldn't also tell *Hello* magazine. Is he being careful and self-censoring, or is that what he would call giving it the full monty?

I notice that my mother will tell perfect strangers the most embarrassing stories about her children. Over the years, at one Majorcan restaurant table after another, old acquaintances and new have been entertained by her unbridled accounts. Nicky seems not to mind this at all, whether he features as the subject of the story or as one of the satellites in a reminiscence that begins, 'My husband…' or 'My daughter…' or 'One day Nicky…' or 'One day Michael…', and ends in peals of laughter. He looks on at her proudly. He loves her and he loves being her son. Her stories put a glow around him. It is uplifting, enriching, being part of what she creates.

Unashamed narcissism has its uses, I think, slightly sourly, reflecting on the good fit between mother and son. But narcissism isn't the only impulse at work because some of the pride depends on belonging, on the fact that the thing created is bigger than the self. The glow comes from the shared history, shared making.

I wonder if I am adding to that or taking away. Will my resolve to write about the family enhance the pride or diminish it, be glue or solvent, or none of the above? Will it matter? Does anybody care? Do I care?

As often happens at this time of year, Mum is fasting. In the Greek Orthodox church, the first two weeks of August leading up to the Festival of the Dormition of the Panagia on 15 August, which Catholics call the Assumption, are a time of strict fasting. The Panagia is the Blessed Virgin, celebrated as the mother of all Greeks. Fasting means abstaining from meat and fish and dairy. Fasting is never easy for Mum because she loves food so much, but she can be resolute. The problem, as we see it, is that she usually fills up on carbohydrates: bread,

Not Speaking

pastries, spaghetti with olive oil. Now, because she's fasting, she doesn't want to go to a restaurant to eat, and time is getting on, so after a quick look round we head back towards Palma. She is dozing. I stare vacantly out of the window thinking about families, mothers and sons.

In chapter six of *The White Goddess*, Graves writes of the annual cycle of growth and decay as expressed in the myth of Osiris, the spirit of the waxing year, and Set, the spirit of the waning year. In this twin-hood, man is divine. But Set murders Osiris every year. So man is only a demi-god; he has one foot in the grave. Woman is divine because she can keep both feet in the same place, be she in the sky, on earth, or in the underworld. 'Man envies her,' Graves writes, 'and tells himself lies about his own completeness, and thereby makes himself miserable.' Woman, meanwhile, worships the male infant; she doesn't worship the grown man. (The worship of the divine child was established in Minoan Crete long before Christianity.) But she retains a passionate interest in grown men because the love–hate Osiris and Set have for each other on her account is a tribute to her divinity.

Graves sees in the rituals and practices of the Catholic Church many signs that pagan beliefs about goddesses were incorporated into Christianity and reworked. He argues that one of the driving forces of the Protestant revolution was hostility towards worship of the Virgin Mary. He doesn't mention the Greek Orthodox Church.

Institutionally, the Greek Orthodox Church is intensely patriarchal. It takes seriously what the Bible says about the necessary supremacy of man over woman, and has no truck with newfangled notions about women priests. In the monasteries on Mount Athos – where Prince Charles used to go for prayer and meditation – women are not allowed to set foot. Robert Graves describes the Christian God as a 'usurping

Majorca: Deya

Father-god' who essentially stole the power of the goddesses, and he saw in medieval Catholicism a Virgin-and-Son dyad that evolved from what he calls Moon-woman and Star-son who are more important than God the father.

We approach a junction and Nicky suddenly swerves off to the right. The sign says 'Andratx'.

'Are you hungry?' he asks me, turning right round in his seat.

It's four o'clock. I'm starving.

'You've got to see Andratx. It's really pretty. Lots of boats and cafés by the water. We'll get a bite.'

'It's four o'clock.'

Nicky waves away concern.

'Aren't you supposed to be back by four?'

'It's OK. We won't be long.'

But four o'clock turns out to be a problem in a different sense. We try several restaurants and in each one the response is the same: sorry, the kitchen is closed. Nicky goes inside to speak with the head waiter. No, not even Nicky can get more than a toasted sandwich and a bit of salad in Andratx at four o'clock in the afternoon.

We sit down to wait and enjoy the view, Moon-woman, Star-son, and me. It's when our toasted ham and cheese sandwiches arrive, just as I'm reminding Nicky that Mum is fasting so she can't eat ham, and he reaches across to open up the sandwich and take out the ham with his fingers, that I notice the little English girls at the table behind us. They're probably about twelve. They're giggling and nudging each other. They've seen Nicky Clarke in Andratx and it's made their day.

Mum eats the sandwich. She explains that she shouldn't eat cheese but the priest has given her permission because she's so old.

Not Speaking

I have tried to find a Greek Orthodox Church in Palma, but failed. There is a Russian Orthodox Church however, and that will do. Rena and I go there one Sunday morning on the bus, a route that takes us through the city to the end of the line.

All the way we talk about fasting. Nicky has been lecturing her about her diet. He has told her she is eating too much carbohydrate and should eat more protein. I have been puzzling over the theological distinction between seafood and fish.

'I thought you said you can't eat fish when you're fasting.'

'Of course not. No fish, no meat, no butter, no cheese.'

'But you had octopus last night.'

'Octopus isn't fish.'

'It comes out of the sea.'

'It's not fish like – *fish* – sea bass, swordfish.'

'You cooked calamari.'

'It's not fish.'

'I don't understand.'

'Never mind.'

Inside the church is cool, darkly colourful. Icons decorate the walls and above us is a glorious dome glittering with gold leaf. As an unbeliever I appreciate it as an aesthetic experience, enjoying the chanting of the priests and the delicacy of the light. I stand straight, my hands out of my pockets. Once, many years ago, a Greek priest in a Greek Orthodox Church in London told me off for keeping my hands in my coat pockets. I was showing a lack of respect, he growled, his surly manner evincing no respect for me. Remembering this – and my annoyance at the time – I feel fraudulent in the company of worshippers.

Never mind. We have made our plans to go to Valldemossa and visit the monastery.

Majorca: Valldemossa

George Sand and Frederic Chopin first met in Paris at the candlelit salon of Franz Liszt's mistress, Marie d'Agoult, on October 24, 1836. They were both celebrities. Sand, who had two children – a boy, Maurice, and a girl, Solange – and was in the process of obtaining a legal separation from her husband, Casimir Dudevant, was six years older than Chopin. Chopin was born in 1810, the same year, as it happened, that saw the birth of Sand's previous lover (well, one of her recent previous lovers) Alfred de Musset, the greatest poet of love in Romantic era France. Chopin, a Polish exile in Paris, told his parents a few days later: 'I've made the acquaintance of a great celebrity, Madame Dudevant, known by the name George Sand.' Chopin's biographers say that she pursued him and he was repelled by her. 'Is she really a woman?' he supposedly asked. Sand's biographers say she was a 'masculine' character, a strong woman, a modern woman born a hundred years too soon, a feminist, a socialist, a hater of religiosity and in love with the idea of progress.

Sand, the famous novelist, and Chopin, the famous composer and pianist, became lovers in the summer of 1838 and shortly afterwards left Paris to spend the winter in Majorca. They were

Not Speaking

hoping for sunshine. Chopin was frail, probably tubercular; and Sand, who told her friends she was willing to take care of him, needed to get away from her son's tutor with whom she had been sleeping and who was tiresomely jealous. They took the children, Maurice fifteen, Solange eleven. They sailed from Barcelona to Palma, arriving on 7 November. It was raining and cold. The children were sick, which was bad enough; but Chopin's sickness was so worrying that nobody wanted to rent property to them and the first landlord who threw them out not only burned the mattress Chopin had slept on but charged them for it afterwards. They had to go deep into the countryside, and that's how they came to rent three rooms in an abandoned monastery in Valldemossa.

In 1838 the Charterhouse at Valldemossa was a three-hour fast drive from Palma along terrifying roads. They travelled in a carriage drawn by mules that galloped down and up steep precipices, through torrents and swamps, over ditches and hedges, into and out of gorges and ravines. The roads were so narrow that two vehicles meeting could not pass. Any journey in Majorca was an obstacle course, they discovered, but since nobody else seemed concerned – least of all the driver who sang the whole time, or sat with folded arms smoking a cigar while one wheel was on the mountain and the other not – Sand decided to be philosophical and contemplate the scenery 'either in expectation of death or in hope of a miracle'.

The scenery was captivating. Sand later wrote that 'nothing could be more beautiful than this neglected terrain'. She loved the uncultivated naturalness, the wild, twisted trees, the thorny brambles, the splendid flowers 'all appearing in the forms God has given them'; the palms and almond trees, the prickly pears, the verdant mountains and tawny rocks, the hues of holm oak, pine, olive, poplar and cypress, and the gorgeousness of the

Majorca: Valldemossa

night, so still, so lovely, that she stayed up till five one morning just breathing it in.

A Winter in Majorca was written as a series of travel articles for a magazine. Sand saw the island's potential as one of the most beautiful and, for French readers of *Revue des Deux Mondes* in 1841, least known places on earth. Switzerland had been drawing writers and artists for half a century. Majorca, in its own way, was no less awe-inspiring, or at least 'picturesque'; it was 'a green Switzerland beneath a Calabrian sky, with the silence and solemnity of the Orient.' Nature 'awaits and welcomes' the visitor in Majorca, Sand wrote:

> There, the vegetation is lofty and strange but has none of the lavishness that often blurs the outline of a Swiss landscape. Rocky peaks stand silhouetted against a sparkling sky, the palm tree leans over the precipice without the wind disturbing its magnificent chevelure, and everything down to the stunted cactus by the roadside, seems to be posing with a kind of vanity to delight the eye.

I liked the idea of the cactus being so pleased with itself it posed for passing tourists, like a celebrity.

Sand depicted herself as the energetic leader of her troop, exploring the island and, to some extent, its history; giving the children lessons; observing what she called 'the natives'; writing and cooking – or supervising the cooking of the housekeeper, Maria Antonia. Sourcing food was a constant difficulty. She was disgusted that instead of butter there was only olive oil – no normal person could eat in Majorca 'unless they liked lard and rancid olive oil'; and pork, for the pig was ubiquitous. 'They treat pigs better than they treat people.' Majorcan dishes were 'hellish concoctions', mostly based on pork and far too full of spices: 'you risk your life with each mouthful.' She loathed the omnipresent smell of garlic. One

Not Speaking

day she bought a huge squid, a 'calamar', its eyes as big as oranges and its tentacles, uncurled, four or five feet long. Not brave enough to try it, they 'paid homage' to Maria Antonia for the way she prepared and ate it with gusto.

I love squid, which the Greeks call calamari, and also the 'charred methods of native cooking' that Sand was unable to stomach, but I know what she means about the preparation. Preparing calamari was a pitched battle in the kitchen sink, although today's squid are less well-grown than their nineteenth-century ancestors. 'You have to dig out the eyes,' Mum said, showing me, after we bought it from the fish counter in the supermarket at Porto Pi. (Sand bought hers from the fisherman on the beach.) And even so it wasn't as bad as preparing octopus. That had first to be beaten hard against a rock and the ink sac removed.

Maria Antonia was religious and greedy. Sand was sickened by the way she put her hands into every dish as she cooked, her fingers nimbly snatching the best morsels from the bottom of the pot without, apparently, getting burned. Pettishly she wrote of her, 'I have never seen a pious mouth as devoted to delicacies', nor a throat 'so capacious for swallowing her beloved hosts' sugar and coffee while humming a hymn.'

Sand's habit of drinking coffee at all hours, rolling her own cigarettes and sleeping sometimes during the days was observed by an apothecary who also lived at the Charterhouse and was at a loss to understand what 'this woman' had come to do in Majorca in the middle of winter. One of the things she had come to do, of course, was to write, and as was usual with her she often worked at night.

Chopin's behaviour evoked no such puzzlement, although how he managed to get a piano up the steep and winding rocky paths baffles me. For Chopin, the Majorca interlude was a productive period of composition. As well as the Mazurka in

Majorca: Valldemossa

E. Minor, op. 41, no. 2, which he called 'Palmejski' because it was written in Palma, he composed two preludes, a ballade, a scherzo and two polonaises. He found time to tutor Solange and defended her against her mother's endless scolding.

Sand found nothing to admire in the Majorcan people and did not hide her sense of superiority. (They, for their part, were probably suspicious of a French woman who wore men's clothes, smoked and was travelling with a man not her husband. Also, the French army's invasion of the island under Napoleon was still in living memory.) There was a storm of protest when the articles were gathered into a book and published in Majorca. The acerbic tone that makes *A Winter in Majorca* so entertaining to read earned her, as she put it, 'a most fulminating and laughable tirade of abuse.' She was unrepentant.

Chopin's illness and their failure to sustain a satisfying relationship is the background story and Sand only partially tells it. He seems to have been peevish; she described him as a 'detestable patient'. They slept apart. Solange, whose relationship with her mother was as troubled as Sand's relationship with *her* mother, watched it all with the cold gaze of an unhappy prepubescent.

It was pleasant to sit by the pool at the Anchorage, or wander down to the strip of beach where the loungers were laid out under the sunshades, and open *A Winter in Majorca*. For several days I was steeped in Sand, and nineteenth-century Majorca, and Chopin the delicate 'wraith' as André Maurois calls him in *Lélia: The Life of George Sand* ('a rather unhappy mortal whose life was but "an immense discord"') but I discovered I had not properly researched the subject when my mother and I drove to Valldemossa. I told her we were going to a monastery and I led her to understand it would be like the monasteries she

Not Speaking

was in the habit of visiting in Greece, a functioning monastery, with monks. She was keen. She liked to enter the atmosphere of devotion, to see and be seen by the men in long robes as she petitioned or thanked the saints. Once, she reminded me, she had thanked the Panagia for giving Tina the child she so badly wanted and which medical men in England had assured Tina she would never have, by going on hands and knees up the long approach to the cathedral at Tinos.

'I couldn't do that now,' she said. 'God understands.'

She appreciated, she said, that we were going to the monastery for her sake, because she was a believer and I, sadly, foolishly, reprehensibly, was not. I explained that although I had no religious motive I did have an interest, and I told her about George Sand and Chopin. Speeding along the smooth highway, I summarised the essential facts: she was a famous writer, he was a famous musician, she had two children, a girl and a boy, he was sick, the weather was bad, the locals suspicious.

'They went in November?'

'Yes.'

'Nicky came here once in November and it didn't stop raining the whole time.'

'That's partly why Majorca is so green and beautiful.'

'And she was looking after her children?'

'Yes.'

'And they were sick?'

'The boyfriend was sick. They were sick too, but not as sick as the boyfriend.'

'What was wrong with them?'

'I don't know.'

'But she had a boyfriend.'

'Yes.'

'And he was younger than her?'

Majorca: Valldemossa

'Six years younger.'

'Only six? That's not very much. And they stayed in the monastery?'

'Yes.'

'They had sex in the monastery?'

'Presumably.'

She smiles.

In Greek monasteries the saints accepted gifts: olive oil, bread, salt. Money would be given in donations and in payment for candles but under no circumstances was money a requirement of entry. It was a shock therefore to arrive at the Charterhouse at Valldemossa and find that there were no monks and we had to pay to go in.

The entry charge caused deep offence. I tried to pay quickly, before Rena noticed, but that was impossible.

'Eight euros?' she said. 'Eight euros! Bloody thiefs.'

She wanted to turn around and go back.

'I want to see inside.'

I picked up our tickets and hustled her through, hoping our eyes would be dazzled by a splendid interior.

We entered a large, plain, high, stone edifice, and made our way down long, empty corridors, the whole covering an area large enough to house an army corps, as Sand had written, without any beautiful architectural features whatsoever. All the way down the corridors Rena sulked and muttered about the 'bloody thiefs'.

'Think of it as a museum,' I said, losing patience and annoyed with myself for not registering what an 'abandoned' monastery meant: no longer a monastery and therefore no monks.

Valldemossa had been abandoned for a long time. The monastery was taken into government hands in the 1830s. The thirteen Carthusian monks who lived there, luxuriating in a generous allocation of space – each was provided with a 'cell' consisting of three rooms, and had a chapel of his own for prayer – had been sent packing, and the estate sold to private developers. Rooms were made available for rent, but the locals, angry at the government, still loyal to their priests, showed little interest. The building decayed. The interior was now scruffy but the views were still magnificent.

The nineteenth-century bourgeoisie of Palma would take rooms sometimes, to escape the heat of summer in the town. Sand thought the coolness of the dark vaulted chapels with their gilt decorations and vulgar paintings an invitation to 'sensual pleasure' rather than asceticism. She pondered the lives of the medieval monks, and could imagine the appeal of monkish solitude in the past, but not in the nineteenth century when social progress was so thrilling, she thought, and humankind had learned the necessity of fellowship with others.

Sand's own sensual pleasures incorporated the intellectual, aesthetic, and maternal sides of her character. She remains famous (or infamous) as an early proponent of sexual liberation for women. But she bewilders commentators – as she bewildered her lovers – because she didn't behave in the ways they expected her to. Alfred de Musset, in Venice with Sand in 1833-34, expressed disappointment that she didn't want 'real hot sex, you know, what you get with sluts'. 'Sluts' were his muses for tender poems extolling the divinity of love. Prosper Mérimée complained that Sand left their bed to go and sit by the fire writing *Lélia*. According to Pietro Pagello, a handsome Italian doctor who was treating the dissolute and abusive Musset for a venereal infection, and with whom Sand had an affair, she was a clever and busy home-maker, adept at sewing curtains, bedspreads, covering a sofa and chairs, who would suddenly leave off sewing or hammering in nails to go to her work table and dash off thirty pages to send to her editor.

Majorca: Valldemossa

'Love of work is my salvation,' George Sand declared.

Freud put love and work together. According to Freud, love and work is all there is, although you won't find the maxim in Freud's writings – it was reported by Erik Erikson as something Freud said. Freud talked of human needs, of satisfaction, fulfilment. These two elements, love and work, were the basis of human satisfaction. Sand's formulation, love *of* work, narrows the meaning. Salvation isn't a word Freud would have used.

What did Sand need saving from? The answer is clear in her many novels and in the prefaces she wrote to new editions. In spite of the extraordinary progress of the times, society was still backward in its ideas about women. Sand was attacked for being anti-marriage. She denied it. She wrote about the frustrations of ardent young women whose romantic and sexual impulses could not flourish in a social order that constrained them. Marriage was the legal, institutional expression of men's rule over women. It told you nothing about women and what they could be. Sand wanted to create heroines in the mould of the melancholy Romantic-period heroes that were so popular, ever since Goethe's Werther in *The Sorrows of Young Werther*, a sensitive artist at odds with a fallen world, or Goethe's Faust, whose spiritual desolation and striving, reckless questioning symbolised the predicament of modern man. Wasn't modern woman in the same predicament? Sand asked metaphysical questions about God, love, the universe. She wanted to comprehend the nature of truth. Was it true that woman's destiny was to serve man? Must women subordinate their desires to male demands? If women followed where their own interests, ambitions and desires led, did they cease to be women?

The first version of *Lélia*, some of which was written during Sand's short fling with Prosper Mérimée, gave a gloomy

Not Speaking

answer to these questions: Lélia ends up strangled to death by a mad priest (maddened by repressed passion for her). Sand rewrote the novel five years later, after her stay in Valldemossa, in the light of the relative success of her relationship with Chopin, toned down the sexual passages and offered a more optimistic solution (of sorts) in a vision of female solidarity in the cloister. Lélia becomes a nun and reforms the church. Since physical love demanded submission to men – and Sand could not envisage ways in which it would not – the only progressive way forward was to remove men from the picture altogether.

Lélia is a feminist novel, and nun-like renunciation is a significant strand in the history of feminism. It's a measure of how hard it has been to factor sexual feeling into women's lives with men, as imagined, lived and told. A woman who behaved with the sexual freedom Sand displayed was inevitably 'scandalous'. George Sand said her novels were not realist fictions; they were fabrications in search of 'ideal truth'.

The Charterhouse at Valldemossa still attracts tourists on the strength of its association with Sand and Chopin, his sickness, her scandal, his music, her books, her opinions of the 'natives'. The three room 'cell' they occupied is clearly marked. I stood with my mother and looked, musing vaguely and voyeuristically on the sex lives of these long dead lovers, and felt first sadness then anger at the waste of women. It enraged me to contemplate the vicious nonsense women have been told about themselves down the ages. It appalled me to register how long, historically, it took for feminism to become established. In Valldemossa I understood how important it was to pay homage to women like George Sand, born Amandine Aurore Lucile Dupin, to thank her for her strength and creativity, her determination, hard work, achievements. For behind the titillating emphasis on the bed lay the larger story. Few women, even those whose ambitions and desires propelled them with the volcanic force of a George Sand, fully realised their potential and even fewer were able to tell the story. Women's lives were meant to be hidden. No wonder, I thought – and now I was thinking about the woman standing next to me – those lives came to be all about subterfuge. Secrecy, silence, subterfuge. Under the noses of the patriarchs you found what satisfaction you could and triumphed in beating a system designed to frustrate you.

Most women accommodated to the system. I included myself in this category, slipping and sliding through much less challenging times than the early nineteenth century when Sand was living or the twentieth century of Rena's life, demurring, obliging, making allowances, pitching tent in the opposition's camp.

A daddy's girl, like so many intellectually ambitious women: thinking as men thought; thinking with men's thoughts; thinking men's thoughts.

It had been so much easier to love our father. 'You're all for your father, all of you,' our mother would say, 'all of you, all the time.'

I think if my mother wrote a novel that imagined an ideal society founded on ideal truth she too would probably make her heroine a nun.

Sexual freedom was not so scandalous in the 1930s when Laura Riding lived in Deya with Robert Graves but she also, seeking truth and dispensing with subterfuge, had her moment of nun-like renunciation. 'Bodies have had their day,' she wrote in 1933, troubled by the subjugation of women in sexual intercourse. What men sought in women, Riding declared, was a completeness they could never attain, for man was the derived rib, the accidental being, and woman the fundamental human. Women should not coddle men's egos, they should not give in to their sexual demands. It was time for the mind to

Not Speaking

rule, and for female minds to break free from the old patriarchal falsities. Riding announced she would no longer have sex with Graves, a matter extensively discussed with their circle of friends and followers.

Riding was a brilliantly original avant-garde poet. Still, she thought truth began where poetry ended and for that reason renounced poetry too. Her views were austere: poetry was not designed to 'give pleasure to the mind,' she wrote, it was 'not an after-effect, not a pleasurable memory of itself, but an immediate constant and even unpleasant insistence on itself.' As for truth, that was not 'a quarry' to be hunted down or pursued. She wanted to 'think *with* truth'. This meant paying attention to language, using words as if they had no experience, ridding them of stale historical and mythic associations. By purifying the language, meaning could be restored. She devoted herself to this task for the rest of her life, after marrying an American, Schuyler Jackson, and returning to America.

How did you think *with* truth? English literary circles largely dismissed Riding as a witch, and even generous-minded biographers lapse into sardonic strain when describing her demands for homage and insistence on always being right. There was money involved in the story, too. To finance their lives in Deya, Robert wrote while Laura decided on the expenditure. Furthermore, in a fiction everybody connived at, the land on which the house – and subsequent houses – was built was supposedly hers. In fact, as an American she could not own property in Majorca; worse, as they later discovered to their cost, they were all deceived and the land belonged to their local agent, Juan Gelat.

I find it hard to warm to Riding, and there is little in her writing to suggest that she wanted me, as a reader, to warm to her; but I feel the pull of what Graves called 'her bladed mind'. She has things to say that I want to hear. I don't know what thinking *with* truth means, but I am sure it would be easier, and more easily explained, in a culture that wasn't fundamentally antagonistic to intellectual women. Because when Riding speaks about truth she means truth about being female. When she declared bodies had had their day she was trying to detach women from a long history of entrapment. She was trying to shift the age-old emphasis and give women some room to breathe.

The Devil in the Room

Over several summers in the white apartment, I discovered my untaught mother's scholarly zeal. She would sit for hours on the sofa, her head bent over a religious book or pamphlet, murmuring as she studied, crossing herself now and again. She compared versions of the stories of the saints and their miracles. Occasionally she showed me portraits of saints. I had thought the icons were generic but she could name them all, her responses quick and assured. This was Stephen. This, Christopher. This, Agatha. Watching her at her devotions made me feel with force her isolation within the family: so many of us, only one of her. None of us could read the books she read, and though we all in different ways at different times made efforts to learn her language, I don't think we really tried to imagine what it meant for her to be the foreigner in our midst.

Rena's command of English remained rudimentary and she spoke with a heavy accent. Having a conversation was always partly an exercise in translation on both sides; it involved repetition, rewording, explanatory asides and blank incomprehension. Technical words – exegesis, for example – often needed no translation. She would repeat the word, giving it a different intonation and sometimes saying 'Ah!' as the meaning became clear. Her thinking was more sophisticated than her ability to express it in English, but it lacked nourishment. Like the Virgin Mary, she kept many things and pondered them in her heart; much of what she had learned as a woman in the world was off-limits for family life, and some of her devotion was repentance.

In large gatherings, when there were many round the table, her histrionic skills made up for limited vocabulary. At these times she generally preferred her offspring not to talk amongst themselves: quick-fire exchanges and complicated syntax left her demanding to know what had been said. Her interruptions conveyed suspicion, as if her inability to understand were a function of our desire to deceive her, as if the English language made us into enemies. Nicky accused her of egotism: 'If it's not all about you, you just switch off'; or, more colourfully, because she did once fall asleep over her soup, 'If it's not all about you it's a head-in-the-soup job.' But there was more to it than that: secrecy and subterfuge had instilled certain habits. In any case, keeping up with the diverse energies and interests of her English children was a challenge. We, for our part, did not look to her for guidance about the world we were entering.

We rarely confided anything about work or school, plans or ambitions. We had no expectation that the social systems, the organisational structures, within which we operated would be understood by her. Elementary details had to be explained. She never grasped the nature of my job, wondering how I could be working if I was at home reading a book, and finding it astonishing when I had a half-year sabbatical that the university paid me my full salary. 'That's clever,' she said, sneering. 'They pay you to stay away and do nothing?' Achievements, similarly, had to be laboriously contextualised. Best was to win a prize: hairdresser of the year, salon of the year; or an OBE, awarded by the queen, which spoke for itself. Having a book published was obviously credit-worthy, but she had no means of discriminating between books; and to say you had been treated to a long and appreciative review in the newspaper, or indeed that you wrote long reviews yourself of other people's books, meant nothing. Hadn't Nicky published a book? And wasn't Nicky in the newspapers all the time?

Failures, likewise, were best left undescribed. Boasting she understood, but admitting that you had failed in something – a relationship, a task, an ambition – diminished you in her eyes. Not everybody was perfect, not everybody was strong, but there was no need to broadcast your weakness to the world.

The easiest measure of success was money. And yet, for all that she loved money – loved to think and talk about it – she had no more respect for people with money than for those without it. And success was not the same as worth. Cheats were successful. Gamblers made money. Her moral compass pointed always towards a God whose judgments were shown by his works: those he approved of he rewarded, the bad he punished. Her long life and good health were clear signs of God's assessment that she was, as she put it, wryly smiling, 'a good girl'. She hadn't always been so, but God had heard her penitent prayers. He looked down on her with indulgence. He knew she had wanted to be good. She had what Patrick Leigh Fermor describes as the Greek 'orientation towards virtue', which, whether it had its roots in paganism or Christianity, exerted a powerful influence, he concluded, on the Greek subconscious mind.

Worldly success for women was measured by the quality of husband they managed to attract. Rena subscribed, in the abstract, to convention: a husband should be tall, dark, handsome and rich. She approved of my husband, John, whom I married in 1977, on these grounds and also because, although

Not Speaking

she didn't understand the English class system, she saw at once that he was 'posh'. In this respect I had succeeded beyond expectations. The arrival of two sons confirmed her in her judgment that John was 'a proper man'. She grew fond of him. It was a sadness to her when our marriage ended some two decades later but she identified powerfully with the spirit in which I leapt into a new life, even if that new life took a form she was determined to consider inexplicable, unnatural, incomprehensible, and so shaming it should never be spoken of except behind closed doors. The fact that my new love was a woman intrigued her and she asked me many questions at the time, such as, 'Which of you is the man?' ('Neither. It doesn't work like that.') 'Has she got a proper job?' ('Yes, she's solvent.') 'Has she always been, you know, like that?' ('No, like me, she was in a long relationship with a man.') 'Has she got children?' ('No, to her sadness, but she's very keen on mine.') 'Has she got family?' ('Yes, she has family in Canada.') 'Have they got proper jobs?' ('Yes, they have proper jobs. Her father was a lawyer and her mother a judge.') 'Why did she leave Canada?' ('It happened. She came to study, and stayed. She's an immigrant, just like you. Well, not quite like you perhaps. But it does so happen that you share the same birthday.') 'Really?' ('Yes.') She shook her head as if that was the most unbelievable of all the unbelievable things I'd told her; and, truly, in the many years that followed she was always surprised to learn that it was Barbara's birthday too when she was celebrating her own. 'I'm not shocked but your father will be very upset,' she said, advising me not to tell him. She also confided that she would have made a better wife to John than I had been. When she met Barbara she behaved towards her with the same outward politeness she showed other girlfriends, boyfriends, wives, husbands, lovers. My father took it on the chin as a done

The Devil in the Room

deal best not enquired into too closely and welcomed Barbara to the family.

In *Roumeli*, Patrick Leigh Fermor tried to sum up the attributes of the Greeks. He listed self-reliance, intelligence, rapid thought, extreme subjectivity, thirst for fame, energy, 'a deep-seated feeling of confidence and of absolute equality not only with other Greeks, but with the whole human race, and of superiority to many', strong family feeling, sensitiveness to affronts, quick temper, and 'scorn for privacy'. He also observed that the Greeks had 'an easy-going moral code' which coexisted with puritanical notions of family honour.

Leigh Fermor had fought alongside Greeks during the Second World War. He appreciated what he termed their ability to create an 'immediate link', friendly and equal, which melted barriers of hierarchy and background. He thought this immediacy, so unlike English reserve, created the sense of being 'in league' as 'fellow-hedonists and fellow-victims' of life. The Greeks, he wrote, believed in sharpening the mind by conversation. 'Talk is an addiction and it is conducted with invention, great narrative gifts, the knack of repartee, the spirit of contradiction, the questioning of authority, mockery, self-mockery, satire and humour.'

I nod when I read these words, sitting on the terrace in the lovely, early morning, Majorcan sunshine. The summary rings true, though he might have added: and a passionate conviction of always being right. Rena's narrative gifts were evident, even in her second language. (She said she learned to speak English after she arrived in England by listening to stories on the radio. She had never had any lessons.) I liked how immediately she engaged with individuals, her pleasure in company (to be told by her that you were 'good company' was high praise), her humorously mocking asides. On good days life was play and laughter. Nicky baited her and she rose to

Not Speaking

the bait. Tina contradicted her and they would shout at each other. Michael teased her, keeping his face straight. There was noisy protestation, contradiction, argument, hilarity. Barbara, observing as an outsider, asked, more than once, 'Why do they have to wind her up so much?'

As a Canadian, Barbara brought some New World freshness to this meeting of two cultures, cockney English and sharp-minded Greek. I, also, occasionally thought, 'Does it have to be so noisy? Can't we have an ordinary conversation, an exchange of views?' But that would have been an entirely different beast, with neither Greek nor cockney in it.

Our hours of quiet study in the white apartment held some of what I yearned for. There was a ritual quality that was deeply pleasurable. When Barbara, an academic and writer like myself, joined us she brought her laptop and worked, as I did, and for the most part we three coexisted harmoniously enough: a man's presence would have required special measures, a woman could be disregarded under the veneer of Greek politeness. At our books we were all at our devotions, us in English, Rena in Greek, mixing up stories with prayers. When I showed Rena the astonishing photograph in Hugo Vickers' book of Princess Alice, Prince Philip's mother, in her full-length nun's robe leading her family out of Westminster Abbey after the coronation of Queen Elizabeth II in 1953, she told me again that Alice was a good woman and always helped the poor, and added, 'She spoke very good Greek.'

I didn't speak very good or even elementary Greek, but I understood my mother's English and her impulse towards virtue better than I had when I was younger. The more time we spent in quiet companionship, the more it seemed the most natural thing in the world to put down in writing the things she told me.

It was not the same as having what I thought of as an

The Devil in the Room

ordinary conversation (whatever that meant in my fantasy) but it was a way of reaching across and recognising the losses on both sides that were the result of language and cultural difference.

One element of my mother's rituals did not please me. Our hours of study ended when she got up from the sofa, crossing herself, and went into her bedroom where she lit the censer. She would come out holding it as the priests did in church, and go through all the rooms of the apartment swinging the smoky incense into every corner.

I tried to persuade her to leave my bedroom out of it.

'Do you have to do that, Mum?'

Yes, she did have to do it, with the gravity of a priestess, all through the apartment.

'It gets the devil out of the room,' she would say, each time I objected.

In July 2009 Tina phoned. She came straight to the point. 'You know that book you're writing? What is it about exactly?'

I denied all knowledge. I said I wasn't doing any such thing and pretended I was no longer interested. Why make trouble? Why go out of your way to upset people? Family matters were best kept private.

She said, 'This may seem a funny thing to ask but has anyone ever said anything to you about Dad not being my dad?'

'No.'

'Are you sure?'

The question frightened me.

'Well, once. I think Linda said something. But I didn't believe it.'

Not Speaking

'Because I've always felt different from the rest of you. I look different.'

'No you don't.'

'You all look like Aunt Vi and I don't. And if Louki wasn't my dad,' she said, the name producing in me a stab of guilty alarm, 'why did I get dragged round to see him every birthday so he could give me fifty pounds, and why was it all hush-hush from Dad? And why do I look like him? And have you seen his three daughters? Fat. Just like me.'

This was a new development.

I wasn't sure I agreed that the rest of us looked like Dad's side of the family, but Tina, without a doubt, looked like our mother. She was the image of the young Rena.

Tina had a request. She had been on the internet, investigating DNA testing. For £250 she could get a kit from the USA that would show degrees of sibling relationship. If Linda and I were willing to participate, she might be able to establish if we were whole or half-sisters.

Of course I said I was willing, but she would have to get it organised quickly. Barbara and I had been invited to go as Distinguished Visiting Professors to the University of Notre Dame in Indiana. We needed to be in place by mid-August and would be in the United States until Christmas. We were busy making plans to go. With any luck, I thought as I put down the phone, the kit wouldn't arrive in time.

Had anybody ever said anything about Dad not being her dad? Who would such an 'anybody' be? Put like that, the question at first formed itself in my mind as an abstract, distant prospect. An anybody, a somebody, who might have heard a story and wanted to make mischief. It was shocking to imagine anybody who knew us making so direct, so personal an attack, especially as Tina and Dad were so close. In fact, it was shocking that Tina could think it. Disloyal.

The Devil in the Room

How could Tina ever think so disloyal a thought? She had gone to such lengths to create her own special relationship with our father, bestowing on him a level of care and affection not forthcoming at home. He'd always had a hankering for country life – tramping in woods, sitting round big fires. Tina gave him that and more besides. When his faults and failings were the theme of our mother's after-dinner (and before-dinner and during-dinner) diatribes, Tina would say cheerfully, 'Don't worry, Dad, you can come and live with me.'

Tina had tried to make everything better.

We all tried to make everything better. Making everything better was a massive cooperative project. It was hush-hush because everything was hush-hush from Dad, as if it was in our power to protect him from his own life, and because we didn't speak about it with each other. The spur was individual; the mode, in different degrees, competitive.

I ask Linda what she thinks. Linda would prefer not to think about it. We're both shaken by this turn of events, feeling the force of Tina's anger. We're hoping we won't be blamed. I can hear Linda's anxiety in her resentful tone. She would really much rather not have to remember these things at all.

I share some of that feeling of resentment, but in me there is an added ingredient. Tina's words, 'That book you're writing…', float free from the confusion of fear and guilt they first induced and give me a lift. I'm excited. I have a book to write.

I coax Linda. We talk for a long time.

She recalls something she assures me that I know. 'You know this,' she says. 'We talked about this. I've told you this before.' It happened soon after Linda married Eddie and had her first baby, Sarah. Sarah was born a year after Tina, and Rena, instead of being a doting grandmother, was a rivalrous mum with a beautiful baby of her own (and a boyfriend). One day she and Linda had an argument, and Rena was telling Linda to be less stupid about life in general and marriage in particular, to instance which she told her about Tina. Rena had found herself pregnant by Louki at a time when she wasn't regularly having sex with her husband. She slept with Bill to cover up the pregnancy. This account, unwelcome to Linda on so many levels, was offered not as a confession or confidence, but in a boastful, self-righteous tone, as proof of female cleverness, male stupidity, Rena's ongoing sex appeal, and Linda's scandalous lack of guile, her refusal to grow up into a proper woman. This was the sort of thing proper women did and it was time Linda learned it.

A feeling of shame overwhelms me. I can't write this down, I can't put this in my book. I don't want this to be the sort of truth I'm telling.

Linda phones Tina and they talk. Linda tries to make things better by assuring Tina it doesn't matter. It makes no difference. It has made no difference to Linda and she has known forever.

Tina is angry that Linda doesn't appreciate what such knowledge means for her. 'How could she know and not tell me?' she asks. She feels let down by both her older sisters. Tina doesn't understand the training in not knowing and not speaking that Linda and I were forced through.

The DNA kit arrives a few days before I am due to leave for America. Mum is cooking a farewell dinner. I meet Linda in the car park of Cropthorne Court, Maida Vale, and a moment later Tina drives up. We sit in the back of her car and she gives each of us a swab that we put inside our mouths. The instructions that have come with the kit are meticulously followed. Labels are filled in. The package is sealed. We laugh. It feels ridiculous and momentous. Then we go upstairs, greet Mum, and have dinner in the usual way.

The Devil in the Room

The results come through to me as I sit in my office overlooking the leafy green lawns of the campus at Notre Dame. Lee has sent them with a note saying that Tina is devastated. They show that Linda and I are 99 per cent likely to be sisters while Tina is 37 per cent or 38 per cent.

Another thing happened while we were away in America. Nicky started saying that his financial advisers were advising that he should probably sell Cropthorne Court.

'And move Mum again?' I couldn't believe it.

'She'll be better off somewhere smaller.'

'Have you told her?'

Nicky hadn't mentioned it to her. Until he did there was no incentive for anybody else to mention the proposal and quite strong reasons to push it away and forget about it.

'There's a smaller flat in Paddington she could have.'

'Have you told her?'

'No.'

There was nothing to be said.

We returned to England at the end of 2009. One of the first things Mum said to me was, 'I don't know what's wrong with Tina.'

The following spring, Tina booked a holiday home in the South of France and invited Mum to come and stay with them for a week. Mother and daughter had been quarrelling about trivial things all winter. It was not many days before Mum's routine criticism, her inability to be pleased – why had they chosen this place, why were they so far from the shops, why was there no café, what kind of holiday do you call this, how much did you say you're paying? – became intolerable. Tina

Not Speaking

exploded. In the screaming match that followed Tina yelled, 'At least I know who the father of my children is!'

'She didn't say anything,' Tina told me, later. 'She pretended she didn't hear anything.'

'Why don't you just tell her?'

'I told her.'

'I mean calmly. Have a conversation. Speak to her.'

'Are you trying to be funny? When did any of us ever have a conversation like that?'

'You could tell her about the DNA test. Give her a chance. Let her know you know.'

Tina let fly at me. 'Did you have a conversation fifteen years ago when you left John and fell in love with Barbara? Did you go and have a coffee and say, "Mum, I'm a lesbian"? I don't think so. As I recall, you asked me, and Nicky, to prepare the ground. We were supposed to tell her that here in England it was all fine. You do know, by the way, that as far as her friends are concerned, you're still married to John? They don't have any gay people in Greece.'

It was true I had depended on my siblings to prepare the ground. Plenty of talk had gone on in the background. The essence of their message to our parents had been: *what's all the fuss about? This happens all the time.* They had absorbed Dad's initial shock and shared jokes with Mum about who did what to whom, had spoken positively about Barbara and generally helped everybody move swiftly on to the new dispensation. By then every one of my sisters and brothers had been through a divorce or separation and change of partners. As Mum said, she was like the queen: the queen's children's marriages broke up but the queen and Prince Philip went on together through thick and thin.

Time passed. Mum continued to say, 'I don't know what's

The Devil in the Room

wrong with Tina', but now she did know, and she was processing it.

Absolute self-belief and a fighting spirit enabled her to maintain the conviction of virtue. Before we went to Majorca that summer I noticed that when I was with her she would now and then mention Louki. One Sunday she happened to meet Louki's cousin at church in Wood Green. She told me about it. He had showed her photographs of Louki with his family. A few weeks later she was in a Greek restaurant off Charlotte Street and a man she knew when she knew Louki happened to be at the next table. They talked about the old days. In Majorca, we went ten-pin bowling with Nicky and Kelly and others and to everybody's surprise Rena not only didn't need to be shown how to do it but turned out to be more skilled than most of the company. She whispered to me as we shared a beer, 'I used to go ten-pin bowling with Louki.'

Squashed into the back seat of a taxi on the way to the airport, she launched into a detailed account of Tina's birth. I asked questions, made notes.

On the plane, there was more. Tina's birth (again), days out at the seaside, a trip to Germany with Louki.

Really? 'You went to Germany with him?'

'We only went for a few days. He wanted to buy a car.'

'How did you manage that?'

She didn't remember how she managed it.

'When?'

She doesn't remember.

'After Tina was born?'

'Of course. We stayed in a nice bed and breakfast.'

'Did you take Tina?'

'No.'

'It was when that man in America was killed. The landlady came with the breakfast and showed us the newspaper.'

Not Speaking

'Kennedy? The assassination of John F. Kennedy? The president? Martin Luther King?'

'Yes, Kennedy, but not the president. His brother.'

'Bobby Kennedy?'

'Yes, his brother. It happened when we were in Germany.'

1968. June 1968. Where was I in June 1968? It would have been the end of my first year at university, two years after Tina was born. So Tina was two, Michael eight, Nicky ten and Paul sixteen. How could she just go away for 'a few days'?

'Your father stayed at home. He looked after Tina.'

'And the others.'

'I wasn't worried about the others, they all looked after themselves.'

'Did he know where you were going?'

'He didn't stop me.'

'So you took a train to Germany, bought a car, and drove it back?'

'Exactly.'

'It must have been a nice break.'

'It was.'

I'm astonished. What did Dad tell the neighbours? What did he tell himself? How did he manage it? How come I didn't know? How come nobody said anything?

He managed it somehow, and the thought saddens me at first until I recall him, happily surrounded by his boys, going down the back steps to fetch something from his shed, vaulting over the back wall to fix the rope in the tree, improvising a cricket pitch in the yard, his grey-green eyes alight and his lean body alert. He had his troop. They looked after him and he looked after them. He was good at that.

They would have enjoyed having the place to themselves.

Where was I? I wasn't part of the troop.

The German trip was 1968. I had left home. But in 1966

The Devil in the Room

when Tina was born I was still living at home, and it disturbs me that when Mum repeats the story of Tina's birth, which she returns to over and over again – the ambulance to Evelina hospital, the baby coming prematurely, and then, following the birth, an incubator for two months – I don't recall any of it. 'I couldn't stay at the hospital,' she says sadly. 'I had to go home. I didn't want to leave her.' She had no choice. 'I had to look after the other children.'

Why don't I recall any of this? I wonder if the pregnancy, as it became apparent, had gathered round itself an aura of disapproving silence, or if my life was simply going on elsewhere. I was living at home, but outward-facing, eager for adventures in the world, expecting exciting things to happen to me. By contrast I have strong memories of her earlier pregnancies when she was carrying Nicky and Michael, and of the household routines that revolved around the boy babies and toddlers.

Did I go to the hospital to visit my new sister during those two months when she was in the incubator? I can't remember.

I ask my mother, 'Did you go to the hospital to visit her?' I don't ask if I went.

'Of course I visited her. I went every day.'

'Did Dad go?'

'Your father didn't like hospitals.'

'Did Louki go?'

'He came to see me when I was in the hospital.'

'Really?'

'Yes.'

'How did you manage that then?'

She shrugs.

'I expect you said he was your cousin.'

I feel cross on Tina's behalf, and guilty.

Mum simply recalls her pleasure in the baby. 'She was a

Not Speaking

lovely little thing. I didn't like to leave her but I had to. The Sister told me to be sure to come back and take her home afterwards. Some women just left their babies. Can you believe that? When I brought her home Michael said, 'If it's a girl you can throw her out the window'.'

'What did Dad say?'

'She was a lovely baby,' Mum says. 'She was very quiet, not like now with her long tongue. You didn't know you had her.'

I remember the night Tina was born, or at least one of the nights when Rena was still in hospital. I was able to join some school-friends on a jaunt. We had decided that the only way to get tickets for Laurence Olivier in Shakespeare's *Othello* – which we'd already seen at a schools' matinee, sitting in front row seats courtesy of the Inner London Education Authority, and which had stolen our senses – was to camp overnight outside the theatre to be first in the queue for on-the-day tickets when the box office opened at 10 a.m.

I don't remember feeling any concern about my mother in hospital, only delight that I was free, and rapture over Laurence Olivier as Othello and Frank Finlay as Iago. Linda must have taken charge, she must have come home from work every night and seen to the children.

As Rena's sphere of reminiscence extended into new pastures, the freedom to speak became invigorating. It was too much for Tina. She was cross with me.

'You've been encouraging her and now she's started she doesn't want to stop.'

Tina, also, had been hearing about Louki.

'Every time I phone her she finds some reason to drop his name into the conversation. I could strangle that bloody cousin in the church.'

Tina decided that if Mum went to stay a few days – as Dad used to – at Billingshurst, and made herself at home, cosily settling into an atmosphere of rural calm, amongst dogs, cats, pigs, sheep and trees, with lovely sunsets to admire and bracing walks across the fields to the local pub, she might hear what Tina had to say to her.

Don't blame me, I thought, if it doesn't work.

Country houses contained no romance for our mother. She could never understand why anybody would choose to live anywhere so far away from everything. But she packed a suitcase and let herself be taken by Michael, who was driving one of his girls to school in Brighton. The visit was not a success. Many things were wrong but the main wrong thing concerned Bill's grave. The patch had been landscaped, there were nice gravel paths and a specially made wooden seat, shrubs, flowers; but it distressed her to note that there was no cross on the grave itself. She complained to Tina. Why was there no cross? It wasn't right. It must mean she didn't love her father after all. Tina explained that she hadn't been able to find a cross she liked, and it was true that she had kept putting off the task because whenever she thought about it she started crying.

'And what about when I die?' Rena said. 'Will I end up in the middle of nowhere without a cross?'

Lee told me, 'Tina can't even go and visit the grave. It upsets her too much. I've had to do all the mowing and clearing myself.'

Rena was resolved. 'I'm going to put it in my will. I'll tell Nicky.'

She continued to talk to Tina about Louki. She couldn't understand why Tina didn't want to meet him. She explained that she could arrange it through the cousin who went to the church at Wood Green. It wouldn't be difficult.

'Don't you think you've done enough damage?' Tina said to her as they drank their coffee in front of the fire.

Not Speaking

'What do you mean?'

'I don't want to see him, and if I did, I certainly wouldn't want to see him with you.'

'Why not?'

'If you want to meet him, that's your business. Don't involve me in it.'

'Me? Why would I want to meet him?'

To me Mum said later, 'I think Tina thinks I might start up something with Louki again. I wouldn't do that. I'm not interested.'

'That's not what Tina's worried about.'

'What is she worried about?'

'I suppose she doesn't know what she'll feel.'

'Why should she feel anything?' The words come out less as a question than as an irritated swipe.

'It's not about *should*.'

'Why should she worry? What difference does it make to her?'

Tina said, 'Can you believe, she's talking to me about Louki as if it's the most natural thing in the world? As if she's telling me a recipe I might like to make. If I live to be a hundred I'll never understand her.'

'What did you say?'

'Nothing. I will never understand her as long as I live.'

'At least she's acknowledging the truth.'

'Not really. She still tells me I'm stupid just like my father and when I say, "Which one is that then?" she takes no notice.'

Dinners and holidays continued. 'What's the lie of the day?' Tina started asking. Rena ceased to wonder what was wrong with Tina. Tina ceased to expect Rena to understand what difference it made to her. Everybody knew about the DNA test; everybody said, in so many words, 'What's all the fuss about? It happens all the time.'

The Devil in the Room

Rena, having asked and been given full details of the DNA test and the scientific proof it had provided, went on the attack.

'Why did you have to send to America?'

'Because that's where the laboratory is.'

'Don't they have that kind of thing in this country?'

'I expect so, but the one I knew about happened to be in America.'

'How much did you pay?'

'None of your business.'

'Tell me. How much did you pay?'

Tina told her.

'You spent all that money! That's typical. You look for any excuse to spend money, any stupid nonsense.'

'It wasn't stupid and it wasn't nonsense. I've got the truth.'

'Truth! Pah!' (This is very dismissive.) 'You just love spending money. You've always been the same.'

'Have I?'

'You didn't have to send to America and spend all that money to find out the truth. I'm sure they're just as good at that sort of thing in England and it would have cost you half as much.'

It's a weekday evening in Maida Vale. Tina has been in town having her hair done at Michael's salon after delivering boxes of the products that he stores in the barn at Billingshurst. Now she's next to Rena at the end of the table. They look so alike sitting side by side, plates pushed away, arms resting on the plastic that covers the hand-embroidered cloth that is put over the dark velvet day-covering on which, for most of the time, the precious framed family photographs are arranged. Their arms are touching.

'I love my Tina,' Mum says to the table at large. She radiates health, pleasure and self-approbation.

'I love the way she tells me off for spending my own money,'

Not Speaking

Tina says. 'Has it ever occurred to you,' she speaks directly now to Rena, laughing, 'I wouldn't have had to spend anything if you'd told me the truth in the first place. And by the way, have you any idea how much Michael is paying for that researcher who's coming here every week? I'd love to know what stories you're concocting for her.'

Tina and Rena on holiday

Our mother's ninetieth birthday was approaching. Michael had commissioned a company called LifeBook Limited to interview her about her life. Over a period of several months a researcher had been visiting on a regular basis. Rena was enjoying the experience. 'She's a nice girl,' she said of the researcher. 'She told me she's a lawyer so I don't know why she's wasting her time doing this.'

'I dread to think what mumbo-jumbo she's writing down,' Tina said.

'*Saklamara*,' Rena replied, using the Greek word that means idiot. 'Why are you laughing? Don't you think I've got a story to tell? After everything that's happened to me, the life I've lived?'

'I just wonder how much sense someone who doesn't know you— she's English, isn't she?'

'She's a very nice girl, educated, polite.'

'How much someone who doesn't know you is going to understand.'

'I've been in this country for over sixty years. Don't you think I've managed to make myself understood?'

'And what she's going to make of what you tell her.'

'She can make what she likes of it. I'm only going to tell her what I want to tell her.'

I didn't envy the researcher her task. Still, I felt reproached by her existence. I had been cowardly and dilatory. What was I waiting for? There was work to be done. It was time to go home and get on with some writing.

Athens

On the volcanic Aegean island of Santorini the beaches are black. Rena's story begins in Santorini, where both her parents were born and married. Her father Evangelos Lignu spent his early childhood in Vothonas, a village built along two sides of a gorge. The family was large (one of the uncles had eighteen children) and reasonably prosperous: they were farmers, grocers, wine-makers and traders who involved themselves in local affairs. But Evangelos did not stay. He had a wealthy godfather who took him to live in Alexandria, a cosmopolitan city with a substantial Greek population. There he fell in love with big city life. He had little education. He became a trader, travelling around the Mediterranean and beyond, dabbling in many kinds of business, taking chances, enjoying risk and freedom. He was in no hurry to marry. When he decided it was time, he returned to his home village on Santorini and made enquiries. In Egypt there had been a mistress but the first quality he looked for in a wife was purity.

My mother's tone is sardonic when she tells me this.

'What happened to the mistress?' I ask.

'She followed him everywhere. She wanted to marry him. They had a child.'

Not Speaking

'What happened to the child?'

'The child died young. After that he felt free.'

'Why didn't he marry his mistress?'

'I told you. He wanted a proper wife. He didn't want a woman who would let her boyfriend in through the back window when he went out the front door. Egypt was very bad for that sort of thing.'

'Really?'

'That was what he said. He loved Egypt. He would play in the casinos. He wouldn't come home for days.'

'Where did he sleep?'

'Where do you think?'

'So he went with prostitutes?'

'Of course.'

'Who told you these things? How do you know?'

No answer.

Later she said, 'Mother told me. Who else? My mother told me.'

In Santorini, my grandfather the playboy heard about 'a good girl' who lived in Mesaria in the centre of the island, about half an hour's walk from Vothonas. Her name was the female version of his, Evangelia – it means good messenger, or the angel that brings good news, as in the evangelist. She was the third of seven children and it was her turn to get married. She had a younger sister who was in love, and eager to marry, but their father wouldn't allow it: the children had to marry in order of age. Evangelia was 'the quiet type', my mother says; she was 'very shy'; she was short, dark, rather stout, 'not beautiful'. She cooked and sewed and showed no interest in men. She prayed in front of the icons. Evangelos went to inspect her. Fittingly, she was in the kitchen doing the washing up when he came. Or she was in church. She was called out. She dried her hands. Or she folded her hands. She was twenty-six. He was thirty-five.

On the day of the wedding two weeks later, 'his family came down from one side of the mountain, her family came down from the other,' and long tables were laid out in the street for the feast. Before anybody was allowed to eat anything after the church ceremony, they had to wait until it was established that the bride was a virgin. The couple consummated the marriage. The blood-stained sheets were produced. After the sheets had been witnessed, guns were fired and celebrations followed.

Two weeks after that my grandfather took off on a boat leaving his new wife alone and upset. She didn't want him to go and she had no idea when he would be back. He reappeared a few weeks later. Her father offered them a small house in Mesaria but Evangelos had decided to make his fortune on the mainland. He wanted city life. It was a twelve-hour ferry journey from Santorini to Piraeus, the port of Athens, a journey from the spectacular scenery of the Cycladic islands with their tiny blue-domed churches and whitewashed walls, their lemon and orange groves, vineyards and gorgeous sunsets, to one of the world's oldest cities, birthplace of democracy and foundation of Western civilisation. There they settled in a good, square house with a flat roof in Kallithea, a village between Athens and the sea. From the roof you saw Athens ringed by mountains like a bowl and the two limestone hills, Lykavittos and the Acropolis, rising high, and the Parthenon changing colour as the light changed through the day.

The house was registered in Evangelia's name. Evangelos bought other houses and launched a variety of business ventures, some of which were profitable, some not. He was often away. A gambler, he loved night-clubs and glamour – one of his failures was a night-club – but there was always

Not Speaking

money. Until there wasn't: he gambled away all the houses except the one they lived in with their children.

There were five surviving daughters: Antonia (Toni), Calliope (Poppy), Irrenoula (Rena), Spirithoula and Fotini. Another daughter, Anna, died young. There was no son. Rena thought of herself as her father's favourite. She adored him.

'Why did your father register the house in your mother's name?'

'Why do you think? He knew he was stupid. He lost all the others.'

'He trusted your mother to look after the money.'

'Of course.'

His gambling landed him in prison for a month. Under the Metaxas dictatorship in Greece in the 1930s there was some attempt to both control gambling and derive taxation benefits from it, and Evangelos fell foul of one of those intentions.

'What did he do?'

'The government told him he had to stop playing cards and gambling at home, but he wouldn't stop.'

'He played at home?'

'At home, in the cafés, in the clubs, he was always playing. Playing and talking, playing and drinking, smoking.'

'Did your mother play?'

'Don't be ridiculous.'

'How old were you when your father was in prison?'

'About fifteen. We went to see him. He was laughing. My mother was ashamed and didn't want people to know but we girls thought it was funny.'

'And when he came out did he carry on?'

'I expect so, but the war changed everything.'

Rena was born in April 1923 and was barely eighteen when

Athens

the Second World War reached Athens at the end of April 1941. Greece had hoped to stay neutral but the Italians under Mussolini had launched an invasion from the north late in 1940. The Greek army, heavily outnumbered, resisted and drove them back over the border into Albania. Hitler sent the Wehrmacht to bail out Mussolini. The Greeks were no match for the Germans, even with some token help from the British. They surrendered. Strategically, however, Greece was unimportant to Hitler's war plans at that time. A full-scale occupation would have drained resources needed elsewhere so a domestic puppet regime under Italian authority, with a Greek general heading the government, was established. Within months the economy had collapsed.

'It says in my book that the Greeks hated the Italians.'

I show my mother Mark Mazower's *Inside Hitler's Greece: The Experience of Occupation, 1941-44* and she smiles at the cover photograph of three helmeted Nazi soldiers posing on the Acropolis.

This conversation takes place in London. We're having dinner in Carluccio's in St John's Wood High Street, which always makes me think sadly of Dad and the way we left him alone the day we began the move into Maida Vale. She has been telling me about her Italian soldier boyfriend whose name was also Carluccio.

'No,' she says. 'That's not true. The Italian soldiers were in the school opposite our house. We could hear them singing. They were beautiful singers.'

'What happened to Carluccio?'

'The Germans put him in a prison camp.'

'Why?'

She didn't know. 'I would have married him.'

'Did you love him?'

'Yes. I had one serious boyfriend, Costas, and I cried for days after that ended. Then when Carluccio was sent to Germany I cried again. My mother said, "Let's see how many days you cry for the next one." She was right.'

'What did she mean?'

She shrugs. Her mother was unromantic; there were men everywhere; why would you cry your eyes out for any man?

'Are you sure he was sent to a prison camp in Germany?'

'He was sent away.'

The Germans were in authority over the Italians who were in authority over the Greeks. It was an uneasy coexistence. 'Perhaps his unit was redeployed to an island?' I suggest, not wanting to think the worst might have happened. We talk about *Captain Corelli's Mandolin*, the film of Louis de Bernières' novel set in Cephalonia under Italian occupation. We saw it at the cinema in Swiss Cottage, a family outing organised by Nicky, and all the way through I remember her hissing loudly, 'That's true, that's exactly how it was.' She reminds me that the Germans killed the Italians at the end of the film.

Hitler viewed his conquered territories as sources of raw materials, food and labour. Greece suffered a catastrophic shortage of food, especially in urban centres like Athens where a fifth of the population lived. The priority for the Germans was feeding their own troops and they weren't interested in helping production and circulation of goods of any kind, they were only interested in systematic plunder and exploitation. Fuel shortages and disrupted transport links meant it was hard to bring food in from the country, and requisitioning combined with inflation to destroy business except on the black market. Meanwhile Greek assets like mines, shipbuilding works and textile plants passed into the hands of the Axis, along with warehouses stocked with olive oil, currants, figs, leathers, cotton and silk. Mussolini himself noted, 'The Germans have

Athens

taken from the Greeks even their shoelaces.' They also presented the Greeks with a bill for 'occupation costs'.

The collaborationist government could neither rule nor feed the country. Mazower writes of administrative chaos, hoarding and pillaging, and the inevitable outcome: famine. The city itself hardly changed in its outward appearance; it had not been bombed. But across Greece, and especially in Athens, there was the worst starvation in occupied Europe outside of the concentration camps. An American diplomat described Athens as 'the abode of hordes of destitute, starving people.' The winter of 1941-42 was 'hell'. The view from Berlin is summed up in a note from Goering to military commanders in the occupied territories: 'I could not care less when you say that people under your administration are dying of hunger. Let them perish so long as no German starves.' And perish they did, even though in international law it was the duty of an occupying power to feed the people under its rule. People fell dead in the streets. The grave-diggers were too weak from malnutrition to dig and the corpses piled up in the corners of cemeteries.

Mazower reflects on the psychological effects of the Greek famine. 'The hell of that winter,' he writes, 'marked the consciousness of all those who lived through it, changing them mentally, morally and politically.'

I read those words and I wonder about the ways the hell of that winter, and the experience of living under occupation, might have marked the consciousness of my mother and changed her.

'It was terrible,' she says. 'People were dying in the streets. People were starving.'

I summon what I know of Rena as a girl growing up in pre-war Kallithea, the middle one of five sisters, with a charismatic charmer of a father – 'Of course he went on having girlfriends,'

Not Speaking

she says when I ask, 'he was that kind of man. Nicky is like my father' – and a hard-working, severely devout mother. There's little to go on. The war dominates her memory. I think of how in England people who grew up in the Edwardian period and experienced the trauma of the First World War looked back to their pre-war childhoods as a golden age, an extended summer. My mother, by contrast, gives the impression that real life only began with the war that brought sequential waves of young men in uniform to be billeted in the neighbourhood and in the school across the road. Of her earlier self she offers scraps. She was tender-hearted (she liked kittens), domestic and religious. She believed in the saints. She saw visions. She claims she liked school but barely attended after the age of thirteen or so. (In later life, noting the pride her children took in their children's educational attainments, the attention that was paid to schooling, she would say bitterly, '*My* education was pushing the pram'.) She was good at housework and loved to clean. She spent several summers in Santorini with relations, but when I show her the map she can't tell me whereabouts on the island they lived. She learned how to sew from Poppy and she made her own dresses, 'but Poppy was better than me'. With her girl friends she went to the open-air cinema and afterwards they dressed their hair in the style of the actresses on the screen. They went regularly to the beach and she liked going in the water, but she never learned to swim.

'What was your mother like?'

'She was a good manager.'

I remember a tyrannical old woman in black whom we were instructed to address as *Yaya*. I was six in April 1954 when my mother returned to Greece for the first time, having left at the end of the war. She brought three children to display, the most important of whom was the youngest, Paul. None of the sisters who remained in Greece had produced any children at all, let

Athens

alone a boy. Poppy, who was settled in Rawtenstall, north of Manchester, had a daughter, Betty, and later would have a son, Steven, who became a favourite of his aunt Fotini, but Paul was the first. The blond-haired toddler was made much of and was soon chatting happily in Greek. He was two and a half; by the time we returned to England in September he spoke no English. 'Your father was furious.'

Yaya ruled the household. I remember absolute imperatives such as having to lie down in the afternoons because it was too hot to go out and the sun would make us mad; because Yaya was sleeping in the front bedroom, we weren't to talk either. I remember feeling under scrutiny. I remember that what we ate wasn't up to our mother and that Yaya kept a close guard on the store cupboards. Helping yourself was theft. Anyone who turned on an electric light after it got dark was screamed at and told to turn it off.

'If she hadn't been a good manager we would have died in the war. My father would have given everything away.'

'What do you mean?'

'My father was generous. He wanted to help everybody. One day we got some olive oil and he started giving it to people in little bottles. My mother stopped him.'

'People were starving.'

'My mother wanted to help people. She did help people. When the nuns came to the back door begging for food we gave them soup. But you had to be careful.'

During the occupation money became useless. Cigarettes were currency, so were olive oil, figs, daughters. The black market was the only market, often run by police and state officials, or the church, all looking out for their own interests. People took for granted the corruption of senior officials. You had to look after your own. Food became an obsession. Even the Germans went hungry. 'Nothing has any importance today

Not Speaking

apart from the question of food – or rather hunger,' wrote a young lawyer, Christos Christides. In the Lignu house in Kallithea the loft held tins of corned beef left behind by the British after their withdrawal from Athens in 1941, ahead of the German invasion. 'My mother used them to make soup. That was why we didn't starve. They lasted a long time.'

Toni was the scholar among the girls, and she had a gift for languages. She had made a special effort to study German and English, finding herself a tutor in Athens and paying for lessons. When the Germans came, Toni went to work for them in an office in Piraeus. 'That helped us too.'

'Wasn't it a problem working for the Germans? Didn't Toni get in trouble later?'

'Of course.'

Some of the German soldiers were staunch supporters of Hitler, but many were not. 'We went out with them. We all did, all of us, all our friends. They were just boys. They wanted to go home. They showed us photos of their mothers and sisters.'

The girls were discreet, they didn't promenade with uniformed Germans, but they were glad to get presents and favours.

Toni was 'clever'. Toni used her position to get food and supplies for Greek prisoners and the Greeks knew this. Once Rena went with Toni to the prison. She opened a door, the wrong door, and they saw older officers, the prison guards, making fun of the portrait of Hitler on the wall. She closed the door quickly, frightened at what they'd seen.

Toni's job gave her other advantages. One day, two German soldiers who'd been drinking in a bar were found shot dead at Nea Syngrou. Under the Occupation, resistance was punished by reprisals. There was a simple scale: for every German, ten Greeks. The Germans came round the houses. 'Toni must have

Athens

known they were planning to come round in Kallithea because she didn't go to work that day. Toni said to us, quick, quick, get out the photos, show them we're their friends. We put out the photographs of us with our German boyfriends.'

'You had a German boyfriend?'

'I told you. We all had German boyfriends.'

The troops came to the house and pulled her father forward. He was to be shot. 'His face was white.' But because the girls were there and pleaded for him, and Toni talked to them in German, they let him off. Later, they all had to go to the square and see the bodies of the ones who had been taken. There were two women among the twenty, and some young boys.

'Didn't you hate the Germans for that?'

'It was war. It was terrible.'

There are a number of accounts in Mazower's book of shocking massacres, whole villages burned and all the men executed, not just ten for every dead German. Mazower writes of 'random and undiscriminating' violence. There was a policy of terror. Much of this was directed at the partisans, the *andartes*, who had taken to the hills and were conducting guerrilla operations. In October 1943, in the northern Peloponnese, the *andartes* captured and killed seventy-eight German soldiers and in reprisal twenty-five villages were burned down and six hundred and ninety-six Greeks shot, including all the men of Kalavryta, the village the abducted soldiers had supposedly been taken to. In Henry Maule's biography of General Scobie I read of 'typical' German savagery. At the village of Kommero, with 'mortars, machine-guns, grenades, bayonets, axes, and knives' the Germans slew two hundred and eighty-five villagers, plus sixteen visiting from other villages, 'raped eight girls, skinned the village priest alive, and thrust burning cotton-wool into babies' mouths. They looted and burned down one hundred and ten of the one hundred and thirty-four houses.' In another village, eighty-seven people were shut up in their cellars and burned alive.

The Greek resistance was active but not politically united. There was EAM, ELAS and EDES as well as EKKA. ELAS was the strongest, and pro-Communist, which was a problem for the Allies, led by the British, who wanted ELAS to be militarily strong but were troubled by the potential long-term political implications. Soldiers in Churchill's Special Operations Executive (SOE) had parachuted into central Greece in the autumn of 1942 and helped the *andartes* blow up a railway. With the defeat of Rommel in North Africa the Allies were planning a landing in southern Europe, so Greece, and its resistance fighters, became strategically important. In fact, the plan was to invade through Sicily and one of the jobs of the British Military Mission was to keep up the fiction that Greece was the intended destination and so decoy Hitler into sending troops into Greece.

In July 1943 Mussolini was unexpectedly ousted in a palace coup and by September the Italians had surrendered. Never having had a high opinion of the Italian military, the German command was not at first surprised to find them selling their weapons and equipment – motorbikes, blankets, boots – to the Greeks, but they clamped down quickly. Weapons were surrendered and the Italians offered a choice: continue fighting under the Germans or leave. Most chose to leave, thinking they were being repatriated. In fact, the trains took them to POW camps. Henry Maule writes, 'The unfortunate Italians were herded away into remote concentration camps destined to be used as forced labour under inhuman conditions, many dying as a result.'

Carluccio? 'The Germans put him in a prison camp.'

I turn the conversation back to Carluccio, hoping that by explaining what I know of the context Rena might remember more. She tells me again: he had a lovely voice, she loved him, she learned some Italian, she cried when he was gone, her mother took the view that she didn't need sympathy and wouldn't cry for long.

Some Italian units resisted and fought against the Germans, most notably on the islands of Cephalonia and Corfu. Cephalonia held out against the Germans for a week. When they surrendered the punishment was 'staggeringly ruthless'. Almost 5,000 men were executed by firing squad. It is a German historian who calls what happened on Cephalonia and Corfu 'one of the most unbelievable war crimes of German soldiers in World War Two.'

I ask again, 'Didn't you have to be careful when you went out with German soldiers?'

'Of course. We were always careful.'

She liked the Germans. They were 'better' than the British – more polite. 'The British!' she would say with an expression of disdain. 'Nothing but beer bottles hanging out of their pockets.'

'I thought the German soldiers were instructed not to fraternise, they weren't supposed to go with Greek women except in official brothels.'

The Germans took the view that the Italian tendency to mix war and sex was part of the problem, making them soft on the Greeks. In Nazi racial thinking, Greek women also posed a threat to the purity of the master race. On the one hand, the ancient Greeks gave birth to civilisation, and many philhellenic Germans were pleased to be posted to Greece where the sunshine was welcome and where, on off-days, they could pursue their archaeological and classical interests; on the other, modern Greeks existed in their imaginations somewhere between gypsies and Jews.

Rena doesn't know anything about this.

Not Speaking

'Why didn't Toni get punished after the war?'

'I told you. She took food to the prisoners.'

'But you told me once she did get into trouble.'

She shrugs. 'Some men came to the house and slapped her about a bit.'

'Were you there?'

'Of course.'

'Were you frightened?'

She wouldn't admit to being frightened. She didn't think any of them had done anything wrong. The war was terrible and they had survived. Nobody died in her family and they never went hungry. The Greek men who came to the house were no better in her eyes than the Germans. They were communists – pronounced 'coo-moo-neests' – which was as good as saying the devil, because they didn't believe in God.

'What about the Jews?' I ask.

'What about them?'

In Thessaloniki, in the north, there was a large Jewish community that had been at the heart of that city's social and cultural life for over five hundred years. It was, indeed, the oldest, significant Jewish settlement in Europe, going back to before the expulsion of the Jews from Spain and elsewhere in the 1490s. In 1943 they were rounded up, over 50,000 people, and brutally transported to Auschwitz where most of them died.

'Did people know about the persecution of the Jews?'

'Everybody knew. Of course they knew.'

She asks if I remember Nina. Nina was a Greek Jew in Athens who had an affair with a German soldier and got pregnant. The baby was taken away, Nina had her head shaved and was sent off to a camp in Germany.

'What happened to Nina?'

Athens

'She survived. She came to London, that's how I met her. She lived near where you children went to school.'

Surrey Square Junior Mixed school, a substantial red-brick, high-windowed, wooden-floored, post-1870 Education Act Board School, built to educate the poor of Southwark.

'Sometimes I took you and went and had a coffee at her house after school.'

Dimly I recall a sharp-tongued woman, small, fierce. I try to squeeze my adult knowledge into the memory from childhood. It doesn't work. I wasn't interested in Nina, as I wasn't interested in any of the Greek women in whose South London houses we were occasionally made to sit quietly, while they talked loudly at each other over coffee and sweet biscuits in a language I didn't understand, about experiences I didn't share.

'Princess Alice hid a Jewish family in her house,' I say.

'She was a good woman.'

'In fact the Greek Orthodox church helped a lot of Jews escape from Greece. The archbishop, Damaskinos, got the Chief of Police to issue false identity papers.'

According to Hugo Vickers as many as 18,500 false identity papers were ordered up. 'There was a campaign, organised through the churches, to hide Jewish families, get them their papers, and get them out.'

'The Italians didn't want to persecute the Jews and nor did the Greeks. It was only the Germans.'

Princess Alice came under some suspicion and was called in by the Gestapo. She pretended she didn't understand what they were saying, and they thought she was a dotty old woman.

'She spoke very good Greek,' my mother tells me, and we talk about Alice and her son Prince Philip. 'Philip tried to learn Greek but he was no good at it, like your father. Your father tried, but he was no good.'

'Greek is a hard language.'

Not Speaking

'I don't find it hard.'

Alice, a great-granddaughter of Queen Victoria, married into the Greek royal family at the age of nineteen in 1903. She had first set eyes on Prince Andrea, or Andrew, in Buckingham Palace and what she saw, she said, was 'exactly like a Greek God', although Andrew's father was Danish and his mother Russian. The royal family was Greek by adoption: in 1863 Prince William of Denmark had been invited to the Greek throne, changed his name and became George I of Greece. In 1867 he married Olga, a Russian Grand Duchess. Olga was intensely religious and lived surrounded by her icons. She was an active philanthropist in the fashion of strong-minded women of the late nineteenth century: building hospitals, establishing reformatories. It was a happy marriage that produced numerous children including Andrew, but George allowed himself 'an occasional relaxation' when he went alone to Aix-les-Bains. He established a strong family identity – regular Sunday lunches for the team – and kept up connections with kin in other royal families: his sister Alexandra married the Prince of Wales and went to England, his eldest son Constantine married a sister of the German Kaiser. The huge family, all mixed marriages, kept tabs on each other – at least, the women did. In part the impulse was defensive: despite their privilege, these were dangerous times for royalty. The Greeks were by no means convinced about George. He reminded his sons, 'Never forget that you are foreigners among the Greeks, and never let them remember it.' He was assassinated in 1913.

'Olga was a good woman, too,' Rena says.

Vickers writes, 'While the Greeks had periodic dislikes for their royal family, they were consistent in their love for Queen Olga.'

After George was assassinated, Andrew and Alice inherited George's house on Corfu, *Mon Repos*, and it was there that

Athens

Philip was born in 1921, her last child, the first son after four daughters. Alice thought of Greece as home. But assassination was followed by abdication and exile: within a short while *Mon Repos* was shut up and the family, after some uncertainty, settled in relatively cramped conditions in Paris, with relatively little money of their own. The wider family saw to it that standards did not drop so far as to threaten the marriage prospects of the older girls.

Something happened to Alice in the Paris years that is hard to interpret. Among its components were political turmoil and the after-effects of war, along with fear and distress at family and national suffering. Like Olga, Alice was an active philanthropist: in the 1912 Balkan Wars she had gone to the front in northern Greece and nursed wounded soldiers in the field hospitals. She had a sense of duty and power. In Paris, perhaps, there was nothing for her to do. Andrew, disillusioned about Greece, settled into a quiet life as a playboy. Alice took to philosophy and religion. She had what is described as a religious crisis, although Vickers also reveals that in 1925 she fell in love with a married Englishman and 'turned towards religion as a safe outlet' for repressed feelings when she gave him up. She became thin and exhausted. She stopped dealing with domestic matters. The children found her strange; she talked about God all the time. In 1928, she was received into the Greek Orthodox church at a private chapel at St Cloud. She had visions. She became a 'bride of Christ'. She believed she had healing power in her hands and would lie on the floor for hours as she received it, or if not on the floor in a hot bath. She worked in a clinic. She wanted to help. She stopped talking to her family. Her mother, Victoria, thought she had 'anaemia of the brain from too much contemplation & starvation', and before long Alice was in a private sanatorium – at first willingly and then, on the instructions of her husband and mother, taken and briefly kept there by force – undergoing psychoanalysis. Her doctor, Dr Ernst Simmel, had worked with Freud and he consulted Freud about what he diagnosed as a 'neurotic-pre-psychotic-libidinous condition'. Freud suggested X-raying the gonads (ovaries) to accelerate the menopause. Other doctors, treatments, diagnoses and clinics followed.

Alice wanted to do good and save the world. Throughout the 1930s she was a lonely and dignified figure, wandering over Europe, thinking spiritual thoughts, cut off from her children, undergoing cures, nervously watched from afar by the guardians of family. She saw nothing of her son Philip. By the end of that decade she was deemed able to look after herself. Her mother considered her 'much more tactful & considerate' and observed that she 'fights against her impulsiveness'. She was 'a bit touchy still', but that was 'natural to her character'. Victoria declared that she respected Alice's determination to live an independent life, 'studying the ways of mankind & its needs & being useful in her own way'. Alice's way was to return to Greece because Philip was, after all, a Prince of Greece (her daughters had married Germans) and he should have a home there; and to found an order of nuns. Shortly after she returned the Second World War began and once again she was able to busy herself nursing the wounded and providing food and clothing for the needy. In 1941 when the Greek royal family – having returned to Greece – went into exile once again, she stayed.

The Germans withdrew from Greece in October 1944. A small British force was sent there under the command of General Scobie. The British were not being sent to fight. Their task was to distribute food, guard supply dumps, maintain law and order and restore communications. It didn't turn out quite like that

Athens

because they ended up having to choose sides in a vicious civil war.

Henry Maule's biography of the General is titled *Scobie, Hero of Greece* and Maule begins by referring to 'the contentiousness of the subject', by which he means the continuing divisions of opinion about whether the British should have supported the pro-monarchists of the right, as they did, partly because of the British family connections of the Greek royals, rather than the communists of the left, and whether right or left, pro or anti monarchy, was the will of the people. Scobie's 'heroism', from this English biographer's point of view, was in helping defeat communism.

The left groupings of EAM/ELAS, well-organised and well-armed, were already keeping law and order in many parts of the country, levying taxes, conscripting the youth. They saw themselves as the legitimate future government and the British, therefore, as the enemy.

Scobie was under orders to maintain friendly relations and keep above politics. It was an impossible task. Earl Jellicoe, also involved in the campaign, admitted, 'Most of us who were there in the autumn of 1944 found ourselves almost wholly unbriefed and psychologically quite unprepared for the realities with which we were soon to be confronted.'

British men encountering Greece and the Greeks often record responses that could come under the category 'psychologically quite unprepared', ranging from the ecstatic to the utterly perplexed and confounded. The Greeks traditionally held the British in high regard. They venerated Byron who went to support Greece in the War of Independence against Ottoman rule (1821-29) and died in Greece in 1824. Byron's fame as a poet had helped turn what was already tremendous British sympathy for the Greek cause into government action and the Greeks were grateful. The British navy had fought

Not Speaking

alongside the Greeks against the Turks. The London Philhellenic Committee backed loans that effectively financed the revolutionaries. Philhellenes celebrated the gaining of freedom in the spirit of Byron's poem, 'The Isles of Greece':

> The mountains look on Marathon—
> And Marathon looks on the sea;
> And musing there an hour alone,
> I dream'd that Greece might still be free.

A free Greece, noble and heroic in the cause of liberty, was the Greece that British men throughout the nineteenth and early twentieth century were psychologically prepared for, especially those with a classical education. Like the philhellenes of the 1820s they for the most part ignored reports of Greek atrocities in the War of Independence, blaming the Turks for everything. Western culture preserved stories about Turks massacring Greeks – as in Delacroix's powerful painting in the Louvre in Paris of the massacre of tens of thousands of Greeks by Turks on the island of Chios. Massacres of Turks by Greeks, such as the extermination of the Turks at Navarino, and the savage infighting between Greeks, were not part of the heroic story.

In 1944 Scobie's troops were enthusiastically received. They were allies, rescuers; adulation met them everywhere; children came up to touch them 'as if we were the heroes of their bedtime stories', as one young serviceman wrote home. There was no hint of the realities that were to come. But as the weapons of the Greek resistance were turned upon each other and the British found themselves caught up in guerrilla warfare, unsure who was friend or foe, the dream faded. Atrocities, terrorist attacks, shootings, forced mobilisation, hangings and throat-cuttings down dark alleys, mutilated bodies stuffed down wells, reprisals and burnings and betrayals multiplied. The cruelty was baffling. In principle, the British were there to support whatever government the Greek people chose; in practice, the politicians did not want to see Communism prevail, as it had done in Bulgaria and Yugoslavia to the north. Was EAM/ELAS a people's party or were they 'hooligans who have got hold of guns'? Were its many members willing or coerced? Were they responsible for mass killings and the 'liquidation' of potential opponents? Opinions differed. Many journalists and politicians in London were outraged that the British army was shooting Greeks; and many soldiers in Greece were astonished that the posting that had been meant to be restful and relaxed had turned into tragedy.

The 4th Infantry Division that assumed control in Southern Greece included the 16th battalion of the East Surrey Regiment. Mobilised at the outbreak of war, the East Surreys had been part of the British Expeditionary Force that went to France in 1939 and had to be rescued from the beaches of Dunkirk in 1940. Incorporated into the 10th Infantry brigade of the 4th Division, the 16th were sent to North Africa in March 1943 where they took part in the Tunisian campaign and from there they went to Italy. After heavy fighting at Monte Cassino and Forli in late 1944, they were sent to Greece as reinforcement for General Scobie. London-born William Clarke had joined the East Surreys in the summer of 1939, before the war began. He was a sergeant-major by the time he got to Greece, serving in the ordnance corps in charge of supplies of every kind ('blanket stackers'), a role that had kept him from the front line and presumably given him some protection in these many theatres of war, although he had very narrowly escaped a landmine in Tunisia that killed a friend standing by him. He was billeted with his company in the school in Kallithea opposite the Lignu household.

Fighting broke out in Athens after a peaceful demonstration

on 3 December left many dead and injured. Historians disagree about who fired the first shot and what exactly was the provocation, but not about the essentials of what came to be known as the *Dekemvriana*, the battles that raged throughout December: it was a struggle for power between right and left, and the British supported the right, meaning that British troops fought against the resistance that had helped defeat the Germans. Many saw the Greek right as collaborationists. The right wanted to reinstate the old monarchical regime despite the social revolution that had taken place. As Justice Emil Sandström, head of the Greek Relief Commission put it, 'hunger, scarcity of all the necessities of life, inflation, the difficulties arising from a state of occupation, terror, the life of privation in the mountains, guerrilla warfare and the collapse of Government authority – in fact, all the sufferings of the Greek population – had a strong radicalising influence on the masses'. Resisting the right was a continuation of resisting the Germans, and few needed to be told that King George II of Greece, in exile, had a German mother and had trained with the Prussian Guard as a young soldier. (Prince Philip had joined the British navy.) No less important was the overwhelming sense of a world gone mad with destruction. In Athens the *andartes* were viewed by some as bandits and lawless criminals: what happened in the mountains and in remote villages travelled to the city as horror stories. Mazower reminds us that in wartime Greece communications were poor; it was 'a world of rumours, confusion, fear and ignorance in which the state and society had disintegrated at a national level and stories circulated locally'. One British officer noted that what he called the 'mountain types' struck terror in city-dwellers.

Kallithea was a leftist stronghold but my mother was not alone in expressing disgust for the activities of the partisans. In the *Dekemvriana* of 1944 she neither knew nor cared about

Athens

the details. When the shooting started the family escaped to the seaside resort of Old Phaleron, where her father had some connections. It wasn't a plan, it just happened.

'How did it happen?' I asked.

'When the shooting started, Toni went mad. She ran out of the house like a mad woman. My mother ran after Toni, my father ran after my mother, we all ran after them.'

'Why Toni?'

'Toni wasn't right in the head after the bombing. A bomb had landed on the office in Piraeus. She came home covered in blood and dust and bits of the building in her hair and crying and shaking. She'd walked all the way, I don't know how. So when the shooting started she went out, out, she just went out, and we all went out. We didn't take anything, not even a pair of knickers. Father knew a police chief, a very high up man, so we went to Old Phaleron, the other side of Piraeus, not New Phaleron, further, and they took us all in. But we couldn't stay there. What were we going to do? We didn't even have any knickers.'

When they returned a week later they found their house had been broken into and jewellery had been stolen. Neighbours told them it was the British in the school opposite who were to blame, or responsible, or just convenient scapegoats. Toni, calmer now and mustering her English, went over and asked to speak to the officer in charge. And thus it was that Sergeant-Major William Clarke, from Blackfriars, London, and his best friend Corporal Walter Smith, from Rawtenstall, Lancashire, neither of whom spoke any Greek at all, first became acquainted with the family into which each was going to marry.

The Lignu household, with its five unmarried daughters, was hospitable. The men found themselves welcomed. There was a barrel of retsina from Santorini on the kitchen table, from which they were offered cool glasses of wine. 'They liked to sit in Mother's kitchen. They liked the wine.' Bill and Walter went out on a few dates with Toni and Poppy. Rena was preoccupied with Fotini, fourteen at the time and ill with what turned out to be appendicitis; Rena spent weeks going backwards and forwards to the hospital. One afternoon, sitting on the balcony, worrying, she had a vision of a saint and ran to tell her mother that Fotini was going to recover, all was going to be well. Bill arranged for them to have a car, with a driver, to collect Fotini from hospital.

'Mother said, "We didn't find the jewels, but we found a man for Toni."' Rena laughs. 'But she was wrong. Poppy went out with Walter and Walter told her Bill was in love with me.'

One day when Rena was in the church opposite, Toni came to her and said she needed to come outside, there was something she urgently needed to say. It was early September. The British had received their orders to leave. 'Toni told me that Bill wanted to marry me.' They had to hurry. He had to go.

'Just like that? But you hadn't been going out with him.'

'I was there when he came to the house. He saw me.'

'But you didn't speak any English.'

'No.'

'And he didn't speak any Greek.'

'No.'

'And he was going out with Toni.'

'Nothing happened between them, Toni said. They didn't do anything. I believe her. Your father was shy.'

'So what happened after that?'

'Toni translated for us.'

'So your whole courtship was a threesome and all in six weeks?'

A shrug.

Athens

'It was the war.'

There is a photograph of Bill and Walter, sitting in chairs on the flat roof of the house in Kallithea, two sunburned, handsome, immaculately uniformed English soldiers in khaki. They're both displaying their rings. They look pleased with themselves and life in general. There's another picture of them with Rena and Poppy, in swimwear, drinking beer and posing on a jeep. ('Your father could always get the beer and the jeep.') In fact, there are lots of photographs as if, once the Germans had gone, there was nothing much else to do. They visited the Acropolis and took snaps, drove out to the beach at sunset. They discussed wedding plans. Walter wasn't sure his mother and aunt back home would agree. He decided to wait. (He would send Poppy her airfare later, with the briefest of notes telling her to come.) Bill was determined to be married at once.

'It doesn't sound like him,' I said.

'He was in love with me.'

Love must explain it because nothing else can.

'We told him our father couldn't pay anything. We had no money. He said that was no problem. He would get the money from England. Nothing was a problem. Everything was fine. He took me to see his senior officer.'

'Why?'

'For permission.'

'You had to get permission?'

'The army didn't like it when the soldiers wanted to marry Greek girls. They always told them to go away for a few months and not see each other and then if they still wanted to marry after that it was OK. But your father was very well respected. They knew him. He'd been in the army a long time and everybody respected him and so nobody made a fuss.'

'Did the senior officer speak Greek?'

'No. He was very polite to me.'

Not Speaking

The war was over and Bill was going home. He had decided to take a piece of the action back with him. Homer writes of Agamemnon, in Pope's translation of the *Iliad*, that his spear-captive Chryseis was a prize, a 'beauteous prize'. Agamemnon was determined to take Chryseis with him on leaving Troy. It is because Apollo demands that he send her back to her father that Agamemnon then commands Achilles to hand over Briseis, *his* prize, prompting the anger of Achilles and his refusal to carry on fighting. Achilles loved Briseis. She is seized, and he is left 'sorrowing on the lonely coast / In wild resentment for the fair he lost'.

Love must explain it because nothing in Bill's life afterwards was ever like that.

The wedding was in Kallithea on 20 October 1945. First there was a Greek Orthodox ceremony, then an English one. Bill wore his uniform (battledress) and Rena a long, white dress she borrowed from a friend, with a pretty veil and white shoes. There was a party and feasting, but she told her mother, 'Don't think I'm having any of that firing guns peasant nonsense just because you were a virgin when you got married.'

Rena explained the 'peasant nonsense' to Bill, using whatever mixture of signs, words and gestures had served them well so far, and he fetched his razor and, kneeling on the bed, nicked his chin a few times. If necessary, sheets could be displayed. They were in a small hotel in Kifissia at the time, so I think it was his idea of a joke or, more likely, he was trying to oblige and had got things wrong.

'Wasn't Toni jealous?'

'Of course. Toni didn't like me. I was my father's favourite. My father was sad to say goodbye to me.'

'And your mother?'

'She was pleased to see me go. It was one daughter off her

Athens

hands, even though the neighbours told her she was losing the best of the five, the one who did the housework!'

The resentment was plain.

'Why did you go?'

She looks at me as if I must be stupid. 'Greece was a mess,' she says. 'He was polite, handsome. I could see he was respected by the officers. He was polite to me. I thought, at least I'll get married. At least I'll have children. What was I going to do in Greece when the men were still killing each other? Who was going to be left for all the girls to marry?'

'But you hardly knew him.'

She agrees. 'I thought if it was no good I could always come back. My father told me to come back. It couldn't be worse than staying in Greece.'

Bill loved the army. He was offered a commission if he wanted to make a career of it. There were two problems: his new wife didn't want to go to Palestine, which is where the army were proposing to send him; and as a working-class boy he didn't think he could cope with life in the officers' mess. Also, his sister back home needed him. He put his name down for demobilisation. They crated up their wedding presents, which included many sets of household linens and embroideries along with quantities of china and glassware, to be shipped to London.

Rena understood that Bill had a number of brothers and sisters in London about whom he spoke with strong family feeling, especially his sister Vi and Vi's husband Joe. This also was a point in his favour, although when the letter arrived from England telling Bill that Joe had been killed in a road accident in Germany, and Bill in his distress wished he could travel home at once and couldn't, because he was still making arrangements for his new wife, he said something that Rena understood to mean he regretted having married because what

Not Speaking

he most wanted to do at that moment was comfort Vi and look after her and her baby.

'He said he wished he wasn't married. He said he wished he hadn't married me.'

'I'm sure he didn't mean that.'

'What else did he mean? That's what he said.'

'He was upset. I'm sure you misunderstood.'

'I understood. He wanted to go back to be with Vi and he couldn't because he married me.'

'That's true, but I'm sure he didn't mean he wished he hadn't married you.'

'Why did he say it then?'

'Because he was upset.'

'Because he was upset about her he had to upset me?'

'I don't think he meant to upset you. I don't think he was thinking about you.'

'Do you think that was right?'

It was a challenge rather than a question, containing within it a lifetime's rivalry with the sister-in-law she hadn't then met.

'Mum, you didn't speak English, and he didn't speak Greek. How can you be sure you understood what he was saying when he was upset about his sister?'

'I didn't need to speak English. I understood.'

Shortly afterwards Bill was on his way back home, having made special arrangements for Rena to follow him by air. Greek war brides mostly went in groups by sea. With Bill's ticket Rena was able to go in a military plane. There were seven officers and seven women – all English except her – seated on benches on either side of a very bare and uncomfortable fuselage. It was her first experience of flying. The weather was bad and the pilot would only go as far as Rome. There they spent the night in a hotel, which was exciting. Next day they flew to Marseilles, where they had

Athens

dinner and made another overnight stop. One of the officers was looking after her ('he was flirting with me'); he made a point of saying there would be dancing after dinner. Up in her room, she started to feel nauseous. She went to bed.

'Were you pregnant?'

'Yes, I was expecting Linda.'

Next day they flew to London. She was taken to a house in Peckham, where she shared a bed with another Greek woman who was due to travel to the north to her soldier husband, and the following day a Greek woman from the Anglo-Hellenic Society ('short, fat, with dark hair') arrived and gave them an introduction to life in Britain. She explained the system of rationing. She impressed on them the importance of queuing and not pushing to the front. She warned them the weather was awful.

Then Bill came to collect her. He was wearing ordinary clothes and a hat and Rena was disconcerted to find that her handsome soldier husband wasn't handsome at all. He looked ugly.

He carried her suitcase, full of pretty dresses. He took her to Madron Street where Vi had kindly offered to put them up in the front bedroom of her two-bedroom flat.

'I knew nothing,' Rena said.

Marrying an Englishman represented an ideal. He would be 'a gentleman'. (She pronounced it 'chentleman'.) She was familiar with the mythology of English manners, with its commitment to decency, fair play, honest and upright dealings. She had heard of Lord Byron. Perhaps she imagined green acres and country estates. If so, she didn't pine for them. Like her father, she liked the city. There was genuine puzzlement in

Not Speaking

her voice when she said to Tina, who was busy all day long, 'What does anybody do in the country?'

Shortly after Rena arrived and began to be acquainted with her new husband's family, the Queen, then Princess Elizabeth, became engaged to Prince Philip. There was controversy: some in England thought Philip's foreign birth and lack of money meant he was, as my mother might have put it, 'no gentleman'. Philip renounced his Greek and Danish titles, converted from the Greek Orthodox church to Anglicanism, became a British subject and took the Mountbatten surname. His uncle Louis (Dickie) Mountbatten had taken a quasi-paternal role in Philip's life up to and including match-making the connection with the House of Windsor (whom he also hoped to persuade to change their name to Mountbatten – Churchill scotched that hope). Philip's sisters were not invited to the wedding in November 1947: it was too soon after the war and their Nazi husbands were not welcome. Alice involved herself in the preparations, staying with her mother in her apartment in Kensington Palace. Afterwards she went back to Athens and wrote her daughters a twenty-two page account of an event that was exciting for all the family.

Alice had a widow's pension in Greece that was just enough to live on, except that she always seemed to need more money. She generously helped others, and then looked to someone else to pay her bills. Her brother Dickie Mountbatten, married to the enormously wealthy Edwina Ashley who had inherited the bulk of her grandfather Ernest Joseph Cassel's vast fortune (he was one of the richest men in Europe and private financier to Edward VII), gave her a monthly allowance, as did her sister Louise. When Alice was on the Aegean island of Tinos founding her sisterhood, she decided she needed her own apartment in Athens and appealed to Philip, telling him it would be a good investment and that it would produce income for him and his sisters when she was gone. Philip provided the deposit. Not long afterwards she decided to sell the apartment and move into a convent. Philip then discovered that his mother had borrowed from a Greek friend who wanted to be repaid. Philip paid off the debt (he was at the same time settling his father's debts) and kept the apartment in his own name for his mother. Like Uncle Dickie, Philip had married a very wealthy woman.

Life was cheap on Tinos and it reminded Alice of Corfu. She had been given a piece of land close to the Church of the Panagia, the most important Orthodox shrine in Greece and the scene of my mother's crawling on hands and knees up the approach to its imposing frontage, petitioning the saints for Tina. Alice had set about raising funds to build a school for religious nurses. 'I love work,' she told Dickie. To Philip she wrote, 'I feel the need of a whole-time job to keep me occupied.' She wore her nun's habit because it helped convey the message about charity, but it was essentially a form of dressing up. Her mystical yearnings went unquestioned, although there were some who found them hard to square with her restless travels, heavy smoking and love of cards. The sisterhood did not thrive. Later Alice wanted to found a Women's University College in Athens. Nothing came of it. She made adventurous journeys well into her eighties and continued to behave in ways that puzzled and sometimes alarmed her family. She combined what Sir Steven Runciman of the British Council considered 'wild dottiness' with 'a sharp intellect and shrewd judgment'.

With Philip married to Elizabeth, and grandchildren arriving, Alice stayed more frequently and for longer periods in London. Her grandchildren were instructed to call her *Yaya*. Charles, born in 1948, recalled that she was very strict, and Anne, born in 1951, that she was not 'a cuddly granny'.

Not Speaking

Had our mother's life not been turned upside down by war and invasion she would surely have married a Greek man, too; or at least, like the Queen of England, a man with significant Greek connections. As it was she had married a Londoner and taken his surname. The William Clarke she knew was a soldier in her land. In uniform, in war, he was one of those who had come to help a beleaguered country. He was decisive and capable. Other men in uniform respected him. She called him an officer, which he wasn't, but he had authority and access to resources so that it seemed he was a man who could make life bend his way. She knew nothing about his background, class or culture before she arrived except that the family he came from was large and 'very poor'; and while Bill spoke warmly about his brothers and sisters, he had no mother living for she had died when he was a child, and he had nothing to say about his father, even supposing Rena could have understood what he said in those early days, because he and his father were not on speaking terms.

London

'What was it like living with Vi?' I often asked, defeated by the challenge of imagining Rena's arrival in bombed out Madron Street at the end of the war.

'I won't say anything against Vi,' Rena said. 'She was good to us.'

Vi had once said, delicately, 'Rena always expected to be number one.'

Not naturally docile but always pragmatic, Rena lived by her sister-in-law's rules while they stayed in the small dark flat. She felt her disadvantage and set about learning the ways of her new country. She picked up some knowledge about English cooking from Vi and experimented with Greek dishes that Bill enjoyed but Vi would not eat. She loved little Robert and looked after him, cooing to him in Greek. Vi told her not to spoil him. 'She hated it when I kissed him.' In the evenings Bill went to the pub. The pub was the family's social terrain. Vi might go too. Rena says she wasn't invited. She stayed at home and listened to the radio.

'You didn't like pubs anyway.'

'I wasn't invited.'

'You should have said you wanted to go.'

Not Speaking

'I hinted.'

'What do you mean you hinted?'

'I hinted I might like a drink too.'

'Is that when he said he'd bring you back a bottle?'

I know this story so well, have heard it as long as I can remember. Whose fault was it that she didn't feel included in the family?

'I hinted I might like a drink too. I meant I wanted to go out and see some company. He said to me,' she imitates, '"What do you want? I'll bring you back a bottle, what do you want, light ale or brown?" Tell me,' she demands, staring me down, 'what could you do with a man like that?'

'He knew you wouldn't like it in the pub. You wouldn't understand what the people were saying.'

'People were very nice to me.'

Sometimes on Saturdays Bill took her to the sumptuous new cinema at the Elephant and Castle, the Trocadero, an outing worth dressing up for. The first time they went she wanted him to buy her chocolates so she whispered that she was hungry. He put his hand in his pocket and pulled out a package wrapped in greaseproof paper: a piece of Vi's bread pudding.

'He didn't know how to treat a woman.'

He didn't have a job. He was lazy, she thought, and content to stay at Vi's waiting for something to come up. In her memory, months went by. In her memory, he drank.

Like all returning servicemen and women, Bill had come back to a changed country and one in which the transition from war to peace was a challenge on many fronts. Almost four and a half million service personnel came home. Finding employment for all those who wanted jobs was not easy, even if the government had declared men were entitled to have their old positions back and married women agreed to give up theirs.

London

Meanwhile, in the aftermath of her husband Joe's death just a few months earlier, Vi was grieving and Bill was feeling the loss. Joe's photograph had pride of place on the mantelpiece.

Bill stored his Soldier's Service and Pay Book with his medals in an old biscuit tin. Along with them went two letters. One was from Major General C. H. Geake, and it was dated 20 December, 1945, which means it must have arrived soon after Bill returned from Greece. Major General Geake wrote to congratulate 7608497 Sergeant William Clarke of the Royal Army Ordnance Corps, 10th Infantry Brigade, for the award of the British Empire Medal (Military Division) for 'gallant and distinguished services in Italy', as announced in the *London Gazette* on 13 December 1945. 'We are entitled, I feel,' General Geake wrote, 'to look back with pride on the achievements of the Ordnance team from Alamein to the Alps which will add fresh laurels to those already gained by the Corps in other campaigns'. On 12 January 1946 Major General Sir Leslie Hamlyn Williams, KBE CB MG, also wrote to congratulate him, having seen his name on the Honours List. Sergeant Clarke's BEM was 'well-earned' in his view and he was gratified 'to see that the work of our great Corps has been recognised.'

Shortly after Linda was born in September 1946 the middle flat next door at number 35, between Vi and Dad's brother Tom, came free. Tom was friendly with the rent collector, Harry Garber, and heard about it at once. Bill and Rena moved in. Like Tom at 37 and Vi at 33 they had two small bedrooms, a tiny living-dining room that was called the kitchen, and a scullery with a cold-water tap where they cooked and washed. The kitchen faced across the basement areas into Vi's kitchen and the lavatory was outside the back door. Steps led down to a small yard where Bill kept his bike and where one of his first jobs was to build himself a shed to keep his tools and repair the

Not Speaking

family's shoes. A wooden fence separated the yards of numbers 35 and 33, but when Bill swept and hosed down his yard he always did Vi's as well, and soon he took the fence away. Across the wall were the large and untended back gardens of shops that fronted Old Kent Road. A tall sycamore leaned towards the houses. Every summer the weeds in the shops' back gardens grew shoulder high.

In this flat where they lived for thirty years, Rena became pregnant at least eight times, giving birth to six children and causing consternation among the wider family. Vi said to her, 'Are you trying to break my brother's back?'

'Your father never wanted any of you,' Rena repeatedly said. 'None of them ever wanted any children. They were always trying to get rid of them. You see those marks on Robert's face? That's where Vi tried to get rid of him.'

Rena's wish to have six children, three girls, three boys, clashed with Bill's vision of a life without any children at all. She recalled how once in David Greig's shop in Old Kent Road she had a dizzy spell – the second pregnancy, me, was announcing itself. 'Everybody made such a fuss of me. People were so nice. There weren't many foreigners then. They brought out a chair and told me to sit as long as I wanted to, and then the boy walked me home. Vi took one look and said, "Are you pregnant again?" Your father went mad. Up and down the room, up and down, holding his head, tearing his hair.'

I'm glad 'people' were nice because it sounds as though the family made their disapproval plain. I'm imagining them consoling Bill who'd come home from the war with a foreign, fecund wife, and three years later was still trying to adjust to civilian life. I think they could have been kinder to the pregnant young mother in a strange land.

Rena brushes such talk aside. On every imaginable count she

London

reckoned herself superior to the people she had come amongst, and the last thing she wanted was pity. She loved babies, she loved being pregnant. It was their problem if they didn't like it.

Ferociously house-proud, she spent her days sweeping, dusting, polishing, cleaning, scrubbing. She would never be found with her feet up, drinking tea and smoking, nor leaning with folded arms in the open doorway gossiping. She shopped and cooked every day, proper meals containing meat or fish, potatoes and greens. Never ever would she give her children bread and jam in place of dinner, nor send them to the pie and mash shop. And she would have died sooner than see them wearing clothes with holes in like the urchins who swarmed in the street. Sewing was her pleasure. She had a Singer treadle machine. She cut and patched, designed pretty outfits, sewed bedspreads, embroidered tablecloths and knitted woollies. She was an excellent manager of money.

'They were jealous of me because I was clever,' she said, meaning Bill's sisters. 'The men saw what a good manager I was.'

Bill had taken a job with a fur trading company, but left soon after. When Linda was born he was working at Caston and Co, a metal work company in Tabard Street. In his spare time he made use of the machinery and discarded metal to make toys, most notably a pram into which Linda put her dolls. By the time I was born in September 1948 the newly built Bankside power station at Blackfriars, close to where he'd grown up, where his father had been a waterside labourer, was taking on men. He became a turbine operator and remained there for 33 years, the entire life of the station.

He was secretive about how much he earned. Rena thought he should give her everything. She hated to think of him standing in the pub buying drinks for family, friends and

Not Speaking

strangers. He was mean at home, she said, and generous abroad. She mimicked him standing at a bar, preening himself and saying, 'What do you want? What shall I get you to drink? Anybody? Drink? I'm paying.'

There was a little dress shop round the corner on Old Kent Road called Rosenberg's. It was when she was politely chatting to Mr Rosenberg one day ('He was flirting with me') that Rena discovered he needed a seamstress. He needed one badly: he had stored a rail full of new coats in the cellar and the hems had been nibbled by mice. 'Such beautiful velvet coats,' she remembered. He gave her one to take away and mend to show what she could do. She cut the bottom off, adjusted the lining, sewed it good as new. Rosenberg was pleased. He came round with an armload. 'Your father was furious.' Rosenberg's coats, piled on the little sofa, the chairs, the sideboard, filled the kitchen where they lived and ate. You couldn't move because of Rosenberg's coats. After the job was done, she had lots of velvet trimmings left over that she sewed onto skirts, cushion covers, jackets.

The money Rena made she regarded as her own. She used some of it to buy treats that Bill's wages didn't stretch to and the rest she saved. She was disgusted when Bill suggested that if she was earning they could share the household expenses. 'He didn't like me working for Rosenberg,' she said, 'but he was happy to take advantage of the money all the same. He wanted to give me less. Like I was born yesterday.'

She was able to make her own decisions about what they needed. Putting down a deposit and paying weekly sums, she bought the gramophone, she bought the television.

The little scullery and kitchen were the hub of the household. Bill took away the door leaving a connecting arch over which a curtain, tied at one side, could be draped when anyone was washing. At Bankside there were state-of-the-art showers so Bill didn't have to wash in the scullery. Rena rarely bothered with the curtain: the sight of her washing herself from top to toe was a familiar one. If someone was washing with the curtain closed, you had to wait; you couldn't go through to the lavatory or the yard, let alone put the kettle on for a cup of tea or make yourself some toast. We were tactful and respected each other's privacy, but not Rena: if you were stark naked she would sweep the curtain aside, no matter who was standing in the kitchen, and get on with whatever she needed to do. A cupboard above the sink held the equipment for washing bodies and a cupboard under the sink stored buckets, scourers, brushes and cloths. Dirty plates and pans were never allowed to stand; all was washed, dried and put away. Along one wall of the scullery Bill put in a cupboard from floor to ceiling, and then hung another over the washing tub. A row of lines stretched the length of the ceiling. In winter, the scullery was draped with damp laundry.

In his shed, Bill set up a vice and a last for shoe repairs. At one end he stacked the wood he chopped for the open fire and at the other, hanging from the ceiling, were metal cans crusted with old paint in which he kept his paintbrushes soft and ready in a thin layer of turpentine. There were always small painting jobs to be done. Nails and screws of every size were in glass jars. The sharp knives with little triangular blades that he used to cut leather were carefully lodged in a rack at the back of the bench. We were not to touch them, but we did. Saws and other tools hung on the walls. The smell of leather mingled with sawdust, turps and paint. In winter it was freezing.

When he wasn't at Bankside, or sleeping, or having his dinner, Bill was in his shed. From his shed he could hear Rena screaming at the children and Vi screaming at Robert. Packed around them were quieter souls. In the basement of 35, below our thumping feet, were an elderly couple who

Not Speaking

wished they could move somewhere else. Above us lived Ted and May Bryant with a teenage daughter who soon left to get married. In the basement of 33 a middle-aged unmarried daughter looked after her parents and worked as a clerk in the civil service; she read cheap American thrillers that she passed on to Vi and later to me. Upstairs at 33 lived Sadie Barnes, a single mother whose daughter, Kay, a few years younger than me, always had sweets. Sadie had a boyfriend who looked unaccountably like Adolf Hitler especially when he was wearing his cinema commissionaire's uniform.

It was Robert who observed the similarity, though that came later when Robert was older and poring over books about Nazi Germany, with their photos of naked women going into the gas chambers. Later still, he began going to a bierkeller near Trafalgar Square and making friends with other men who were fascinated by Nazi regalia and SS terminology. By then he was working as a porter at Covent Garden. He arrived so early in the morning that the silk-scarved night revellers with their plummy voices were still on the scene, devotees of the Opera House and Drury Lane theatre who loved rubbing shoulders with the true working man and who knew you could get a drink in the pubs in Covent Garden at 4 a.m., despite the licensing laws. Robert occasionally came home with theatre tickets he had been given and which he passed on to me. He was a reader with a keen interest in ancient Rome, especially emperor Nero, and he lent me a copy of Suetonius's *The Twelve Caesars*. It was from Robert that I first heard about Robert Tressell's *The Ragged-Trousered Philanthropists*, the novel about painters and decorators in Hastings that working men really did pass from hand to hand; and it was through Robert that I first read *Fanny Hill, or Memoirs of a Woman of Pleasure* – a book he had some hesitation about letting let me borrow, and some anxiety that my dad would find out, insisting I keep it hidden and give it back to him in a few days. I was troubled by my desire to read John Cleland's 'dirty' book. I thought there must be something wrong with me that I wanted to read what boys and young men like Robert were reading.

There were neither dividing walls nor doors between the middle flats and upstairs. Sounds travelled up and down, and across the basements to next door. From the kitchen of 35 you heard everything that went on in the kitchen of 33, and vice versa — all the more so when what was going on was Sadie hanging out of her window to shout abuse at Vi, or Vi knocking Robert round the room (till he got too big), or Rena taking off her slipper and belabouring one of the children. But there was also wit and laughter. I remember the ache of laughing. Robert made us laugh so much we begged him to stop. He got that from Vi, but he was funnier than her, quirkier, more dangerous.

Robert was a heavy, pasty, lazy boy, and Dad was all for sport, but Robert's wicked way with words, his peculiar take on life, reminded him of Joe. He wanted to be a father to Robert. 'You would have loved Joe,' Dad used to say to us. 'Joe was so quick. Joe had an answer for everything. If Joe had lived…'

He often said this. 'If Joe had lived…' Joe had been a bookie's runner. 'He would have owned a string of betting shops, and Vi's life,' Dad would say sadly, 'would have been completely different.'

We had the sense that we had been deprived of the most glamorous, the most important person in our family. And because Dad so admired Joe's ability with words — 'You could listen to Joe all evening, you would never get tired' — I felt this mysterious loss acutely, the power of Joe's personality, the absence of his presence in our lives.

Not Speaking

'If Joe had lived, Vi would have been walking round in furs.' Instead, she worked as a lunchtime waitress. She gave Robert his breakfast and saw him off to school then got the bus up to the Strand. She had a cleaning job as well. She was up at 4:30 a.m. to catch the early-morning cleaners' bus into the City, home to change into her waitressing outfit, off to the restaurant by 10 a.m., back for an hour's nap at about 3:30 p.m., and then, sometimes, out again to do evening cleaning. Once a week she went to Bingo and once a week to the Lemon Tree in Covent Garden to drink stout with Joe's widowed mum, who lived in the Peabody buildings, and Joe's sister Lil.

At Bankside the men worked shifts so Dad was often at home in the daytime. My early childhood memories of him, when it was Linda, me, and Paul, are full of activities. He took us to the park, played football and cricket, taught us to roll over and stand on each other's shoulders, wrestled, boxed and swam (always the swimming), let us wobble about on his bike while he steadied the handlebars and gripped tightly the saddle, but I don't recall a single moment when he looked at one of us and spoke a word that was about us personally, or that acknowledged our part in the love and happiness he so evidently felt.

He rarely sat down and if he did we climbed all over him and played with his hair. His hair was very straight and black. He put Brylcreem on and combed it slick. We shaped it lovingly into points and nonsense. He never let his hair grow long (he was ex-army in his attitude to hair, as Nicky was to discover). He would sit patiently, amused and pleased at the petting.

We were street children and mostly we played outside. All along Madron Street children were told to go out and play. Nobody wanted children in the house, making a noise, getting under their feet. Boys like my cousins Kenny, Tony, Peter, Derek and Robert, and my brothers, played football and cricket, chased each other round the block, through the estates, along the back wall. Little gangs of boys crouched in the gutters playing marbles, or hovered together near the wall of the Two Eagles to play flick cards. Girls played running games too, racing to the lamp-post and round the block, or tin can tommy, and rounders, but generally we played hopscotch, marking up the paving stones with chalk, and two balls – games boys never played, just as girls never played football. I began a training programme for Paul: he was a boy, he could be a famous footballer. It wasn't clear what I could be.

At school I understood that I was clever and that being clever was a good thing given my background. It meant the possibility of escape. At home there was no privacy and rarely any peace.

One day the Sunday School arranged an outing. We were taken to spend the day with a congregation in Thames Ditton. Each child was allocated to a particular household where we were given lunch. Linda and I, as sisters, stayed together. A kindly couple welcomed us and we were introduced to a girl about Linda's age who, after lunch, took us into the garden and showed us her pogo stick. I thought I had never seen anything so exciting in my life. And the idea that you might live in a house with a bathroom, and a garden, and a pogo stick, in a neighbourhood sweet with the smell of blossom trees, with parents who enquired gently and politely about your thoughts and feelings, and listened to your reply, was intoxicating.

In 1802 William Wordsworth was travelling up from Dover and heading back to his beloved Lake District. Passing through London, he was stunned by the beauty of the city in the early morning light. He stopped on Westminster Bridge to admire the view and wrote a sonnet that begins:

Not Speaking

Earth has not anything to show more fair:
Dull would he be of soul who could pass by
A sight so touching in its majesty:
This City now doth, like a garment, wear
The beauty of the morning...

I could imagine Wordsworth stepping out of his carriage and marvelling at the 'ships, towers, domes, theatres, and temples' glittering in the smokeless air. (London in 1802 without smoke meant it must have been unusually early.) The mighty heart of the city was lying still. Everything was asleep, even 'the very houses', and Wordsworth, best known as a poet of 'Nature', registered a calm that was so deep it eclipsed even the calm he felt when ranging the hills and valleys of Cumberland.

My father loved London, too. He grew up near the river, played on its banks, and at fourteen would walk daily over Blackfriars Bridge to his first job in a fur trading company in the City. It was reading Wordsworth that gave me the idea of getting up early in the morning and taking in the sights. I would creep out of the house at 5 or 5:30 a.m., and stand on Westminster Bridge, London Bridge, Southwark Bridge or Tower Bridge, testing my far from dull twelve-year-old soul. Once, I joined Vi and travelled on an early morning cleaners' bus – a raucous affair. I could imagine Wordsworth through his poem. It was much harder to imagine my father and his father, his mother, brothers and sisters, all of whom were familiar with that same skyline of towers and domes, theatres and temples, and the great river in every kind of light.

My grandparents were married in a church very close to where Wordsworth noted the beauty of the morning. It was one hundred years later, 19 August 1902, and the wedding took place at Christ Church, off the Blackfriars Road.

Thomas Henry Clarke, aged twenty-one, gave his

profession on the marriage certificate as 'waterside labourer'. His father was a cooper – making and repairing wooden barrels. The Thames was still a working river and the Clarkes, father and son, were among the many thousands who lived off it. Barrels were needed to ship goods, wet and dry; waterside labourers were needed to unload barges that brought up the raw materials and goods from the docks downriver to be stored in wharves at Bankside.

Jenny Meakins, aged twenty, had 'no profession' and probably kept house for her father, a chair-maker who had come to London from Wales. Migration into London from depressed rural areas had helped bring about a huge increase in population. The Meakins lived at 4 Brunswick Place. Henry Clarke (as Thomas Henry was always called) lived at 6 Hatfield Place. I am able to find out almost nothing about the young couple, my grandparents, but I do know something about where they lived. These Southwark addresses featured in a book published that year, Charles Booth's *Life and Labour of the People in London*.

Charles Booth, a successful ship-owner who wanted to understand about misery and depravity, conducted a survey of the poor in London. He was inspired by an earlier enquiry that had received wide publicity in *The Pall Mall Magazine* in 1883, Andrew Mearns' *The Bitter Cry of Outcast London*, and the Royal Commission on the Housing of the Working Classes that had followed. In *The Bitter Cry of Outcast London*, Mearns vividly described the 'pestilential human rookeries' that served as homes for the abject poor: stinking courts, dark and filthy passages swarming with vermin, rotten staircases up which investigators fearfully trod, blackened walls and airless overcrowded rooms. Tens of thousands of inhabitants, Mearns wrote, after explaining that he had toned down the 'horrors and infamies', were crowded together in the slums 'amidst horrors which call to mind what we have heard of the middle passage of the slave ship'. There was a 'terrible flood of sin and misery' and it was rising as the poor became poorer: 'seething in the centre of our great cities, concealed by the thinnest crust of civilisation and decency, is a vast mass of corruption, of heart-breaking misery and absolute godlessness.' Mearns appealed to Christians to act. The problem, he assured them, was not that the poor had a natural propensity to sin; the problem was casual or no employment and low wages. Even those working seventeen hours a day were earning barely enough to eat. Rents meanwhile in these 'fever dens' were high.

Charles Booth, walking and noting what he saw, avoided the rhetoric of seething masses and godless infamy. His was the tone of the scientific investigator attempting to describe and classify. *Life and Labour of the People in London* ran to seventeen volumes altogether, a remarkable achievement. I imagine Booth in a top hat and a buttoned-up jacket, holding his notebook and pencils as he went purposefully into the rookeries. Hatfield Place, where Henry Clarke lived, was a 'flagged passage' filled with bare-headed children – Booth noted that they were 'hatless', and that most of the doors were open, suggesting that the children ran in and out of each others' homes. He saw what he judged 'a few fairly comfortable families', but they were the exceptions; the majority of the households were 'poor and very poor.' Stepping into nearby Running Horse Yard, mostly untenanted and turned into stable lofts, Booth talked to a fat man who had lived there for forty-six years who told him it 'used to be very rough'. Pursuing his way down narrow alleys that gave access to small courts and yards all crammed with families, Booth marked the area down in his lowest category: vicious, semi-criminal.

London

These passages, places and yards are gone now, but Charles Booth drew sketch maps and they have been digitised by the London School of Economics, custodians of the Booth archive. Booth's map shows that Hatfield Place and Brunswick Place were close to each other. Also nearby was Mander Place, a small cul-de-sac off Union Street, where Henry and Jenny Clarke settled after they married. There were nine dwellings in a terrace along one side of Mander Place. Henry and Jenny took number 2. The houses each had three small, squat rooms, one above the other, and a yard at the back with a cold-water tap. There was no running water inside, no bathroom, no flushing lavatory. Booth talked to a woman in Mander Place who paid seven shillings a week in rent. He talked to another woman who told him the houses were 'rabbit hutches' and that they swarmed with black beetles and bugs.

Some photographs were taken in 1912 of nearby Ladd's Court and Taylor's Yard. There were three houses in Taylor's Yard and twenty-four people in the photograph, fourteen of them small children. Ladd's Court was much the same. The photographs, from the London Metropolitan Archives, appear in a collection, *Panoramas of Lost London*, and the editor Philip Davies comments of these images, 'The large number of people gathered outside their homes bears witness to chronic overcrowding and high levels of deprivation.' What he calls the 'squalid mass of dingy streets and sunless alleys' was among the worst housing in London and had the highest concentrations of poverty.

When Booth walked down a street or passage he made an estimate of the kind of work people did and the income they probably lived on. His sketch maps were colour coded. Black was the lowest, the habitation of casual labourers, 'loafers' and semi-criminals. A dark blue stripe indicating the very poor meant families who lived on casual labour and experienced chronic want. Their income would be less than eighteen shillings per week. Light blue meant poor: these were carmen and waterside labourers like my grandfather, and they probably earned between eighteen and twenty-one shillings a week. All were under the poverty line.

'How does a working man's wife bring up a family on twenty shillings a week?' asked another middle-class social observer in 1913. Maud Pember Reeves was a feminist and Fabian socialist, whose politics gave her an interest in poor men's wives. Pember Reeves helped run a study of the daily lives and budgets of working-class families in Lambeth between 1909 and 1913, later published as *Round About a Pound a Week*. The area chosen for the study stretched from Kennington Lane to Lambeth Road and Walworth Road; had they extended it just a little bit eastward they might have included Mander Place. The subjects of the study were what was known as the respectable poor, whose wages ranged from eighteen to thirty shillings a week. The men, it was found, worked generally as 'somebody's labourer, mate or handyman'. They were young men, with growing families. The wives were 'quiet', 'decent', and the children were 'the most punctual and regular scholars, the most clean-headed children of the poorer schools in Kennington and Lambeth'. (Being 'clean-headed' meant they weren't crawling with lice.)

Maud Pember Reeves established that seven or eight shillings was the standard rent for three rooms, noting that it was a third of a poor man's income whereas a middle-class man was unlikely to spend more than a sixth of his income on rent and rates. And the housing for the poor in general, she wrote, was 'wretched': 'dark, damp rooms which are too small and too few in houses which are ill-built and overcrowded'. Adding that 'above the overcrowding of the house and of the room comes the overcrowding of the bed – equally the result of poverty, and equally dangerous to health.'

Henry and Jenny Clarke's first child, Thomas, was born in 1904. He was followed by Arthur, Nellie, Rose, and Violet. On 20 June 1918, their sixth child William was born, and two years later, Louise, the last. All seven grew up at 2 Mander Place and all reached adulthood, the younger ones living exceptionally long lives: Vi and Lou lived into their nineties and Bill into his late eighties.

At Mander Place the room on the ground floor was the general living area where the family cooked and ate and crowded round the fire in winter, and the two rooms above were the bedrooms: the boys slept with their father on the first floor and the girls with their mother at the top. There is a lot about sleeping arrangements in *Round About a Pound a Week*, the 'overcrowding of the bed' being of particular concern to reformers. (The reformers would all have been familiar with the language of *The Bitter Cry of Outcast London* with its 'horrors' and 'infamies'.) In the households visited by the investigators, one bed for four people was commonplace, as in one of a list of examples cited: 'Man, wife, and five children; two rooms; one bed, one sofa, one perambulator. Wage 22s. One bed for four persons across window in tiny room; perambulator for baby by bed; one sofa for two boys in kitchen, also tiny.'

Maud Pember Reeves was concerned about the lack of fresh air and the spread of infection. She worried about the difficulties of washing and about inadequacies in diet. She was a propagandist for porridge who, like her fellow investigators, had to learn by slow stages why poor women did not feed it to their families. The reason? It was hard to cook porridge without burning it and ruining a precious pot, and porridge was not considered palatable made without milk. The ending

Not Speaking

of one woman's 'long and patient explanation of why she did not give her husband porridge' was quoted verbatim in *Round About a Pound a Week*. It went like this: 'An' besides, my young man 'e say, Ef you gives me that stinkin' mess, I'll throw it at yer.'

When I read this it made me laugh because our father was a great enthusiast for porridge. It would 'stick to your ribs' he would say and keep you going. He made it with milk and sugar and served it with a sprinkling of mixed spice from a little pot. In our family he was usually the person who made breakfast, a meal he treated solemnly: 'So long as you've got a good breakfast inside you, you can get through the day if you have to.' Hence, porridge, toast and jam, egg and bacon if we wanted it.

I picture Maud Pember Reeves in a tweed skirt suit and a hat. She was observant, sympathetic, unpatronising and appalled – as much by the stoicism of the women as by the conditions they lived in. Her tone accommodated humour but not unmentionables like real violence, or incest. She was in any case anxious to squash negative assumptions. She was noticeably keen to insist that in the families studied few men had money to spare for drink, indeed many were teetotallers, 'and some did not even smoke'. Knowing the propensity of her own kind to judge, she pointed out how 'fatally easy' it was to label all poverty the result of 'drink, extravagance, or laziness', adding: 'It is done every day in the year by writers and speakers and preachers, as well as by hundreds of well-meaning folk with uneasy consciences.'

To support his growing family, Henry Clarke did a variety of labouring jobs, as well as working on the waterside and on the river. He was a porter at Covent Garden market, he was a painter and decorator, and he taught himself shoe repairing. On the ground floor at Mander Place, he set up a cobbler's bench with a last for fitting the shoe on. Dusty boots and shoes were quickly despatched for they were needed. His tools – pincers, hammers and tacks and the very sharp, short-bladed knives used for cutting leather – lay ready to hand.

I talked to my aunts Vi and Lou about their mother and father and how they lived at Mander Place. All my information came from them because my father was not forthcoming; and the poor in the early twentieth century didn't, on the whole, leave records. We know what middle-class visitors with their notepads observed and wrote but we usually don't know what the subjects of their social investigations thought and felt.

'Our mother,' Vi said, 'was quite genteel.'

I (being a middle-class investigator) find this surprising, and am at a loss to imagine my grandmother bringing up her seven children in a 'rabbit hutch' of a dwelling without sanitation that also served as a cobbler's workspace. What would it mean to be 'quite genteel' in the circumstances? But according to *Round About a Pound a Week* there were many women like her whose lives were hard – 'over-burdened' is the word used – but whose natures were not, who fed, cleaned, clothed and organised their broods, who battled with dirt and bugs armed with a bucket and a bit of soap and soda, who carried water in and out and up and down, who sewed, darned, made, mended, patched, knitted, sat up with sick children, worried about making ends meet, took care of their pots by not cooking porridge, had few comforts and almost no scope for aspiration, and who yet retained a sense of dignity.

Depression was the problem. Pember Reeves and her investigators noted in their observations that the drabness and monotony of daily life tended to drive out whatever 'spark' might have been there at the beginning. Of one woman, Mrs L., we're told that she was, 'gentle and always tidy, always clean', but her manner was 'very depressed'. A Mrs S. loved

Not Speaking

her family, we learn, 'in a patient, suffering, loyal sort of way' that irked the observer and, the observer opined, could not have been 'very exhilarating' for the children. Children, kindly and patiently treated by these mothers, seemed as they grew older to lose 'the joy of life'; they accepted limitation and disappointment as their lot.

History does not record if the children at 2 Mander Place were oppressed by their mother's tidiness, gentleness and patience. Lou, the youngest, remembers only that her mother was 'a lovely lady – too good for my father'.

Lou tells me about the woodyard, and I wonder if that is the sawmill which Philip Davies in *Panoramas of Lost London* says was adjacent to Taylor's Yard and overshadowing a blind alley. There was also an egg factory across the way. Lou remembers she would be given a basin and told to go over and ask for cracked eggs. It was sixpence for a basin of cracked eggs. (In *Round About a Pound a Week* one woman paid threepence for 7 cracked eggs.)

From Mander Place you got into Borough Market, and then on to Southwark Cathedral where they went to Sunday School. On the way to the Cathedral was the soup kitchen: 'beautiful soup they used to do for the children, a penny halfpenny.'

When I ask about her father, Lou hesitates then says, 'Well, of course, he drank. They did in those days.'

I know this very well. Henry Clarke, 'the old man' as his children called him, was a legendary drinker, which didn't stop him living until 1956; while Jenny, gentle genteel Jenny, worn out by child-bearing and domestic violence, was committed to Cane Hill Mental Hospital in 1927 and died there of heart failure in 1930, at the age of forty-eight.

I wrote to Cane Hill hospital asking if they had records about Mrs Jenny Clarke and received a letter telling me there was no surviving paperwork, but they could confirm the dates of admission and cause of death.

Drink wasn't the cause of the poverty but it was a trigger for tragedy. I asked Vi to tell me what happened to their mother. She didn't want to because she found it shameful. Nevertheless, one evening we sat by the gas fire in her council flat on a newly built, attractive estate near London Bridge, designed to accommodate older single people, where she'd recently moved, and Vi told me. She said sternly, 'It may not do you any good, but it is right you should know.'

It was Christmas Eve, 1926. My father was eight, Vi twelve, Lou six, but Vi doesn't mention Lou nor any of the older siblings, only herself and Billy. 'The old man came home drunk and in a foul temper. Well, that wasn't unusual. He was ranting and raving about something or other, I don't remember what. He started beating her about. As usual. That was what he did. But that time, what was unusual was it was early in the day. I was there. Your dad was there…'

Vi is only telling me this from a sense of duty. 'There isn't really much to tell,' she says reluctantly. 'The old man told us to clear off. He was really wild that day. And something got into our mother. She was such a gentle, proud person. Normally she could control him well enough, she knew how to handle him. She understood him. She loved him. But that day was different. He snatched up a knife from his bench. You know, a little cobbler's knife.'

I knew exactly. Our father's sharp cobblers' knives with their triangular blades, that had fascinated us as children.

'She picked up a chair to defend herself – and us I suppose. I don't know how it happened exactly, but without meaning to, when she was defending herself, she pushed the chair at him and one of the chair legs went into his eye. It split the pupil.'

'She blinded him?'

'No. They took him to hospital.'

'What happened?'

'He got better, she didn't.'

'What do you mean?'

Vi didn't want to tell me. 'She couldn't live with what she'd done, dear. She locked herself in the upstairs room, her face to the wall, and wouldn't come out. The old man wrote to her from the hospital begging her to visit him. He didn't blame her but she blamed herself. His brothers blamed her too. They went round to beat her up. Tom and Arthur saw them off. In the end, months later, she was taken away. I don't believe she ever forgave herself. She died of grief and shock. She was such a gentle, good person.'

After a pause, Vi said, 'It's not nice, is it?'

It took me a long time to recover from hearing this story. I didn't tell anybody about it for a while, and when I did I noticed that I was as reluctant as Vi was to embellish it. I didn't ask my father if or what he remembered. Nor did I ask Vi to tell me more or tell me again, yet I longed to know what it was like in that dark mean house. What happened in the months that followed, before their mother, weeping and going quietly mad, was 'taken away'? The girls must have tried to speak to her. They must have taken food up, emptied the chamber pot from under the bed. They must have slept beside her.

I wonder who called in the doctor, how much it cost in that pre-National Health Service era, how and when it was decided she should be removed to a mental asylum, and which stigma was worse, her mental breakdown or his alcoholic violence.

When I talked to Lou about her childhood she didn't mention the events of Christmas Eve 1926 and the months that followed, and I didn't know if she knew that I knew. I asked her about life in Mander Place without their mother and the first thing she told me about was the shoe repair.

London

Shoe repairing features among my earliest memories too. When I was a child and my father was down in his shed at all hours mending shoes for the whole family I liked to watch him. His movements were fluid: cutting leather, spitting tacks out of his mouth into his left hand, placing them accurately with his thumb and rapidly knocking them into the shoe with his hammer, tap, tap, tap, till there was a neat horseshoe shape of dots. It was lovely. Then I would follow him upstairs into the scullery where he heated the soldering iron on the gas ring and finished the job off, quickly sealing the joint and giving the shoe a good black edge. The finishing had to be done quickly, which meant standing in the scullery in the midst of whatever mayhem, keeping the babies at bay, avoiding the wet laundry.

'Billy would come home from school and there'd be shoes to mend,' Lou said, 'and he'd find Father drunk again, so he and Vi would do the shoes.'

Lou's job was to take the mended shoes to the customer and get the money. 'They'd invariably say they'd pay later. I could never insist. It's no wonder I still hate asking anybody for money.'

'Billy used to have to do the shopping,' she told me. 'He had to go down the Cut to buy meat before he went to school. This already made him late, and often when he brought it back the old man would tell him it was too fatty and he'd have to go again and change it. Eventually the school realised why he was late so often and stopped punishing him for it.'

Dad told a similar story about being selected for the school cricket team. He was supposed to stay behind after school for practices and matches, but the old man wanted him home to do the chores and if he was late he beat him, and as his father's beatings were worse than the school beatings, he went home. But he was sad about the cricket.

'He had a terrible time,' Lou said.

Not Speaking

I never understood why he didn't explain to the school, why he had to wait for them to work it out.

'In those days you didn't,' Lou shrugged.

Dad's stories were about games in the streets. Playing cricket, Tom hit the ball one day when a neighbour was walking along holding a jug full of beer: the ball hit the jug and then went on to smash the window of the Sunday School mission house on the corner. Mr Smith who ran the mission (bringing God to the heathen) – 'a lovely man' according to Lou – came to find out who'd done it but they'd all 'scarpered' and one of them, Tommy Morgan, quickly sat down at his little piano and started playing, pretending ignorance.

I'm intrigued by the little piano. Booth doesn't mention anything of the sort, though he does talk about birdcages: a birdcage in the window signified a street with some 'fairly comfortable' families.

Nellie, Rose and Vi took charge of the household. They were all capable, and Vi was a fighter. ('Vi was a fighter,' my father would say, and a soft look would come over his face.) The older girls protected Lou. She describes how one night they were in their bedroom on the top floor when the woman next door – 'a biggish woman' – 'went out the window'.

'What do you mean 'went out the window'? Do you mean she threw herself out?'

'My sisters wouldn't let me look. I don't know if she fell or… I suppose, yes, I suppose she threw herself out.'

Saying this, Lou echoes my words listlessly, as if they were not the words she would have chosen or likes.

I'm struck by 'went out the window'. It is so like 'went out the door'. But this window was on the top floor, and I wonder how often women 'went out the window' in these vile back alleys and if that was implicit in the unease investigators like Maud Pember Reeves felt when they found themselves encountering one depressed wife after another.

When we were children Vi used to come over by the back stairs from her scullery next door, lean against the sink in our scullery, light up a cigarette, and tell us about the old days. Vi did the voices and the silly walks. She laughed at everything. Vi was the 'rebel' and the entertainer. When Vi was fifteen or sixteen, Lou tells me, she wanted to go to a dance at a place on Southwark Bridge, and announced that she intended to stay till the dance ended. Her father said she had to come back by a certain time. 'He was always strict with us girls.' There was a confrontation. Vi argued and insisted she would stay out as long as she wanted.

'She was standing with her back to the front door,' Lou says. 'I'll never forget. The door had one of those big old-fashioned locks. The old man drew back his fist to punch her, but Vi ducked, and his fist smashed into the lock.'

Vi went to the dance. She also, more surprisingly, won the argument because Lou was sent after her to tell her she could, after all, stay till it ended. An excited Lou had run all the way, carrying what she thought was welcome news, only to be blithely dismissed by her older sister. Vi had every intention of staying, no matter what.

'I was a bit put out she wasn't more grateful.'

Lou finds nothing odd in this memory. Her father was 'strict' with his girls as, in her eyes, a father should be. She has a much softer version of him than I've been used to hearing. 'When the old man was sober he'd make us lovely dinners, stews and things.'

Vi once corrected me sharply when I talked about 'the London poor'. 'We didn't think we were poor,' she said. 'There was always enough to eat. On Sundays there was always a roast.'

Not Speaking

'We loved him,' Lou adds. 'And when I got married and had children I understood more what he had gone through.'

Of her three brothers Lou was closest to Arthur. She met her husband, Reggie Pollard, through Arthur. Arthur was a wood machinist, a frame-maker, working for H. J. Searles, chair makers, in Old Kent Road. Arthur, married and living near Walworth Road, drank in the Roebuck in Trafalgar Street. The Roebuck became a regular haunt. Lou shows me a photograph taken there one evening: Lou and Reggie, Arthur and Edie. I'm startled by how glamorous they look. It reminds me of the photograph of Tom and May's wedding which was published in the *South London Press*. How did that happen?

Lou laughs. 'Tom always liked to make a splash,' she says.

'But how did it get into the local paper?'

Lou doesn't know.

Before the war, Lou and Reggie lived at 7 Madron Street. Tom was already at 37, with May and their son, Kenny, and Vi at 33, married to Joe Putnam. Bill had been working as a journeyman plumber; he lodged with Vi when he was in London. Nellie had married Harry Vinnicombe and moved to Bermondsey, to 34A Thorburn Square, a basement flat, where they lived till their old age. Harry's sister Jessie lived above. Nellie and Jessie, best friends (as Vi was with Joe's sister Lil), worked together at the Peek Frean biscuit factory. 'Most people in Bermondsey worked at Peek Freans,' Lou says, and when she says it I remember the sweet custardy aroma that floated from Clements Road to our school, Aylwin, in Southwark Park Road. Depending on which way the wind blew, what you had in the air was biscuits or malt or the smell from the Bermondsey leather tanneries.

The wives all worked: they were early morning cleaners, factory hands, waitresses.

'When war broke out,' Lou says, 'Reggie joined the

merchant navy as a gunner. Harry Vinnicombe was in the navy proper. Billy was already in the army, so was Joe. Tom couldn't enlist because of his leg.' Tom had lost a foot in a tram accident. 'Arthur was rejected because of perforated eardrums. He joined the police reserves. Sometimes it happened that Reg, Harry, Joe and Billy found themselves in the same place during the war and then they would move heaven and earth to meet up and have a drink.'

It strikes me as unlikely that they would ever have been in the same place at the same time but Lou insists it did happen.

I don't ask Lou why Bill joined up before war broke out.

I remember having one conversation with my father about his early enlistment. We were talking late at night, and he immediately tried to retract what he said. The memory of what happened existed for him in the category of 'not to be spoken', and like much else that he recalled it lacked narrative coherence. I understood he had quarrelled with his father. He was twenty. What was it about? Who knows? His father threatened him with a knife.

'It wasn't so bad. The old man couldn't help it.'
'What did he do?'
'Nothing really.'
'But you had a fight?'
'Not a fight exactly.'
'You quarrelled. And he picked up a knife?'
'Well, he was always like that.'
'Threatening you with knives?'
'No. Not that. Not as bad as that. But that night I just thought, I've had enough of this.'
'So you went and joined up.'
'I had enough. It was the last straw. I didn't want anything more to do with him. So I went and took the King's shilling.'

Lou remembers something else. 'And then your father was

Not Speaking

missing after Dunkirk and we thought he was dead. And then he turned up. And then the old man was proud of him.'

Dunkirk we've all heard about, how he was on the beach and was one of those rescued by someone in a small fishing boat; and then, because everything was so chaotic and nobody knew where anybody was, once safely ashore he took advantage of the opportunity to wander about the countryside for a few days before reporting in.

'Billy was the only one of his sons fighting for his country. Our father was proud of him. He did look handsome in his uniform.'

'Did they make up their quarrel?'

Lou can't answer but wants me to believe they did. Dad had never said his father was proud of him.

I ask Lou, 'Where did your father go when everybody else moved to Madron Street and Walworth Road and Bermondsey?'

She doesn't know. She was busy being a new mum.

'He was somewhere in the Borough, doing shoe repair. He got himself a kiosk that he worked from. Reg called it a shop, but it wasn't. When I went there, pushing the pram, I couldn't even get it in. There was just room for him to sit.'

Lou was working as a cleaner at Guy's hospital in the early 1950s when her father was diagnosed with throat cancer and had a tracheotomy. That was when he moved to Madron Street. Vi, the rebel, took him in. Lou tells me about a crisis early in his illness when they took him to Guy's and heard an unsympathetic doctor say to a nurse, 'Give him some morphine and send him home.' Lou, indignant, told the doctor, 'We love our father and we only brought him here because we were worried.' She says she spoke quietly and didn't forget her place – especially as she worked there. 'They sent him home in an ambulance.' Once he was settled, Vi offered the ambulance men a cup of tea. The old man had been put to bed in the front room, where Bill and Rena had stayed during the first year of their marriage. Vi went in to him and came out ashen. 'Oh my God, it's like a slaughterhouse in there.' He had burst an artery. Because the ambulance men had stopped for tea, they were able to deal with it.

My grandfather lived another five years. My only memory of him dates from this period. We children were told that he had a hole in his windpipe and that was why he always wore a white choker. He couldn't talk. There was something funny about his eyes. He was a looming, ill-tempered and frightening presence, living next door to us.

I tried to get Lou to tell me something about how the family reacted when Bill brought Rena home from the war. It was a question too far.

'Don't you remember anything?'

Lou tells me about taking her new sister-in-law down East Lane market. Rena was interested in the stalls selling fabrics. Apparently there was an uncomfortable moment when a stallholder became angry because the foreigner was fingering his cloth. 'Of course, in her country that's what they did,' Lou says politely.

She says she still can't always understand what our mother says when she's speaking.

'Could you understand her at all at that time?'

'Well, she didn't speak any English,' Lou says.

Derek, my cousin, chips in gleefully, 'I remember her shouting at you lot.'

A flash of annoyance goes through me. 'All the time,' I say.

'All the time,' he repeats, enjoying himself. 'Couldn't understand a word, mind you.'

I think how much I envied English friends and relations their

Not Speaking

quiet, English houses. Then I recall Vi and Robert and their screaming rages.

Rena knew the old man had been 'rough' with the children but she approved of the respect they showed by taking care of him. He knew something of Greece: he had been a soldier in the First World War, stationed in Thessaloniki. He recognised some Greek words; he liked Greek food and encouraged her to cook it. There was a thread here, connecting her to her home, that must have been comforting.

Vi helped deliver the babies born at home: me, Paul, Nicky, Michael. She developed a special tenderness for Nicky. As soon as he could crawl he began spending his afternoons in her lap. He would see that her kitchen light had come on, meaning she was home from work, or he would hear her go out the back door to the lavatory, and he was off: down our back stairs backwards, as he'd been taught, across the yard, up her stairs on all fours and through the door into her scullery and kitchen. They fell asleep together.

In 1961 there was a horse running in the Grand National named Nicholas Silver. Vi put a bet on him just because of the name and he won. She came over with her winnings and we were all jubilant.

Rena was a proud mother. Walking along, pushing the pram with Nicky or Michael in it, she swung her hips and pouted, and men whistled. 'You see, even with all of you, I can still turn a man's head.'

As the two red-headed boys grew, the 'overcrowding of the bed' became a problem. Linda, Paul and I shared the back bedroom. Linda's bed faced the door, its head pressed up against the cupboard. To open the cupboard you had to move Linda's bed. Mine was alongside but facing the other way, and Paul's bed was next to mine. No more than eighteen inches separated them. Beside each bed was a cabinet with two drawers, one for neatly folded underwear and socks, the other for blouses and shirts. Woolly jumpers and skirts and dresses were stored in a tallboy along with terry nappies, towels, baby clothes and boys' shorts, and piles of pressed bed linen. There was a chair in front of the tallboy (to open the tallboy you had to move the chair) and Linda and I, after passing the eleven-plus and getting places at Aylwin Grammar School, laid our school uniforms out on it nightly: green skirt, cream shirt, green tie, green jumper, white socks, green jacket with the school badge on its breast pocket, and green velour hat. We had two shirts each, which were always washed and ironed and in our drawers by Sunday evening; we could choose if we changed our shirt on Wednesday or Thursday. I don't recall ever going to my drawer and failing to find a school shirt when I needed it.

On the tallboy, Rena arranged her icons. Every night before she went to sleep she came into our bedroom, lit a candle and prayed, standing at the tallboy, crossing herself, whispering.

Under our beds we each had a pot. The back door was bolted at night and, anyway, nobody wanted to go outside to the toilet in the dark. In the mornings we emptied our pots, hurrying to get it done and over with, the homely smell of urine mingling with cold lino and the tang of the outdoors off Dad's bike as he carried it through the kitchen and down into the yard when he came in off the night shift.

Nicky and Michael slept in the front room, squashed in cots, one each side of Mum and Dad's double bed. In the middle of the night they would often get up and come to us. Nicky was bony. Linda would say, 'You go into Norma's bed.' She didn't mind Michael because he was chunkier. A bunk bed was installed and Nicky graduated to the back bedroom but

Not Speaking

Michael stayed in the front. When Tina was born, six years after Michael, the problem got worse. Tina, after she came back from the hospital in the summer of 1966, slept in a pram at the foot of our parents' bed. Luckily, Linda was getting ready to marry Eddie in September and leave home. Another bunk bed was purchased. A year later I went to university.

'We could have bought a house,' Rena declared. 'We should have bought a house. When Michael was a baby I saw a house I wanted your father to buy. It was where the sixty-three bus turns off the Old Kent Road, going to Peckham, right by the bus stop. It was a lovely house, big, like the ones in Greece.'

'How much was it?'

'Two thousand pounds. A big white house. In fact it was two houses together. We could have lived in one and put someone in the other.'

That would have been a plan.

'I told your father. I offered to go half and half with him. We could buy it together. But he was so obstinate.'

'He was scared.'

'He was obstinate.'

I was surprised my mother had that kind of money in 1961.

'I was always making money. I had plenty to do for Rosenberg. There was a good dress shop next to Woolworths that gave me work. I was quick. When I said I would do something I did it. You know the two brothers in the dry cleaner's near East Street?'

'No.'

'Yes you do. I did some work for them. And the same day Michael was born they came to me. Desperate. It was only hand sewing. Please, they said. I could do it sitting up in bed. I got nine pounds that day when Michael was born.'

'Nine pounds? In a day? In 1960? That was half a week's

wages. Are you sure it wasn't nine shillings?' In my first job, in publishing, in 1970, I earned £20 a week.

'Are you calling me a liar? I'm telling you, they were desperate.'

'Maybe they gave you a big tip because you'd just given birth to your fifth child an hour earlier?'

'Very funny.'

'So what happened about the house?'

'I said I would buy it by myself. I went to a lawyer.'

'How could you buy it yourself?'

'I had some money from Greece after my father died. Not much, but some. It was my money.'

'You went to a lawyer?'

'I went to a lawyer in Peckham. It cost me three pounds.'

'What did he say?'

'He told me I couldn't do anything without your father.'

I'm reminded that Linda, after she married Eddie in 1966, was shocked that she couldn't even get a public library card without her husband's signature.

'Perhaps if I knew more I could have done more, but I knew nothing.'

In the 1950s and 1960s, married women who worked outside the home were not generally admired. A married woman's job was to look after her husband and his home. A married woman could not get a mortgage to buy her own home. She could not sign a hire purchase agreement. My mother bought the gramophone and television from the local shop by putting down a deposit for half the sum and promising to pay the rest in weekly instalments. Had she defaulted, the local shopkeeper would have had no legal comeback. Effectively, in spite of the Married Women's Property Act, 1882, a married woman was not considered to have her own income. For tax purposes, for example, the earnings of a working married woman were considered as part of her husband's earnings. Hence, the tax form was sent to be filled in by the husband who was legally obliged to declare his wife's income and assets.

'Every year your father went mad because I wouldn't tell him how much money I had.'

'Why wouldn't you tell him?'

'Are you trying to be funny?'

'It was the law. He had to fill in the tax form.'

'That was his problem. It was his country. Nothing to do with me.'

Linda came with me to visit our eldest cousin, Arthur's only child, Jeannie – or Jennie – who still lived in the flat off Walworth Road that her parents had lived in, where she'd grown up and where we occasionally visited as children.

The Church Estates property – social housing, built around central communal areas, with trees and seats testifying to a society that once wanted to take care of its own – was being sold off.

Jennie was local in an old working-class, Old Labour way: a governor of the school and active in the church, she had worked for the Labour Party in its head office in Walworth Road, her daughters had flats on the same estate and her grandsons lived in her building. For all of them, family and neighbourly contact was close and constant. Every evening the grandsons checked in with Jennie and Bob, bringing a dirty shirt for the wash – a happy arrangement that suited them all. There was a budgie in a cage on a table by the window.

Jennie had her father's marriage certificate and showed it to me. On 22 October 1932, Arthur William Henry Clarke, aged 26, married Edith Maud Warner, aged 28. He was a 'rough carpenter', she a 'kitchen hand'. Tom was Arthur's witness. His father seems not to have been there. Why not? We don't know. Edith's father, Herbert Warner, was already dead. The couple both gave the same address: 106 Upper Kennington Lane. Jennie said, 'They might not have been living together. In those days they were strict about parish boundaries. That was her address, it probably wasn't his.'

I was impressed that Jennie knew this.

Bob, who no longer went out because he was crippled with arthritis, had a phenomenal memory for pubs. We remarked on how many pubs there were near Madron Street: two in Madron Street itself, the Two Eagles and the Surrey Arms, and so many nearby in Old Kent Road. Bob named them fondly: the World Turned Upside Down, the Dun Cow, the Red Lion, the Swan, the Green Man, the Thomas a Becket. 'That was a Meux's,' he said of the Thomas a Becket. I remember it as the boxing pub, the one with a gym upstairs where Henry Cooper trained. He recalled their own local, the Roebuck. And when we talked about photographs Bob said, 'All the pictures taken with pints in hand,' and laughed. Arthur was a great drinker. So was Bob. Bob and Jennie met when Jennie was working behind the bar of the Queen's in Neate Street. They married in 1959.

The pub was the centre of social life. The men sank pints chased with whisky, the women sipped gin or port and lemon or halves of mild, or Guinness or stout (supposed to have medicinal qualities). They talked and laughed noisily, sang as the evening wore on and closing time suddenly came upon them, and staggered home.

I murmured that our mother found no pleasure in this.

'Your mum went once or twice,' Bob said kindly.

'She wouldn't have understood,' Linda told him, meaning not just words and gestures but the codes of behaviour.

Not Speaking

I told them what we had been told over and again about how Bill, who counted out his pennies so carefully when he was giving our mother her housekeeping money, was transformed into Maecenas, or his modern equivalent, Onassis, when he was in a pub. I acted out Rena acting Dad, an Englishman at a bar, his fists full of fivers, eyes wildly searching for new people to buy drinks for. 'Jack! What can I get you?' 'Jim, what are you having?' I told them Mum preferred to stay home, plaiting rag rugs from offcuts of material from coats she'd shortened and hemmed – 'so that the children, getting out of bed in the night, didn't have to put their feet on the cold lino' – and nursing her resentment.

They smiled, unsure how to react.

Jennie remembered her father earning £3.10 shillings per week at a time when they were paying 19s 6d in rent. So they moved and found a flat for eight shillings per week. She was born in 1936 so she's probably remembering the post-war period. During the war, when Arthur was in the police reserves, there was talk about the reserves being the 'soft' option. I wonder how much of that talk came to Arthur from his own father. Jennie remembered how hard it was in the bombing. She wasn't evacuated because her mum didn't want to let her go and Edie wouldn't leave London without Arthur so they all stayed. There was an air-raid shelter at the back – 'spotlessly clean', Jennie said – but the smell of crowded bodies was too much for her. It got to the point where she would retch the moment they stood at the top of the stairs, so Edie took her back up to their flat saying, 'If we go we'll go together.'

Arthur saw terrible sights. Once, near Madron Street, he saw the body of a pregnant woman, sliced down the front, the foetus visible. Many times he had to dig in the rubble of bombed houses. 'They wore out their uniforms,' Jennie said.

'There was nothing you could do. You just had to get another uniform.'

Edie worked at Booth's gin company, bottling. One day she came home from work, stood on a chair to fix her blackout curtain and fell off, drunk from the fumes.

I wanted to find out about the older generation, our great-grandparents, or the brothers who went round to beat up our grandmother after she stabbed our grandfather with the chair leg, but it was hopeless. Arthur never talked about his childhood. Jennie knew nothing about any great-uncles or aunts she might have had, although her father had a cousin, Charlie Clarke. She thinks Arthur was born in Islington. Bob says, 'People were secretive about their families in those days.'

Jennie knew our grandmother died at a relatively young age, and had been told she 'went a bit funny around the change of life.' She knew about the house with its three rooms one above the other, and the way all the boys slept in one room, along with their father, and all the girls in another, with their mother.

We talked about the hospital at Cane Hill. Jennie, the first child of our generation, was named after her father's mother. 'The family didn't like me being named for her,' she said. 'They thought it was unlucky. That's why I was always called Jeannie.'

Linda said, 'Dad wanted me to be christened Jenny too, but Mum put her foot down and said no.'

Jennie didn't know about the knives or the chair leg, the fracas involving the old man's brothers, the hospital, the letter, the breakdown. She thought her grandmother ended up in a mental hospital because changes in her body – the menopause – affected her mind. She thought it was 'women's trouble'.

'He was violent,' I said. 'He was a drunk, and he was violent.'

Nobody liked my saying this.

Not Speaking

After an uncomfortable pause Bob said, 'Arthur's ears. That's why Arthur's ears were so bad.'

Arthur and Edie's wedding photo was above the mantelpiece. You could see Arthur's crooked ears sticking out. I remember them. Jennie said matter-of-factly, 'Dad always said his ears were bad because of the number of times he got hit when he was a boy. He had perforated eardrums, you know.'

'A clip round the ear,' Bob said, and laughed.

'It's not just Dad's family that was violent,' Linda says when we talk about it later. She's cutting out a shirt that she's making for me. Behind her in her workroom upstairs in her house at Winchmore Hill is a pile of jeans that she's altering for Nicky.

Our mother took immense pride in being a good mother and in her eyes that included beating her children into submission. Her rage knew no bounds. Answering back was the greatest crime, though stealing pennies from her purse almost matched it. Words of defiance, some affront to her dignity – a dignity almost mortally wounded by the day-to-day experiences of marriage and family – would unleash violence.

In our house, the child run down to a corner of the room was a recurring scene. She would come at the offender teeth bared, arm raised, in her right hand her shoe, left palm forward, fingers spread to push obstacles (smaller children, furniture) out of her path. Hair was pulled, heads hit, the shoe used as a weapon. It was always waiting to happen. Out of the ordinary clamour would arise a hot and sudden explosion: accusation, red-faced denials, heart-rending physical closeness, screams and tears. Someone had to admit they were wrong. There had to be recantations. And then the panting exhaustion, quiet and dreamy with righteousness and guilt.

London

The violence was not something we talked about amongst ourselves. Our mother's stories of how she administered wrathful, chastising subjugation embarrassed us, though she was proud of what she did, and she never, ever, changed her mind about that.

Michael, when he became a father, said, 'We were lively, clever children, cooped up in that tiny flat. No wonder.' He was trying to understand stories he was forced to hear, which his mother enjoyed rehearsing. When Michael was three, he climbed up the kitchen curtains and they came ripping down. Rena beat him so hard, she would recall ('Only on his bottom, not on his head or anything like that'), that even she was frightened afterwards. 'You slept so long,' she would tell Michael gaily, 'I thought I'd hurt you seriously.'

After we became parents ourselves, it was tense around the table when she launched into these tales. Attempts to mount a counter-thesis, to say, 'We don't agree with hitting children,' 'it doesn't do any good hitting children,' 'we didn't like being hit as children,' got nowhere. The stories were shaming and so was our inability to say that we'd been hurt and that damage had been done.

Once our mother was boasting to a friend about how quiet and well-behaved her children were when she took them visiting and the friend said, 'One look from you and of course they're quiet. You frighten everybody.' When Rena recalled this remark it made her laugh. 'I had a terrible temper,' she said complacently.

When Paul was twelve he put on a show of bravado one evening as she was going out, all dressed up. She had told him he was not to have a friend round, a particular friend she didn't like. (She never liked other children to be in the house, not trusting them.) Paul said, 'You can't stop me. I'll let him in after you've gone.' She attacked him with her handbag and beat him savagely, so that he would know, forever, never to think he could defy her even if she wasn't there.

By then she wasn't there most evenings.

For six years Paul had been his mother's darling, the first boy in a family of girls. Nicky's arrival, followed two years later by Michael, changed all that. It might not have been so traumatic for Paul if Rena's affections hadn't also been redirected, in the intervening years after Michael's birth, away from home. By the time Paul was twelve Rena had had it with being a dutiful wife. What Paul was defying that evening and what Rena was defending couldn't be spoken by either of them.

There were other Greek women who had married English servicemen, living in Camberwell, Peckham, Kennington. They bought olive oil, Greek coffee and cakes from a shop in Soho, met at the Greek Orthodox church in Bayswater, or at the embassy which ran a weekly social club for mothers with small children, or at each other's houses where they talked loudly over each other, Rena's voice rising above the rest in emphatic declamation. Slowly, gradually, she had created her own social circle. Her friends had names like Koula, Soula, Sminnie, Poppy, Lucy, Helen, Stavroula, Christina, Maritsa, Maria. Their husbands were variously Albert, Alfie, Charlie, John, Tom, Jim, Joe, and almost never to be seen. When an English husband did appear alongside his Greek wife it was likely to be at a wedding or a christening, and he would look awkward and at once constrained and constraining. Blankly sitting at a large table loaded with titbits, politely addressed as 'Mr John' or 'Mr Jim' in the Greek way by people whose English was poor and whose respect for the host country might at times seem questionable, they were rarely at ease.

Bill found such occasions boring and embarrassing.

'Your father was shy.'

Rena said she enjoyed herself more when she didn't have to worry about his reactions.

'Everybody was always polite to him. Everybody respected him, but he wasn't comfortable.'

I'm sure he resented feeling like the foreigner in his own country. Sublimely convinced of British superiority, 'foreign' in Dad's eyes meant inferior.

It was at a Greek wedding in North London that Rena met Louki. She was sitting at a table with her friend Helen and some other women. No men. Louki was Cypriot, recently arrived in London, the cousin of another friend. He was twenty-four, much, much younger than her, had a girlfriend with whom he lived, and a small son. He was a pleasant, round-faced, well-dressed man with a penchant for gold jewellery, and he liked dancing. They danced at the wedding. He told her he had to take his girlfriend home but he would return. He did. They danced some more.

'How old were you?'

She shrugs. I work it out. 'You were forty or thereabouts.'

'I was sixteen years older than him.'

'Didn't his girlfriend mind?'

'You don't have to feel sorry for her.'

'Why not?'

'I wasn't the first. He was a womaniser. He had plenty of other women, but with me it was different.'

Louki was making money as a gambler. He operated out of a café near the Elephant and Castle where men – some, like Louki, recent arrivals – played cards for surprisingly large sums. Rena began to help out at the café, 'making the coffees', and being with Louki.

'How did you manage that?'

I know part of the answer: Linda and Norma. After school,

Not Speaking

in school holidays, at weekends, child-care was a matter-of-fact aspect of our lives. It was no burden. We doted on our baby brothers and took pride in being efficient little mothers. Dad's shift work routines meant we often had the place to ourselves. Through peaceful afternoons we played records, built castles out of coloured bricks and raced toy cars on the linoleum in the passage. I cut up card into little squares and drew a letter of the alphabet on each square. We spread the squares out on the table. Nicky learned to read, choosing a letter, making up words and sentences.

Late at night Louki took Rena to Greek restaurants and Greek clubs in Fitzrovia. Their favourites were Anemos in Charlotte Street, where Rena sometimes sang, and Maxim's, where Helen worked as a waitress. They drank retsina, ouzo, and whisky with Coca-Cola; they ate grilled fish, moussaka, rosemary-scented lamb, dolmades, stuffed peppers, stuffed tomatoes.

'What was his girlfriend's name?'

'I can't remember.'

One damp day when they were walking together at the Elephant and Castle, Louki's girlfriend appeared and lunged at Rena, pulling her hair. She got a good grip. Freeing herself, Rena hit back hard with the umbrella she was carrying. A proper fight ensued.

Rena said indignantly, 'She knew he had other women. She didn't care about them. It was only me.'

'Why was that?'

'She knew it was serious.'

'Did you love him?'

'Yes.'

'Did *you* care about the other women?'

She doesn't answer. She tells me she had a good time. 'He was generous. But he wasn't the sort of man you left your husband for. One day he had a hundred pounds, the next day nothing. He was a gambler – cards, horses. He was just like my father.'

Louki's girlfriend pursued Rena. She practiced voodoo on her. 'One day I opened my door and there was a pile of sticks and pins and rubbish on the mat and a stupid note.'

'What did you do?'

'Nothing. I cleared it up and threw it away.'

Then she got a letter she couldn't ignore. It was a summons to attend Tower Bridge Magistrates' Court. She was being charged with common assault against the peace.

'I wasn't surprised. I was expecting it. She said she was going to get her solicitor and take me to court because I hit her.'

'With the umbrella.'

'Yes.'

'You went to court?'

'She hit me, she started it.'

'You went to court?'

'I hid the letter. Your father didn't know anything about it. I had to go to Tower Bridge court on a certain day. I put my best clothes on. I was very polite. She was there with her solicitor. I took no notice. I showed the judge where she grabbed me by the hair.'

'And?'

'The judge could see, looking at us.'

'What could he see?'

'She was a rough sort of woman.'

'What do you mean?'

'She was from the village. She was shouting.'

'And the judge?'

'He was flirting with me.'

'Really?'

Not Speaking

'He said, "Go home". He wasn't going to have an argument about it. He just smiled at me and told us to go home.'

'And was that the end of it?'

'Of course.'

I am reminded of a London court case, Muilman v. Muilman, that ran on for some decades in the early eighteenth century. A courtesan named Constantia Phillips, otherwise known as Mrs Muilman, exerted her powerful charms on a judge and described the case in her memoirs in 1748. Constantia Phillips/Muilman went to court to prove the validity of her marriage to a wealthy Dutch merchant, Henry Muilman. She did so because she had been arrested for debt, had indeed been in prison for two years. She argued that these debts were properly her husband's. According to the law, as she sweetly explained, a married woman was like an infant, she could do 'no Act or Deed to her own prejudice', and that included racking up debts. As well as displaying her wit and determination, 'Spirit and Fortitude' (she badly needed the money), Phillips made sure she dressed to impress 'the Gentlemen of the Law': a low-cut dress, diamond earrings, buckles, lace. At the sight of her 'lovely form', the judges 'rose from their Seats to salute her' and fretted about whether she was sitting in a draught.

I decide to research my mother's dealings with 'the gentlemen of the law'. I want to know the date the fight happened, the date of the court case and the girlfriend's name. The registers recording all the cases that passed through Tower Bridge Magistrates' Court are in hefty folios in the basement at London Metropolitan Archives in Clerkenwell. There's no index. The archivist looks doubtful. 'There's a lot of them,' he tells me. 'How many do you want me to bring up?'

I guess that the incident happened early in the relationship. I begin with a volume covering early 1961 and work steadily forward. Each time I finish a volume I take it back to the desk and the archivist hands over another one. I spend a full two days turning the pages, running my finger down the handwritten columns. Various entries catch my eye. In November 1963 Christos Evangelides, aged twenty-two, a waiter, was fined £5 for breaching the Betting, Gaming and Lotteries Act passed that year, by 'gaming by playing with cards and coin'. Was Louki's gambling café illegal? Playing cards for money wasn't an offence in itself, but it was illegal if done in a street or public place, and Christos (evidently Greek or Cypriot) contravened section 34 (1) of the Act. He got off lightly; he could have been fined £50. Legal or illegal, Louki was probably prepared to risk a £50 fine given the money he was making.

At last, when I'm starting to flag and think the whole exercise pointless, I find what I'm looking for. There they are. The case was heard on Monday, 4 January 1965 and the fight took place on 27 November 1964. To my surprise both women are there as claimant and defendant in two separate entries one after the other. The 'Nature of Offence or Matter of Complaint' in both cases was the same: 'Did assault and beat her against the peace.' The girlfriend's name is given as Bordellou or Bordellon Antoniou (I can't read the handwriting). I take a photograph of the entry and I'm glad I found it, but it leaves me feeling flat.

In 1914 Cyprus had become part of the British empire, making Cypriots British subjects. In the mid-1950s migration from Cyprus increased in consequence of the violence following demands for independence, and it peaked in 1960 when independence was achieved. Most Cypriots went to London. The men congregated in cafés – many of them were working in the food industry, like Christos the waiter; the women were likely to be in sweatshops sewing dresses for small clothing outlets. Gambling was a common pastime. Louki's gambling success gave him the capital to start up another operation.

London in the early 1960s was the scene of the minicab wars. Until 1961, licensed black taxis held a monopoly. Taxi drivers had to undergo a rigorous self-education of streets and noted buildings and pass a demanding test called the Knowledge. Eddie, Linda's husband, was a black cab driver. It was Eddie who had encouraged Paul to do the Knowledge and become a cabbie. By the terms of the 1869 Carriage Act, only licensed taxis with a registered driver with a badge could roam the streets and 'ply for hire'. However, there was no law against carrying people and taking money so long as no touting for custom had taken place. With an office, and a phone, and a team of drivers, a company could provide a car service. The minicab boom began.

Together with a cousin, Louki found premises off Charlotte Street and launched a minicab company, naming it Urgent Car Service and installing an illuminated sign. (The sign was still there in Tottenham Street, W1, until very recently.) They had a small kitchen, a room with a large street map on the wall where the drivers sat, and a bedroom.

Business was quiet during the day but in late evening and after the pubs closed at 11 p.m. it was brisk. Louki, who drove a majestic coffee-coloured Wolseley, picked Rena up most evenings. He would turn into Madron Street from Old Kent Road at about 8 p.m., after Dad had cycled off for the night shift. He never parked, just waited in the middle of the road. From her dressing-table in the front bedroom Rena had a clear view and the moment the car nosed round the narrow turn she dabbed an extra bit of perfume behind her ears, checked her lipstick, straightened her seams and went, earrings flashing, high heels clacking.

Louki's drivers were Greek Cypriots like himself. They passed the time while they waited for jobs playing cards. They had cash in their wallets from their fares. Rena presided, taking calls, managing the drivers, making coffee. The men liked to give her presents. When Louki dropped her home at four or five in the morning, her handbag with its lipstick, chewing-gum, hankies and perfume would also be stuffed with money. The money went in the bank.

Sometimes she arrived home just as Robert was leaving for work. Robert dubbed her Cinderella.

Sometimes as she got into bed Michael woke up and wanted to play. 'He was a little monkey like that,' she recalled fondly.

She had no qualms, apparently, about anything. She weathered her husband's pain and humiliation – neither of which were words she would have used. 'He didn't like it,' she admitted, 'but he didn't stop me.'

Or, 'He didn't like it, but he liked the fact that I had the money.'

Or, 'He didn't like it, but I was finished with your father by then.'

She trusted Linda and me to look after the young ones. She never went out without feeding everybody properly, washing up and putting the dishes away. Nothing was neglected. Everything, as she said, was where it belonged.

We thought it was wonderful to have the place to ourselves. We took a sadistic pleasure in making Paul go to bed, which he wasn't always inclined to do. We locked him out of the kitchen and he would howl and rage in the passage, flinging himself at the door and furiously working the handle up and down until he exhausted himself. Had the cupboard under the stairs not been full of coal I'm sure we would have enjoyed throwing

Not Speaking

him in there. Eventually he would give up and cry himself to sleep.

It was usually quiet by about 10 p.m. and then I had the pleasure of getting my books out and spreading them over the dining-room table.

Occasionally, Mum liked to take Linda and me with her on a night out. Sometimes Helen or another friend came too. We'd sit dressed up at a table at a Greek club and Louki would say with lordly largesse, 'Order whatever you want,' and she would hiss, 'Don't you dare tell anybody how old you are, or I am, or anybody is.'

We colluded and kept our mouths shut, and felt a little self-contempt. Greek women, it seemed to us, were obsessed with questions about age. Now it strikes me as characteristic that she would want to parade us, her almost-grown daughters, while facing down impudent reflections on her age and behaviour.

There was romance in transgression, hers and ours. In my first job, at a small publishing company in Soho, I got to know some local writers and artists including Martin and Fiona Green who lived in Tottenham Street and whose children, as it happened, were friends with Helen's children. They were customers of the Urgent Car Service and were intrigued by Rena, remarking on her queenly bearing and ability to resist their charm. Some reflected glory came my way. It didn't work in reverse, although my friends knew many giants of arts and letters, and if a denizen of Fitzrovia's 1950s glory days dropped into the Fitzroy Tavern we'd hear again about Dylan Thomas and how Fiona sat on Caitlin's knee. They were all, in Rena's view, drunks making fools of themselves at two in the morning.

One option was to be proud of my independent mother who

was resolved on self-determination and refused to accept the domination of her husband. But that wasn't how she saw it.

'Your father,' she repeatedly explained, as if it was a fact we were finding hard to absorb, 'didn't know how to treat a woman.'

Among her models for how a woman should be treated was Melina Mercouri in the film *Never on Sunday*, a big hit in the early 1960s. Mercouri plays Ilya, a prostitute in Piraeus, beautiful, exuberantly in love with life, warm-hearted, and with much more natural wisdom than the American philosopher – mockingly named Homer – who undertakes to teach her the 'real' meaning of existence as outlined by Socrates, Plato and Aristotle, the pure Greek classical heritage he idolises. In scene after scene, the American is made to look clownish while the Greek men who crowd round Ilya/Mercouri understand how to relish life in her presence, either by dancing, or singing, or swimming, or just gazing in adoration.

Ilya knows her Greek myths, and holds her audience spellbound. They accept her variations. When she tells the story of Medea, who kills her children, she changes the ending. Medea cannot kill her children, she is a Greek mother and loves them. In her version, they go to the sea-side.

As for logic, that was invented by Aristotle who said women weren't capable of it. Mercouri pouts at the mention of Aristotle. 'I hate Aristotle.'

I knew what my mother meant when she said, 'Sometimes I see myself in the woman in the film.' Like the woman in the film, she changed the facts to suit her. 'She wasn't a prostitute,' she said of Ilya, the whole point of whose presence in the film is that she is a prostitute. 'She never went with any of the men.'

Ilya not only goes with the men but adores going with the men. When the fleet comes in she's in a frenzy of joy. That the tart loves her work, and will go with a man who offers less money just because she prefers him, is one of the sentimental messages conveyed. It is an aspect of her abundance. It demonstrates her autonomy. Ilya's love of money is a component of her sexuality: money and sex meet when men and women come together. Homer understands none of this but the Greek men do and are excited by it.

Much of *Never on Sunday* is given in Greek with English subtitles. It was probably the first spoken Greek Rena had heard on film since leaving Greece. The music, by Manos Hadjidakis, celebrated taverna life and bouzouki-playing. It became immensely popular in England. In restaurants like Anemos, English tourists could relive their enjoyment of Greek island holidays, smashing plates and dancing the tsamikos, or, after *Zorba the Greek* in 1964, the syrtaki, feebly copying these great originals as the American philosopher does, and, like him, expecting their homage to be appreciated.

When I watched *Never on Sunday* I saw in Ilya my mother's vivacity and zest for company and in Homer my father's well-meaning, misguided, hopelessly decent efforts to please her. No intellectual, Dad tried to hold the whirlwind using the tools that came to hand: British reserve, resentment, rage and restraint, along with a dash of xenophobia. The appeal of the film for Rena must also have been in the way it reversed her situation: here it was the man, from a powerful country, who was among foreigners and struggling to adjust to their cultural ways.

Paul remembered these years with bitterness towards his sisters, especially me. He wrote from Hastings, 'I still remember bouncing on a bed in Madron Street during a pillow fight between you and Linda, and as soon as I laughed, everything stopped and you told me I was getting too excited. I was having fun and you screwed it.'

'We didn't have much help, growing up,' I wrote back.

He answered:

There were a lot of us in a small space. It was lucky that the younger ones, me, Nicky and Michael had the gardens at the back. You took up most of the living space for your studies. You had the table and the flaps were always opened. It didn't leave much room. Without that garden at the back things may have been very different for all of us, and you. We did have support but only from Dad. Dad always attended our school open days. He took an interest. What did Mum do? Nothing! Now she's prancing around her successful offspring like a strutting pea-hen. When you and Linda left home things took a turn. Dad was working most nights, Mum was whoring it up in Goodge Street and I was left to change Tina's nappies and put the boys to bed. I was fourteen years old. Give or take. When I got the chance to go outside, I watched all my mates playing while I rocked a pram. There are many things that you are probably not aware of.

There were two tables for me to work at in Madron Street, the drop-leaf dining table in the kitchen, where the television was, and the Formica-topped table in the scullery. The bedrooms were too cold to sit in during winter but in summer I perched on the edge of Mum's sewing machine, crammed up next to her dressing-table with its perfumes and vials, avoiding putting my feet on the treadle, and improvised a desk, arranging my books on the bed, the dressing-table stool, the cot.

Nobody questioned the virtue of my 'studies', and I thought only of how unfair it was that luckier people, like prisoners for example, or nuns, had whole rooms to themselves and no babies to look after.

Later, I would often spend the evening in Fitzrovia when

Not Speaking

I was working in Dean Street and living in a shared flat in Clapham. I sometimes took a Greek coffee with Mum at midnight at the Urgent Car Service, with or without my drunken friends. Nicky was twelve or so then, Michael ten, Tina four. My memory is that the children still at home, including Paul at eighteen, lived in a war zone, but as I'd never had a conversation with any of the boys about it, nor mentioned Louki's name, nor Stavros who came after, I knew nothing about how it felt to them.

It is true that I didn't give one thought that I can remember to who, after I'd left, would be looking after the children. But my friends from university tell me I talked about home and siblings all the time.

Dad's brothers and sisters had a powerful sense of identity as stalwart South London working class. They had survived the Blitz and won the war. They would say things like, 'We look after our own.' And (proudly), 'We came up from the gutter.' They believed in being cheerful, having a drink and a laugh – and possibly a knees-up – after the day's work. They drank in pubs their father and his father had drunk in and where other clannish families gathered, in the Borough, Old Kent Road, Elephant and Castle, Walworth Road. They quarrelled and fell out, fell back in, spread malicious gossip, helped each other, were rivalrous and disparaging and profoundly bonded. The familiar 'we' signalled an inclusive ethos. The family, it seemed to say, could provide everything; it was a world in itself.

When Bill brought a Greek wife home from the war, it was a challenge. I know this by inference and induction, not because I was told: Rena's arrival and assimilation into the Clarke clan never featured among the stories. Tact, discretion, the mixture of admiration and alarm she seemed to provoke, kept people silent. What they might have said amongst themselves I didn't ask. Rena's difference was a fact of life that Rena's children were born into.

The texture of daily experience inside our home was a composite we absorbed as we grew, now English, now foreign: language, food, values, behaviours. All institutions outside the home were English: school, church, Sunday school, hospital, although we did occasionally go to the Greek church in Moscow Road, Bayswater. School and university were for me intensely, purely English, and personal; a separate sphere, full of adventures that I told Linda about. I didn't think of my sister as being half Greek. When I closed the front door behind me I closed it on the Greek part of my life and had no reason to think she did otherwise – had I thought about it at all. The mixture didn't show and it had no meaning. It wasn't hidden; it just wasn't there. I assumed the same was true of Paul, Nicky, Michael and Tina.

I came to understand that I was wrong, as I came to understand that my impulse to write about the family had as much to do with separation as belonging. As a child, my imagination had dwelt on escape. My future would be elsewhere, following a path laid down by school, not home. The younger generation of my siblings also imagined futures for themselves outside the range of family expectation, if it makes sense to talk of expectation at all. All three became rich, which was certainly a fantasy. Unlike their older siblings they resisted the logic of separation. The more their lives diverged from their family origins – as they sent their children to private schools, bought large houses and expensive cars – the more their behaviour, it seemed to me, reproduced patterns they had grown up inside. Their habits, too, were clannish and inclusive. They worked together, regularly dined together, went on holidays together – skiing in the winter, Majorca in

Not Speaking

the summer. Much of this activity revolved around the two fixed points towards and from which the energy ran, where meaning and value were assigned: Rena and Bill, Mum and Dad. Far from weakening as years went by, the child-parent bond strengthened. Mum and Dad also worked, dined and went on holiday with Nicky, Michael and Tina. (They didn't go skiing, though not for want of being asked; it wouldn't have surprised me to hear that Mum was going to cook for them in Courchevel.)

Dad, determinedly and programmatically unobservant and taciturn, believed silence was golden especially where speech might cause 'awkwardness'. After he died it was startling to realise how much he had acted as a screen, traditionally protective, shielding his wife from his world and his children from his wife. As our mother's husband he had soaked up a violence of emotion and expression that to her was daily fare; and had digested herculean quantities of his own anger and shame. He brought to the marriage his experiences of violence and a placating impulse that was easily mistaken for weakness. Sometimes it *was* weakness – he was often out of his depth. One reason it came as a surprise to realise how important his presence had been is because it required conscious effort to think of them as a couple at all. Once when we were talking about this Nicky said, 'Was there a single day when they weren't doing silent indifference or all out war? They should have gone their separate ways, not stayed together for sixty years.'

But stay together they did, sort of. In the end, your parents' marriage is unfathomable, unknowable. This very mystery keeps the conversation alive and there were many such conversations in the aftermath of Dad's death. At first our exchanges had a cohesive effect on us. As in all large families, we discovered there was a central pool of shared knowledge and many uncharted rivers, hidden rivulets and tangled streams. It was comforting that our experiences of our parents had been so similar; or, as Paul expressed it, 'it was good to find that you all felt the same way as I did', a formulation that revealed how inside the citadel of self every child is an only child. At the same time it was disquieting that so little of what we had experienced had been spoken. Just as there was no model of happy coupledom for us so there was no model of speaking about feeling. In itself this was not unusual in post-war British households. But even the conversations after Dad's death, in the tell-all culture of the new millennium, kept to navigated routes.

More mysterious, perhaps, was the Clarke clan's silence on the subject of Rena's nocturnal comings and goings between 1961 and about 1985 (when she gave up boyfriends and sin for God). Not one of Dad's brothers and sisters who lived so close to us said a word, so far as I know, to any of us then or later. If it was hard to imagine Rena arriving in bombed out Madron Street after the war, it was even harder to make sense in family terms of the years that followed her meeting Louki, the ending of that relationship after thirteen years, and the beginning of an equally long and no less steady relationship with Stavros. The clan's silence was an aspect of sibling-service. It was what they did to help a brother who had always, and would always, help them.

Hastings

Paul's one-bedroom flat in St Leonard's is on the sea-front. The rooms are small and poorly furnished. He has everything he needs, he says, and the little balcony is sheltered from onlookers so he can sunbathe naked. His monthly rent is deducted from his benefits, an arrangement that suits him. It's years since he drove a taxi but he could still direct you around London if he had to, and if you didn't rush him by butting in and thinking you knew better.

He doesn't go out much. His feet hurt. It is a ten-minute walk to the café that Linda's ex-husband Eddie runs, the Love Café, and anyway Paul has quarrelled with Eddie and won't go there. Since his marriage broke up he has had little contact with his two sons, Ben and Oliver. He feels aggrieved that they have not tried harder to keep in touch with him. 'They know where I am,' he says stubbornly. 'They should pick up the phone.'

Tina unpacks the groceries we have brought. Olive oil, washing-up liquid, tins of tomatoes, fish and beans, spaghetti, rice, cheese, hand soap, more hand soap, shampoo ('Is that Nicky's shampoo you've got there?' 'No, it's Michael's'), eggs, cuts of Tina's home-reared pork ('you can freeze these'), biscuits, chocolate, cake.

Not Speaking

'No vodka, then?' Paul says, smiling. He knows what Tina thinks about his drinking.

'No vodka.'

Tina puts on a pair of yellow rubber gloves and begins spraying Paul's kitchen surfaces with an antibacterial cleanser. 'I'll make tea in a minute, if you want to sit on the balcony and talk. Keep your clothes on, Paul.'

Across the busy road, beyond a car park, under a dull sky, the sea stretches before us, flat, grey, uninteresting. Still, it is a sea view, and to the left, craning my neck, I can see Hastings, where the land rises and there's a green hill. 'Have you seen those fishing huts in Hastings Old Town?' I ask, remembering the tall, thin, black structures built in neat rows on the beach, and trying not to start a quarrel about Paul's attitude towards his sons. The net huts were for storing fishing gear and were originally on posts in the sea. Now English Heritage has them Grade II listed, all fifty or so of them. It's early in the day. We could walk down there and have a look. I'm sure his feet don't hurt that much and it would do him good.

No, Paul doesn't want to walk.

'We could buy some fish.' The Hastings fleet still goes out from the Stade, as it has done for centuries, and brings in mackerel, herring, Dover sole.

No, Paul doesn't want to buy fish.

The truth is, he isn't feeling so good, he explains. Partly it's his feet, partly his digestion is bad. He lights a cigarette. I fiddle with my phone, checking to see what time the fish shops close and whether the net huts are open to the public. Surely a walk would be the best thing.

'You are wrong,' Paul says to me, 'if you think I'm going to tell you I had a miserable childhood. I don't know about you, but I had a wonderful childhood.'

'I didn't say you didn't.'

Hastings

'When I look back all I remember is good things. We were very lucky.'

Tina is scrubbing the mugs. I'm reminded of Mum, in Majorca, squeezing washing-up liquid into the bottom of a glass and sponging it vigorously then rinsing it a long time under the tap. When I get my tea it smells of detergent.

'We were lucky we had the back gardens and all that freedom. It's not like it is for kids today.'

Paul wants to help me write my book. He thinks it's important. He's been writing his own book that he doesn't want to show me, although he has sent versions of it to Tina, Linda, Nicky and Michael.

I ask him if he feels half Greek. He tells me he feels more Greek than English and that he is passionate about Greece and its people. 'In Greece the family stays together. Even though a son or daughter has their own house, the parents are always close by and playing a part. Children don't leave the nest, not like in our culture. When we leave, we leave, and there's no way we're coming back.'

'Do you think that's a good thing?'

'What?'

'What you just said.'

'Which bit of what I just said?'

'About the family staying together and everybody playing their part.'

'I spent two years living in Greece,' Paul says, side-stepping the subject and addressing me in a princely manner. 'The Greeks are just normal people.'

After the divorce settlement and the sale of his house in Bermondsey, Paul took all the money that was left and went to live on a Greek island until it was used up.

'What were you doing in Greece?'

'Living. They know how to live in Greece.'

Not Speaking

'Drinking,' Tina says.

'It was a good life. I want to be buried there.'

'Who's going to organise that then?' Tina asks, quick as a flash.

I'm jealous of Paul's two years. I think I would have liked that life, a writer's life on a Greek island. To hide my jealousy and avoid contention, I praise him. 'At least you learned the language, which is more than anyone else did.'

'In spite of Mum.'

'What do you mean?' I know what he means.

'Ask Tina. She had the same experience. You would think Mum would want us to learn her language but she did everything she could to block it.'

It's a hard language, we agree.

'It was my first language,' Paul says. 'Don't forget that. I was lucky. I had an advantage.'

In the foreign office, where command of languages matters, Greek is considered much harder than other European languages and those who master it are accorded the same sort of respect as those who can speak Mandarin or Finnish.

'Mum's Greek is street Greek,' Paul declares. 'It's fluent, but the more I learned the more I realised, it's just street Greek.'

'It's not her fault she didn't have an education.' Tina wants to be fair. 'Anyway, everybody in Greece speaks street Greek, and everybody makes grammatical mistakes.'

Children in Greece have to work hard learning their own language. The grammar is difficult, pronunciation has to be perfect and it matters where the stress falls. If you stress the wrong syllable in one word of an almost perfect sentence you may not be understood, or you may be saying something you didn't intend.

The history of the Greek language as used today is bound up with Greece's political history. Since 1976, the official state language of modern Greece has been the spoken language, or demotic – street Greek. That decision came after a century and a half of controversy, going back to the founding of the modern Greek state in 1832 at the end of the war of independence. Throwing off the Turkish yoke, some people wanted to purge the language of what they saw as corruptions. They wanted to leap back over the centuries of occupation and return to ancient beginnings. The language of ancient Greece represented purity; it was the true language, unadulterated. Unfortunately, it was not what people spoke. A compromise was achieved in the introduction of a formal, written language, modelled on ancient Greek, named *katharevousa*. Writers were urged to produce great works in *katharevousa* so that the highest standards of prose and poetry would filter down into the vulgar demotic speech of the people in the streets and 'correct' it. Poets, novelists, historians and philosophers would be 'legislators', it was claimed, an idea taken directly from Byron's friend Shelley who named poets the 'unacknowledged legislators' of the world. But the filtering down process didn't work; the distance between *katharevousa* and demotic widened and the controversy continued into the twentieth century. From 1967 to 1974 Greece was a military dictatorship ruled by right-wing colonels who insisted on the virtues of *katharevousa*. The downfall of the hated colonels marked the end of the reign of *katharevousa*, and the fight went out of the fight over language.

'Every time I tried to talk to Mum in Greek she laughed at my pronunciation,' Paul says, laughing.

'It was worse than that,' Tina adds. 'Don't you remember how she ganged up with Fotini and taught us all the wrong words for things?' I remember this. They thought it was funny to hear obscenities on the lips of the innocent. '"Vagina" was her favourite. I would think I was saying "let me see the picture" or "give me those scissors" or something, and what I was actually saying was "let me see your vagina". How was that supposed to be funny? I didn't even know what a vagina was and they were falling about laughing. You couldn't trust anything they said.'

Tina and Paul exchange memories about being in Greece on summer holidays, staying with Yaya, or taking a boat to one of the islands. Sometimes Fotini went with them. They mingled with other relatives and friends.

As first-born son and in the absence of his father, I reflect, Paul would have been the most important person in the family on those Greek holidays. Plenty of homage must have come his way. His importance, symbolically, was over and above that of his mother, the third daughter in a family of five girls. At the same time it would have been constantly made clear to him that nobody in his life was more important than his mother.

Was it gift or penalty, being the first-born son? Which bit about it made Paul feel more Greek than English, I wonder?

In England there were plenty of boy cousins – all Dad's siblings had boys except for Arthur, Jeannie being our only female cousin – but I don't recall there being a fuss in the family about boys as such. Historically the boy child mattered in English law because of primogeniture: the inheritance went to the eldest son. Younger sons got nothing and that's why they went into the army or the church. My mind wanders off and I think about Jane Austen and the problem of primogeniture in English families, and how it often ruined the eldest son. Tom Bertram in *Mansfield Park*, for example. Of course this only affected gentry and aristocratic families: there had to be something to inherit if you were going to be ruined by its loss.

Rena went twice to visit Paul when he was living on Paros.

Hastings

Jane Austen never left England. Within England she travelled more than people often think, living in Bath and Southampton as well as Hampshire, and visiting Kent and Derbyshire and London. She came from a large family, too.

'Mum must have appreciated being in Greece with you,' I suggest, 'and you being at home there and speaking Greek and everything.'

'Umm,' Paul says.

The moment I say it I remember her dismissive tone. Paul had been out of favour because he took himself off, with a girlfriend he'd met in the pub, leaving his teenage boys to be cared for by their mother. I recall being told that Paul did 'nothing' all day long. On her return, when I asked what they'd done, Rena reported witheringly that they'd done nothing. Paul was writing a book. 'He's writing a book all day long, nothing, he's doing nothing, and drinking.' She didn't approve of the girlfriend, the girlfriend was 'even worse than Paul'. Was she writing a book too? The whole exchange made me uncomfortable. I was writing a book. Jane Austen wrote books.

Paul says, 'I did try to have conversations with Mum in Greek. She wasn't interested. I told her once that I was speaking and writing to Fotini from time to time and she said, "What do you want to speak to *her* for?"'

Tina says, 'She was frightened you'd hear a different story.'

'I thought she'd be pleased, but she never had a good word to say for her sister.'

'She was frightened you'd tell Fotini a different story.'

Tina gathers up the cups. Her expression is unreadable, although I can see she wants to leave. Perhaps we should go and buy fish.

Rena never encouraged outreach within the wider family. Language was a barrier, and the fact that none of Rena's sisters in Greece had children played its part: for us there were no

Not Speaking

cousins whose stories might inflect our mother's versions of events. There were no Greek cousins in 1954 and still none in 1962, by which time, on Rena's second return visit home, she arrived in full panoply with five children, three of them boys.

We had cousins in England who were half Greek: Betty and Steven, Poppy's children with Walter, but we didn't see them often. Poppy's English had a northern burr, picked up from Walter's family and in the markets in Rawtenstall and Bacup where she sold cloth. Betty spoke Greek; Poppy didn't laugh at her pronunciation. Betty and Steven holidayed in Athens with their mother, they stayed with Yaya, were close to Fotini and Spirithoula and Toni, and felt the sense of belonging that Paul so badly wanted and that I never felt.

'I wasn't allowed to give the taxi drivers tips either,' Paul added.

'Nor was I in Majorca.'

'All very well for her, she was sodding off on the next boat, but I was living on Paros and my name was mud.'

'You were writing,' I say, 'and improving your Greek.'

'I was trying.'

'Doing "nothing".'

'What did she expect you to be doing on a Greek island?' Tina says impatiently. 'There's nothing to do anyway except swim.'

Tina, whose father is Greek Cypriot, who speaks a little Greek, who wants to go home now she's cleaned the kitchen.

'It was a good life,' Paul insists.

Our visit leaves me edgy and unsatisfied. Paul is right that I want him to help me write my book but I don't know exactly what I want from him and my efforts to steer the conversation go nowhere. He's not abrasive, he appears receptive – in fact, he overacts his readiness to listen – but the smile on his face tells me he's waiting to show me how wrong I am.

Hastings

I think of him as having been damaged by being the eldest son, but he doesn't think that. He knows about Louki but will not sully the moment by speaking about him. He finds fault with women, I notice: his mother, his ex-wife. Dad glows in the memory; Dad was 'a diamond'.

He's pleased with us for coming to visit him. He didn't need anything, he has everything he needs, but it was nice of us to bring gifts. He expects Tina to bring presents: she is the one who phones him, who keeps in touch. She likes to look after people, he says.

When we leave he tells me again, 'You are wrong if you think I had a miserable childhood. I had a wonderful childhood.'

Marylebone

When I was a child Greece was a distant land. In 1954 it took us five days to travel there, by train and boat. In 1962, our second trip, it took three days, by train. In the late 1960s and 1970s Paul, Nicky, Michael and Tina went several times all the way by coach, long, sweaty, tedious journeys. These were the cheapest methods, but even so. How did Rena manage it? In 1954, we went in April and stayed until September – six months. In 1962 we stayed three months.

I ask her, 'How did you manage it?'

'I told you. I always had money. I always worked.'

'Sewing?'

'None of the English women could sew. I started sewing for Rosenberg a year after I came to England. And then the other dry cleaners heard about me, and the neighbours. I did everything, hems, zips, brassieres, curtains. A shilling here, half a crown there. I put it all in the bank. That's how I did it. Not like you people nowadays.'

We're sitting in Michael's salon in Marylebone and Michael is blow-drying her hair. She no longer lets him colour it and it is almost completely white now, as God intended. They've spent the morning going round the banks reviewing and

Not Speaking

refreshing her accounts. I've spent the morning in the British Library.

'Not like you people nowadays,' she repeats, in case we missed it. 'Six holidays a year and eating in restaurants all the time. No wonder,' she gives Michael a look in the mirror, 'you haven't got any money.'

'Even so,' I say, 'I still don't get how you managed it. In 1954 you had three children.'

'I worked, and I put it all in the bank.'

I still don't get it.

'I hadn't seen my family for eight years. Your Uncle Tom felt sorry for me. He tried to give me two hundred pounds, secretly, without telling anybody.'

'Did you take it?'

'No. He was sorry for me because I hadn't seen my family for so long.'

I still don't get how she managed it. She tells me she couldn't afford to fly but it wasn't expensive to go by train and coach.

'And you took all the food,' Michael says. He remembers the later trips: bags rammed with plastic containers stacked with meatballs and hard-boiled eggs and cheese and tomatoes. There were loaves of bread, tins of cakes, biscuits, fruit. 'How on earth did we carry it all?'

'We managed. We bought yoghurt at the stations. The boys would come up to the windows. Sometimes we had dinner on the train. You never went without.'

'And all the suitcases, the bags?'

'People helped. People were kind.'

'Men?' I say, because I know.

'Of course. It wasn't my fault I was beautiful. Don't judge me now I'm an old woman.'

'In 1954 Dad came out to Athens for some of the time,' I tell

Michael, who wasn't born then. 'I remember being excited that he was coming and sad when he left.'

'It wasn't my fault,' Mum says to Michael.

She thinks I'm criticising her. 'I didn't say it was.'

'Your father only had two weeks' holiday. He had a good job at the power station. They let him have a bit extra and he came for three weeks. Then he went home.'

'Loaded down with olive oil.'

'In 1954 you couldn't get good olive oil in this country. They sold it in the chemists to put in your ears, like a medicine, in tiny bottles.'

'How many tins of olive oil did he carry home?'

'I can't remember.'

'He redecorated Madron Street while we were away, fresh paint, fresh wallpaper all through, and I remember you going mad when we came home because the cooker wasn't spotless.'

'He had no idea about cleaning.'

It's quiet in the salon and for once Michael has time to talk. One of his juniors brings Rena a carrot, apple and ginger smoothie from the new café-bar downstairs, with a slice of dairy-free, gluten-free, sugar-free banana and almond cake. She takes a sip of the bright orange drink through the straw. I break off a bit of the cake. It's good.

'Why don't you get them to bring you one?'

'I just wanted to try it.'

'You people are all the same, always picking at food.'

'Us people?' Michael says.

'I still don't get how you managed it,' I say, thinking about 1954, post-war London, rationing (which was still in force until that summer), Old Kent Road dress shops, Walworth dry cleaners, three children aged three, six and eight, and Dad's family. Tom's gesture touches me.

'You were ill after Paul's birth,' I remind her. That was December 1951.

'I was depressed.'

The local doctor arranged for her to go, with baby Paul, to a convalescent home run by nuns in Kent where she stayed for two weeks. Welfare services sent someone to us each morning, an upright figure in tweed, wearing a beret. My earliest memory is my dislike of this stranger who placed the cushions wrongly on our little settee.

'Tom told your father I was missing my family. He told your father I needed to go home. I was homesick.'

'And you had a son to boast about.'

'I wanted my father to see Paul. What's wrong with that?'

'Nothing.' She's cross with me. 'Did you take lots of cash sewn into your skirt?'

'Don't be ridiculous. I didn't need lots of cash. I had some traveller's cheques and I stayed with my mother. My father was always giving me money, taking me into Athens to buy things for the children. My mother cooked and my father was always giving me money. My sisters were jealous. Toni was so jealous she said she hoped the ship would sink and the train would crash and the aeroplane fall out of the air, that's how jealous she was.'

'She wanted you to die?'

'Every time. She was the same when Poppy went with Betty and Stephen. Just jealous.'

'So she cursed you?'

My mother's back stiffens. Michael pauses, blow dryer angled away. 'I gave her one slap,' she says firmly. 'I pulled her hair. I told her she should just shut her mouth if that was all she had to say.'

'One slap?'

'I slapped her good and hard.'

'You had a fight?'

'I slapped her.'

'That's interesting,' I say, energised, 'because I read this book called *The Slap*, about a Greek family in Australia, and a little prat of a boy who gets slapped at a barbecue, but really it's about how you don't slap people in Australia, and now I'm reading *Dead Europe*,' I produced the book from my bag, 'by the same author, Christos Tsiolkas, and it's about an Australian who's visiting the home country, Greece, and one of his cousins, Giulia, keeps slapping him all the time. It's amazing. Every time they meet she slaps him round the face.'

'I read *The Slap*,' Michael says, back at work with the dryer.

'Did you like it?'

'I felt like I knew the Greek mother.'

'Me too.'

'I could hear her speaking.'

'Me too.'

'What was that all about then?'

'I wonder. Have you read *Dead Europe*?'

'Is Europe dead?'

'Some people think it's going that way.'

Mum mentions the Cypriot financial crisis. She is an avid watcher of Greek television news. Images of anxious people standing outside banks, unable to draw out their own money, have become familiar; and now, in Cyprus, the government has closed the banks and 'stolen' people's money.

'Thiefs,' she says. 'It's disgusting.' She tells us that the only place to live, where people behave with respect for the law, where you can trust the banks and the authorities, is England.

Images of demonstrators clashing with police on the streets of Athens have upset her. She doesn't know what to believe. Are people really starving? Friends have had their pensions cut.

Not Speaking

But she says you can never trust Greeks, and last time she was in Athens the restaurants were all still full. Meanwhile, it is reported on English television, as I tell her, that rich Greeks are buying up properties in Maida Vale and St John's Wood.

Michael understands economics much better than I do but I don't know his views on the Greek crisis. Greece, the country I used to think of as a distant land – and in more than a geographical and historical sense since our Greece of Mum's family, neighbouring children, dusty roads, local beaches, sweets on the balcony, watermelon, searing heat, strict rules and fierce contestations was not the Greece my classics teacher enthused about – had suddenly leapt into prominence. Newspapers and television were full of the Greek crisis. It was no longer distant: people I knew who knew nothing about my connection to Greece were speaking to me about Greece.

They were saying unflattering things: that the Greeks were lazy and corrupt, irresponsible, untrustworthy. Greek debt was astronomical: spending had boomed between 2000 and 2007 on the back of foreign capital, and repayments proved 'unsustainable'. Having entered the Eurozone, Greece did not have the option of devaluation to bring the debt down.

One of the ways in which the Greek government had apparently been corrupt since about 2000 was by hiring Goldman Sachs bankers, at fees of hundreds of millions of dollars, to devise ways of hiding their actual level of borrowing. Goldman Sachs came up with a useful scheme: the cross-country currency swap. Billions' worth of Greek debts and loans were converted into yen and dollars at a fictitious exchange rate and magically lowered. A secret loan of 2.8 billion euros also helped bring the figure down. It was 'predatory lending': Goldman got 600 million euros, a decent sum by any reckoning. Later, the Greeks admitted they didn't understand the complex financial instruments in play; at the time they were cock-a-hoop. Christoforos Sardelis, head of Greece's Public Debt Management Agency, described the relationship with Goldman Sachs as 'a very sexy story between two sinners.' But when bond yields plunged, Greece found itself trapped inside a deal that meant their debt almost doubled. By 2005, the 2.8 billion had become 5.1. Mario Draghi, head of the European Central Bank, was then managing director of Goldman Sachs' international division. His concern was to save the banks. Greece's debt was 'restructured' and the 5.1 billion locked in. The debt went on growing.

Greece and its high deficit were profitable for banks like Goldman Sachs, and when the newly elected government of Andreas Papandreou announced an auction and sale of government bonds in January 2010 the take up was enthusiastic. 'Greece looks bust' declared the *Economist* in April that year. Rich Greeks rushed to put their savings elsewhere. In 2010 and 2011, Greeks were the biggest property buyers in London next to Russians and Arabs.

A bailout programme initiated by the so-called Troika – the European Commission, the European Central Bank and the IMF – in May 2010 gave Greece a loan, a staggering 148.6 billion euros, of which some 106.5 billion went to servicing the debt and recapitalising Greek banks. The 42.1 billion left over mostly went towards financing the government budget deficit. There was nothing to spend on growth. Further, the loan had conditions: Greece was required to introduce austerity measures, cutting public sector salaries and pensions by 40%. These recessionary measures devastated the Greek economy.

The loan was impossible to pay back. It had become a monstrous sum. Even the IMF argued for debt reduction. In Greece it started to be said that the loan was illegal: it had been agreed because the statistics – Greece's capacity to pay back – had been fudged; and it had been driven by the desire to save

Not Speaking

German and French banks. It began to be said that Germany, the strongest state in the EU and the country pressing Greece hardest, had its own history of debt. Those who examined the question discovered that, as German economic historian Albrecht Ritschl put it, Germany was 'the biggest debt transgressor of the twentieth century' as German debt had been forgiven after the Second World War. Ritschl declared that Berlin's intransigence and demand for obedience from Athens had no moral basis given Germany's own history as 'king of the bankruptcies'.

It began to be said that Germany should pay back the money extorted from Greece during the war, including the forced loans extracted from the Bank of Greece in 1941–43. In response to being called 'lazy pigs' and compared unfavourably to disciplined, hard-working Germans, some Greeks pointed out that Germany, responsible for the deaths of millions of people in two world wars, not to mention the genocide of the concentration camps, had its debt cleared and was allowed to become an economic powerhouse, while Greece, the country that gave the world democracy, freedom, philosophy, science, arts and literature, was being punished and traduced.

It was said that the Troika were the new Nazis, and that the conditions imposed on Greece were a modern version of wartime occupation. Far from asking for the debt to be 'forgiven', in fact, Greeks should be seeking reparations.

Some people were also saying that if the European Union was really a union, and if the Eurozone had any meaning as a common currency, then all participating nations should help each other. They should think of each other as family.

It was noticeable that the Greek expatriate elite kept a low profile in these exchanges. Money poured into London and disappeared in property, or to Switzerland and into banks. Some people asked why enormously rich Greeks – the

Marylebone

shipping tycoons, the dynasties and clans, smart Greek royals-in-exile who hobnobbed in top circles, jet-set socialites and party-goers – were so unwilling to help. Did they have no national feeling? Didn't they want to strengthen their country? Were they content to let ordinary Greeks suffer? Why were they so tax averse? There was no rush of wealthy Greeks onto television and radio networks to explain their point of view.

And then the unthinkable happened. An election was called in late 2014 (by then, Greek government debt was somewhere in the region of 300 billion euros) and the Socialist party, Syriza, was voted in. Alexis Tsipras ('that coom-oon-eest' in my mother's words) became Prime Minister. Not long afterwards, in a spirit of helpful cooperation, HM Revenue and Customs in Britain started drawing up a list of Greeks who had bought properties in the UK so that the Greek government could pursue them for tax evasion.

What does Michael think about all this? He shrugs. He's not surprised, but exactly what he's not surprised about – tax averse wealthy Greeks or meddling HM Revenue and Customs – isn't clear to me.

Michael was a keen memorialist of his own and his parents' lives. With Nicky's help he assembled old photographs and made a splendid display at Rena's ninetieth birthday party at the Elysee restaurant near Charlotte Street. More photographs were taken at the party; and in the Elysee's upstairs room a photographic studio such as might be found at a funfair was set up, with hats and wigs and funny noses, beards and moustaches and giant spectacles, miscellaneous accessories and make-up. All the guests were invited to go upstairs and play.

It was Michael who had initiated and supervised the LifeBook autobiography project, helping out where necessary.

Not Speaking

The researcher found the task challenging, but accumulated plenty of notes. These were organised into fourteen more or less coherent chapters told in the first person. Michael edited the manuscript and selected photographs. Each of us was asked to contribute a page or two of our own memories to serve as an introduction. Lavishly illustrated, *I Was a Greek War Bride* by Irene Clarke ran to 140 pages. A dozen or so copies were printed.

It was strange to hold in my hands a book with my mother's name on it as author. Books, I had thought, were my world and her world was something else. I leafed through the introductory pages. Linda wrote about Mum's sewing ('My own love of pattern cutting and sewing comes from watching Mum cutting out dresses for us and sewing them on her treadle sewing machine') and cooking. My entry began, 'You never would take no for an answer', and went on to eulogise her vitality. Paul reflected on the contrast between 'the good life' in Greece and post-war London. Nicky lovingly described a 'matriarch' who was always busy cleaning, cooking and sewing; and recalled journeys to Greece and 'Mum's handling of various situations', including German customs officials. Michael wrote of her 'strongly held, highly focused opinions and inflexible habits' and her devotion to her children, and signed off as 'My Michael'. Tina commented on her 'amazing' life and observed that it competed with any modern story, 'full of love, tragedy, survival, happiness, betrayal'.

The narrative voice in the body of the book was distinctively that of my mother with her idiosyncratic idioms, sometimes half-corrected by the researcher who then provided impeccably grammatical sentences Rena would never have uttered. Well-known anecdotes often made only partial sense on the page, but cumulatively the meaning was clear. It wasn't mumbo-jumbo, but some of the statements were shocking:

Marylebone

'My children... don't believe in anything, maybe money and business'; some perplexing: who is the Jehovah's Witness mentioned on p.115? The book was a valuable document, with all its factual inaccuracies, false tones and glaring omissions.

The launch party for *I Was a Greek War Bride* was a private affair in St John's Wood. One Sunday evening in spring 2014, we gathered at Nicky's house. All the contributors were present, along with a scattering of grandchildren. The books with their attractive, pale blue, laminated covers were piled up alongside Nicky's many piles of art books, design tomes (including some large ones by Kelly Hoppen), illustrated histories of music, fashion, film and hair, and precious signed copies by famous friends. The champagne was in the bucket. Olives, nuts, dips and crudités were set out.

Rena wore the dress she wore at her ninetieth birthday party that Nicky had chosen and bought. As she had written in Chapter 14, 'Happy 90th Birthday', 'On the morning of the party Nicky had five different dresses delivered to my house, each costing around £400, as well as three pairs of shoes and some blouses.'

To the sound of champagne corks popping we congratulated our mother on her book and insisted she sit and sign copies. The dining table was laid. We would eat later.

'You must sign it.' I showed her where. 'These will be collector's items when you're famous.'

'She's already famous,' someone murmured.

'*Saklamara*,' she said.

A pen was found. She signed awkwardly in a mixture of Greek and English script: I. Clarke.

A formal group photograph was taken. Rena told us we were stupid but enjoyed the joke – she had been to a book launch or two – and the fuss. Mostly, as always, she was pleased to be at the centre of a family party.

Not Speaking

In years to come when we were all gone – I reflected portentously, two glasses of champagne later – the volume I held in my hand would serve to convey the sound and fury, by which I meant drama, of her presence.

Did her book bring our worlds together? No, that would have been a convenient, sentimental truth, and I didn't feel it. Her book related to books as I understood them in the way John Gay's *The Beggar's Opera* related to Italian opera. It was *The Rape of the Lock* not the *Iliad*. Authentic pastiche. The analogy didn't really hold, but the subversive undercurrent, the need to speak in code to deflect the retributions of power, the background facts of secrecy and self-fulfilment, human passions, human boastfulness – these were all present in my mother's book.

Did her book do justice to her story? No. Later generations, our children's children and their children, picking it up, would need to have things explained. Exegesis would be needed.

Exegesis, a Greek word and one we both knew: the explanation or critical interpretation of the Bible, a seeking of truth.

I could provide exegesis. I could be a faithful scribe. I could fill in gaps, settle tricky points of dogma, elucidate variant texts and manoeuvre between vested interests. I could tell her story; even, I *should* tell her story. Or should I?

We were sitting side by side on the sofa when Nicky and Kelly called us to the table. Vast dishes and platters of meat and vegetables were being carried in from the kitchen. Red wine was already decanted. The crystal glasses and silver were reflected in the huge mirrors. The stag with its big antlers was mounted on the wall, its blind eyes seeing nothing. I began to get up, but before I could do so Mum dug her elbow into my arm and whispered, pointing at the book in my lap. On the flyleaf of my copy I wrote down what she told me that evening in St John's Wood, the last time we were all together at Nicky's, six months or so before the great quarrel about housing erupted. 'It's not lies,' she confided, 'but it's not the whole truth. If I told the truth everybody would run away.'

I understood her fear. I felt it myself. The devil was in the room. There were so many reasons not to write, not to fix these stories in print. But here was Rena's version, potentially for public consumption, in hardcover. Here was her book, in her voice, with her name on it.

Books spoke to other books; books gave birth to books. Rena had given me what Pope said Homer invented, a new and boundless walk for the imagination: her story. It was a gift. I loved it.

After the party, waking up in Tottenham and getting ready to go to work, the fear returned and with it forebodings of loss.

St John's Wood

The move out of Cropthorne Court, Maida Vale, to the new apartment round the corner was accomplished by January 2015 with maximum effort and ill temper and against the background of the Greek crisis. Nicky probably endured more than most, as seemed fitting, but everybody could point to a bruise or two on body and soul.

By finding the new apartment and signing the rental agreement (£2390 per month) for a year, Nicky put himself in pole position. He wanted to regard the move as a wholly practical matter. He had imagined us acting collectively, working in unison and pooling our resources after the example Dad set when he made himself available to Nicky, to Michael, to all of us, and in the spirit of sibling-service. 'Come on guys,' Nicky said, or words to that effect. 'I need you to help me with this.' He expected to draw on the blind belonging that was the unstated Clarke family ethos. 'We look after our own,' as Vi used to say. Vi looked after Nellie when she was paralysed after a stroke; Dad looked after Vi when she went into the home in Peckham. They had looked after their own through their poverty-stricken childhood and the Second World War. Now, the words sounded hollow. Poverty was not our problem,

Not Speaking

though we joked about Nicky's 'poverty' when he raised the subject of moving Mum, especially when, gathered around his dining table in opulent St John's Wood, we heard in the next moment about a skiing holiday that was being planned or a picture he intended to buy. Michael thought Nicky looked after his own interests only too well. Nicky thought Michael was jealous of his celebrity. And Tina had come to understand that she didn't belong to the Clarke family at all. Threads had loosened, plates had shifted, deep-seated forces were unleashed.

It was not obvious that there was a connection between Nicky's resolve to get his finances sorted and Tina's attritional combativeness ('Lee tells me just to forget about it, but I can't'), except that they both focused on one old woman. Rena's final years, the comforts of her widowhood, were at stake. Or, what was at stake was a primal competition for blessing, the need to be beloved above all others, to be number one.

When some of us wondered how the not speaking had happened – or rather, the too much and too virulent speaking in emails around Christmas 2014 – we rehearsed the known facts: he said this, she said that, this was unforgiveable, that was outrageous, inflammatory, unacceptable, disgusting. Accusations of lying had gone back and forth. Insults were flung.

Friends said, 'Siblings do fall out, you know. It isn't so unusual.'

I didn't know what Tina wanted, nor did I know what was making Nicky behave the way he was behaving, but they mirrored each other in their intransigence and they went to war. The war satisfied something in each of them, possibly the unconscious desire to destroy the family myth.

It wasn't really about the money, and it was about the money. Two thousand, three hundred and ninety pounds divided by six came out almost exactly at £400 each. I noticed that Tina, who refused to 'cooperate', went out of her way to buy expensive things for Mum that often added up to £400 a month. Michael began making plans to convert the property next door to his salon into a one-bedroom granny flat. If she agreed, he would move our mother there and absorb all her living costs. He would not participate in Nicky's scheme. The granny flat was his answer, although he needed the space for an office for his staff.

'Nicky promised her a home for life,' he repeated. It was like a mantra.

He understood that those of us who were swayed by Nicky's arguments acted out of what we thought were Mum's best interests but in his view we were mistaken.

Michael had for some years hoped to be able to purchase the adjacent flat upstairs too, above the new property, and if he could bring that deal off – if his brokers could raise enough loans, if the owner would sell – he would be able to achieve both ends: an office and a granny flat. Although property prices had risen astronomically in recent years, he explained to me, servicing the debt had not become commensurately more expensive. Interest rates were low. His brokers needed to find about a million pounds. He seemed to think they could do this.

'Really?'

'It won't be easy, but I think it's possible.'

'And move Mum again after we finish moving her now?'

'Why not?'

It didn't bear thinking about. 'She's ninety-two.'

'She's strong as an ox.'

'Even so.'

'We shouldn't have to be doing it at all,' Michael said angrily, returning again to the story of Cropthorne Court and how, in 2005, he had understood it was to be a shared purchase, and

Not Speaking

how Nicky and Lesley had gone ahead without including him. 'We thought Mum *had* a home for life.'

She never believed that, I thought, remembering how she changed all the locks, remembering all the talk about being thrown out onto the streets of Maida Vale.

'She had no security of tenure,' Michael said. 'It was all Nicky's gift.'

'It was family.'

'Twice I asked Nicky to sign a document giving her secure tenure.'

'A tenant's agreement.'

'Yes.'

'I know.'

'A simple one-page document. He wouldn't sign it. He swore he would never evict his mother, as if it was disgusting of me to even think it. As if I was the person behaving badly by suggesting she should have the protection of the law.'

And what defence would law have been against a mother's love? I didn't say it. Mum was going willingly.

'What we've been pitched into now is not a viable arrangement,' Michael went on, more calmly. 'If she lives ten years she'll run through all her capital. Or if something does happen to her, she won't be able to live alone. We need a long-term solution, and throwing money away in rent is not a solution.'

It might not have been a solution but it was the situation we were in. The people throwing their money away were: Mum, Linda, Nicky and me.

There wasn't a single moving day. Rena's possessions were transported bit by bit. The empty rooms in the new apartment, which looked quite spacious before we began, filled up with ugly black bags. 'I'll sit down quietly and put everything away later,' she said whenever anyone suggested it would be a good

St John's Wood

idea to put the clothes in the fitted wardrobes so that the space could be cleared for the arrival of chests of drawers, tallboys, beds and armchairs. 'I'll do it later. Quietly. I'll sit on the stool and do it later.'

She wanted to iron everything before she put it away.

She went on sleeping in the old flat for weeks after most of her things had been bagged and taken. She couldn't cook because all the kitchen equipment and most of the crockery and cutlery had gone. The walls were bare. The curtains had been taken down. I bought food from a deli in St John's Wood High Street and we snacked as best we could: bread, cheese, ham, artichoke hearts, beetroot salad. There was no wine. I went out to Tesco Metro, which I could see from the window, and bought little bottles: rosé for her, red for me. One night we went to the Everyman cinema, also now visible from the uncurtained window. The cinema had a convenient lift up to a pleasant bar. We saw the film and afterwards ate in the bar.

Pole position was unenviable when it came to negotiating between the owners of the flat, the porters on site who supervised storage, and Mum and her things. And then there was the table. Nicky reminded Mum that he had offered to buy her a new, round table. She didn't want a new, round table. She wanted her table, the one still in the flat he was moving her out of.

We stood in the new sitting-room. We contemplated the space.

'There isn't room for it here,' Nicky said. 'A round table,' he showed her, 'will fit perfectly in the alcove.'

He didn't bring her table. He dragged his feet.

('Nicky still hasn't brought my table.')

Kelly's Dad helped him bring the sofas, armchairs and glass cabinets ('the bloody glass cabinets') and once they were in place it was clear to Nicky that his original insistence on a round table was demonstrably correct. He measured out the alcove. He showed her again. He repeated his offer.

'Are you going to bring me my table or am I going to ask somebody else?'

'There isn't room. It doesn't fit. Nobody will be able to sit round it.'

'I don't care.'

'It won't fit in the space.'

Nicky brought the table at the end of another day of heavy lifting. He reassembled it. It was an awkward job. The table extended from the window almost to the back of the sofa.

'You can't walk round it,' he said.

'That's because you've left all that space by the window.' She began pulling and pushing at the table.

'Look,' Nicky said, fully prepared to disassemble it. 'The porters can store this one in the basement. We won't throw it away. But I'll buy you a new one.'

'I don't need a new one. This one is fine,' she said.

'It's not fine.' He was tired. He was losing his patience. He showed her how he could only just squeeze by between table and sofa, and the sofa couldn't be moved because it was already wedged in with the armchair and the second sofa (which it was impossible to sit on because the coffee table stretched along its full length). 'How's anybody going to sit round it?'

'Don't worry about that. I'll worry about that.'

'There's no room for people to sit.'

'It's fine.' She was losing her temper.

'I'll buy you a round table.'

'I don't want a round table.'

'We won't be able to sit here.'

'Then you won't be able to sit here. It's not my fault.'

A few days later she said to me, 'I'm so worried about Nicky. He's got high blood pressure, like your father had. When he

St John's Wood

loses his temper, you don't know what might happen. He doesn't look well.'

'He's feeling the strain.'

'Don't upset him. Don't say anything to upset him.'

'I haven't said anything to upset him.'

We were eating tinned fish and a salad of lettuce and cucumber. I was crammed up against the table edge, sitting on one of the velvet plush dining chairs, and if I moved I hit my knee on something hard. On the floor behind me a narrow mat had been laid in a space that was too small for it and its long side lay uplifted along the back chair legs so that if I tried to get out, I couldn't. Most of the table surface was still occupied by extraneous objects: at my left elbow rose a mini mountain of knick-knacks and photographs. Other ornaments were piled on the floor.

'He's right, Mum. There's no room for people to sit.'

'There's plenty of room. Stop complaining.'

Much remained to be done. The icons had to be mounted on the bedroom walls. Extra shelves were needed in the kitchen. There was no cupboard for mops and brooms and nowhere to put such a cupboard. The oven, for some reason, was a mystery. Nicky had shown her several times how to turn it on, Kelly had demonstrated, I had demonstrated, Nicky's PA Lucie had demonstrated, Tina had explained, Michael drew a diagram, but still it was a worry. 'I can't get a leg of lamb. I'll ruin it. I can't make the moussaka. I'll spoil it.'

It was easier to eat out. We investigated local pubs, drawn instinctively back to Maida Vale rather than St John's Wood. Unless it was raining, we walked. ('It's good for me to walk.') Rena put the strap of her heavy leather bag over her head so that the bag rested on her chest and took one of the fine sticks Nicky, or Michael, or Tina, had given her. Shoes were a problem. I'd stopped nagging her about the fact that most of

Not Speaking

her shoes were too small for her ('they're not too small, it's just that my feet are swollen') and unsuitable for winter wear.

'If you were American you'd wear trainers.'

'I'm not American.' She was wearing gold sandals.

'It's freezing outside.'

'Never mind. Let's go.'

'You can wear my shoes if you want.' I was wearing black trainers.

This was an offer too far. She would never wear trainers.

'Anyway,' I said, 'what's wrong with your feet?'

'It's nothing. A sore on my toe.'

'Haven't you shown Lisa?' Lisa was the talented manicurist at Michael's whose deft attentions kept my own ingrown toenail under control.

'I'll show her next time. Come on, let's go.'

Linda joined us for a burger and chips at the Warrington, a spacious Victorian pub 'lovingly restored to its former glory' with stained glass windows and a marble fireplace. We assessed the fireplace. Michael's fireplace in his salon was nicer, we agreed.

'Your father would have liked this.'

I think Dad would have preferred the Warwick Arms down by Warwick Avenue tube, but it was comforting to imagine him standing at the bar, getting the drinks in.

Tina joined us at the Robert Browning in Clifton Road, a blunt alehouse, distinguished for me by being named after the Victorian poet although it has since changed its name to the Eagle. As we went in I noted the portraits in glass of Browning and Elizabeth Barrett Browning in the windows. Browning had settled in Warwick Crescent in 1862 after the death of Elizabeth Barrett Browning in Florence the previous year.

'Childe Roland to the Dark Tower came.'

'Who?'

St John's Wood

'Childe Roland to the Dark Tower came...' I couldn't remember any more lines, or indeed much about Browning's poem.

'What dark tower?' Tina mentioned the series of novels by Stephen King.

'No. "Childe Roland to the dark tower came, / His word was still 'Fie, foh, and fum / I smell the blood of a British man." Shakespeare,' I said. 'Robert Browning took the line and wrote a poem called "Childe Roland to the Dark Tower came", which is one of the few poems I know of Browning's, but I can't remember any of it.'

'Right,' Tina said. 'What are you going to eat, Mum?'

I quickly googled Robert Browning and found the poem. The opening line made me laugh out loud.

'What are you laughing at?' Mum asked suspiciously.

'It's just a poem.'

'What's so funny?'

'Nothing really.'

'Then why are you laughing?'

Tina raised an eyebrow.

'It's just an old poem and sometimes, without meaning to be, they're funny when you read them now.'

'Go on, read it,' Tina said.

'The poem is about a knight, that's Childe Roland, "Childe" meaning knight, who is disillusioned with life and is on a sort of final quest, for the dark tower. We don't know what the tower is, all we know is that others have tried, and Roland, who's given up on hope and doesn't even think he could cope with success now, wants little more than to give the quest a decent shot. He needs to reach the tower for the satisfaction of ending.'

'To get closure.'

'Yes. And the way is desolate, and ugly, and mean. Nothing

grows on the plain, and everything he passes is horrible. There's an old horse he thinks has been slung out by the devil, and a wheel like the wheel they used to use for torture.'

Mum wasn't listening any more.

'The opening line is, "My first thought was, he lied in every word..."'

Tina laughs. 'Who?'

'Some old cripple who's given him directions.'

'Not his mum then?'

'Roland doesn't believe him. He thinks he's just having a laugh, but actually, they were the right directions.'

'What are you talking about?' Mum asked.

'I'm telling Tina this pub was named after a Victorian poet who lived round the corner. In fact, he's a very interesting poet because he fell in love with another poet, Elizabeth Barrett, who was much more famous and successful than him, and she lived around the corner from Michael, in Wimpole Street. They ran away together. To Italy.'

'What were you saying about his mother?'

'Nothing about his mother.'

'*The Barretts of Wimpole Street*,' Tina says. 'Mum would probably like that. I'll see if Michael can get it so she can watch it on his big screen.'

'Please don't.'

There are several film versions of the dreadful 1930 play by Rudolf Besier, all unbearable.

'Charles Laughton and Norma Shearer?' Tina is looking at her phone. '1934.'

'That's the first one. Then in the 1950s there's another one with John Gielgud playing old Mr Barrett who doesn't want any of his children to marry.'

'Is Norma Shearer who you were named after?'

'I have no idea. I'm pretty sure it wasn't Bellini's opera.'

St John's Wood

Idly, for no particular reason, I google Bellini's *Norma*, a great hit at La Scala in 1831 with a libretto by the poet Felice Romani and based on a play of the same name by Alexandre Soumet. It's set in Gaul in either 50BCE or 50AD and Norma is a Druidic high priestess. At the same time she seems to belong in an ancient Greek tragedy, specifically *Medea*, although Norma – who has two sons – only threatens to cut their throats. Maria Callas was the most famous Norma in the twentieth century. She also sang Cherubini's *Medea* and featured in a film of *Medea* by Pier Paolo Pasolini.

I click on a link and suddenly Callas is singing for us, the soaring notes of 'Casta diva' from *Norma* causing one or two heads to turn in the quiet pub.

'Sorry, I didn't mean to do that.'

Mum knows all about Maria Callas because Callas was Greek and, as it happens, her exact contemporary.

'Wasn't she married to Onassis?' Tina asks.

'Not married,' Mum says. 'She was his girlfriend. He treated her very badly.'

'Remember what you used to say when we wanted something? "Who do you think I am? Onassis's daughter?" And then,' Tina says indignantly, 'you named me after her!'

'No, that was his wife. But you weren't named for her.'

Aristotle Onassis, a Greek shipping magnate, was one of the world's richest men in the 1950s and 60s. His name and his yacht, the Christina – named after his wife, Tina – signified unquantifiable wealth and limitless pleasure-seeking.

'Her mother's name was Evangelia, which is the same name as my mother.'

'Whose mother?'

'Callas of course. Maria Callas. She was in Athens in the war.'

'Did you hear her sing?'

Not Speaking

'Don't be stupid. Anyway, she left at the end of the war. She married a rich Italian old enough to be her grandfather. She didn't love him, but she loved his money.'

'She wasn't born in Greece,' I say.

Maria Callas was born in New York City to Greek parents who had only recently immigrated. They were an ill-assorted couple and in 1937 the mother returned to Athens with her two daughters, Maria the younger then about thirteen. It was in Athens that Maria trained and made her professional debut in 1941 to an audience largely composed of Italian and German soldiers. Some of them she went out with. Biographers, queasy about Maria's fraternizing with the enemy, suggest that her pushy mother forced her into it as a way of getting food and money for the family. Or rather, Maria, whose hostility towards her mother and sister was uncompromising, said as much. In one simple summing up she explained the matter: 'Everything I did for them was mostly good and everything they did to me was mostly bad.'

From about 1952 she refused to have anything to do with her mother and sister.

'Her mother put pepper on their lips when her children told lies. It's a Greek punishment, apparently,' I announce.

'Who told you that?'

'I read it here.' I hold up my phone.

'Sometimes you read some really stupid things.'

'And when Maria was born her mother didn't look at her for four days because she was so disappointed she wasn't a boy.'

'That's nonsense. She must have looked at her if she fed her.'

'Her little boy, her darling Vassily, had died a few months earlier. She wanted a son.'

'Your father was the same. After I had you he went mad. He thought it was going to be nothing but girls, just like my father.'

'And like Michael,' Tina said. Michael's four children by his first partner, Frances, were girls. And now, married to Gaby, he had twin sons, James Artemis and Jack Alexander, born in September 2014.

Rena adores the twins. They are the first male grandchildren since Tina produced Devan in 1997, the first twins, and they take the total of grandsons to nine. (There are five great-grandsons thus far.) The fact that they are boys, and that two arrived at once, seemed obviously the work of Providence. Rena had prayed – not specifically that Gaby (who was herself a twin) should bring forth twins but that Michael, who had expressed a wish for 'a couple of boys', having fathered four girls, should get what he wanted. God had seen what was needed in the situation and acted accordingly. 'After all, Michael's not as young as he was. It was better to have them both at once.'

Rena is impatient to be done with the trials of house moving so as to spend more time with the babies.

'I know it's not right, and I'm not saying anything against the girls, but you can't help loving the boys more.'

'It must be Nature,' Tina says drily.

'Or culture.'

Or maybe it's just Rena.

'How many granddaughters and great-granddaughters have you got?' Tina suddenly asks.

We count them. Sarah, Tellisa, Tishian, Angelica, Christiana, Tatiana, Alexia: seven granddaughters. Jodie, Milly, Esme, Clara: four great-granddaughters. 'That's eleven second-class citizens,' Tina says. 'Add on your three daughters, and that's fourteen human beings in your family alone you've consigned to the second class. Are you proud of that?'

Rena ignores her. 'Maria Callas married a rich Italian but she didn't want to help her mother.'

Not Speaking

'Why was that, then, I wonder?' Tina asks, sifting through her recent photos of the twins to show me, because the truth is we are also a little besotted.

'She had a terrible temper,' Rena says.

'She was Maria Callas,' I say. 'She was a diva, a prima donna. There had never been anybody like her. They thought she'd been sent from God, "La Divina", divine, a miracle. She was the greatest soprano of all time.'

Rena is not impressed. She folds her arms. 'She told her mother to jump in the river and drown herself.'

'Really?'

She nods.

'Wow.'

'She told her sister to throw herself out the window.'

'Are you sure?'

'Of course I'm sure. You don't think I'd make it up, do you?'

'Didn't Onassis marry Jackie Kennedy?' Tina asks.

'That's right,' Rena says quickly. 'And he was already after her before her husband was killed.'

'Before Kennedy was shot?'

'Onassis was chasing after her. He had her on his yacht.'

'Really?'

'And then when the brother was killed, she didn't care any more so she said yes.'

'What?' Tina says.

I explain. 'Bobby Kennedy was shot when Mum was in Germany, with Louki, buying a car. After you were born.'

'That's right. The landlady came in with the newspaper.'

'Bobby Kennedy was Jack Kennedy's brother. They were both shot.'

'And you love America so much,' Rena says, mostly to Tina who has been spending longer and longer periods in the apartment they have rented in Los Angeles so that Lee, who has a green card, can network and get more and better film jobs – and secondarily to me.

'What's that got to do with Maria Callas?'

'Onassis was a womaniser,' Rena exclaims. 'He was a typical Greek man. His wife understood that. You don't think she didn't know about Callas and all the others, do you? But Callas was different.'

Tina is lost. 'What do you mean she didn't care any more? Who didn't?'

'Jackie Kennedy, keep up.'

'Callas loved him,' Rena says. '*She* understood as well. She understood. He let her sing. But anytime he wanted her she always went to him. He had to come first.'

'Is that because he was a man, by any chance?'

'He was a Greek man.'

'That's ridiculous.'

'I'm telling you what happened.'

'It can't have been like that.' I tell my mother she is wrong. 'Callas was a professional singer, a serious artist. She had to learn her parts, rehearse them with the other singers and orchestra, and then be where she was meant to be by going to the opera houses and performing. That's what being an opera diva means – hard, demanding work, to a schedule that's set for maybe years ahead.'

'He was a man. He had to come first.'

'Do you mean that if she was booked for a run of shows at the Royal Opera House and Ari's yacht happened to dock at Southampton and he wanted her she would drop everything and go?'

'She would. And that was the problem with Jackie Kennedy. She didn't understand she'd married a Greek man.'

'Why was that a problem?'

Not Speaking

'It wasn't a problem for her. She didn't care. It was a problem for Onassis.'

Now I'm lost. 'How so?'

'Onassis made a mistake. He was stupid. He wanted to be the big man and have the most famous woman in the world on his arm but she didn't care, she was American, she did what she wanted.'

'Wasn't Callas more famous than Jackie Kennedy? Or at least, more talented?' It annoys me to be putting them in the same sentence.

'She made him famous.'

'Callas?'

'Callas, of course. She made Onassis famous. That was after she lost a lot of weight and was slim and glamorous. But he was stupid. She loved him, she thought he would marry her, she did everything, but secretly he was making plans to marry Jackie Kennedy. And at the same time as well,' she suddenly remembers, 'he was having sex with Jackie Kennedy's sister.'

'No!'

'Yes.'

Callas had, still has, legions of adorers. (Few have anything good to say of Onassis.) Googling Callas is like entering a shrine, a cathedral of love. I spend happy days trawling the web, watching documentaries, listening to Callas in a variety of roles. On stage she was mesmerising; speaking to camera in interviews she invariably looked shifty. She'd been taught how to sing and act; nobody taught her how to be a celebrity. Her big eyes, big mobile mouth, big nose filled the screen – she was hardly a beauty, it seemed to me (the adorers would disagree), yet intensely dramatic; full of life and at the same time forlorn.

There was newsreel of opera-lovers crowding into the opera houses of London, Milan, Venice, Paris, New York to see their divinity, and news reports of cancelled engagements.

St John's Wood

At a gala performance of *Tosca* in London in 1965, Queen Elizabeth and her ladies emerge from limousines, fur stoles around their shoulders, tiaras glittering. Callas sang *Tosca* that night, but cancelled the rest of the booking. In Paris the same year, she sang the first act of *Norma* and then said she was exhausted and couldn't go on. She had a reputation by then for being difficult. Sometimes she didn't show up at all for scheduled performances. As a diva, she was expected to be temperamental; but the feuds, the harsh things Callas said, the way she quarrelled, surprised even the cognoscenti. In interviews, you can see cultivated upper-class Englishmen like Lord Harewood delicately treading around these issues, trying to work her out, hoping not to provoke an explosion.

Callas declared that marriage was the most important thing for a woman. Perhaps, interviewers like Lord Harewood suggested, she could be thought of as two people? Yes, she was two people, she agreed: Callas the artist, and Maria the woman. Callas the artist was dedicated to music 'like a priestess', and worked immensely hard mastering difficult roles and insisting on perfection. Maria the woman wanted 'to live a human life' as a woman.

She wanted Onassis. She had fallen in love with Onassis.

I think it's a pity she didn't fall for Franco Zeffirelli, who spits nails when he speaks of Onassis, although it's true that like many of her adorers Zeffirelli was gay.

Her life, she implied and others said, was a tragedy. She died young – at fifty-three, heartbroken. But Maria the woman had already killed Callas the artist: the weight loss that turned her into Audrey Hepburn and opened up the doors of high society took away some of her vocal range and power. (She lost forty kilos in one year. Some said she swallowed a tapeworm.) She would have given it all away to have Onassis forever.

'My work is alone,' Callas says in one of the interviews,

Not Speaking

explaining that the career she chose – or that was chosen for her – was 'the programme' her mother had devised. 'I was made to sing... and I hated it.'

There was 'no communication between my family and me,' she declared in 1971. The bitterness with which she spoke of her family was public knowledge, and yet none of my research – which began to border on the obsessive – yielded a convincing explanation for what had been a complete and, as it seemed to me, unusual break with her mother and sister. Already in 1945 when she sailed from Piraeus to America to renew her American citizenship, Maria refused to let them come to the port to wave her off. Her mother, she claimed, favoured her elder sister who was prettier and thinner. Maria planned to find the father her mother had left behind, a man described by Evangelia as being 'like a bee: to him every woman was a flower over which he must hover to sip the sweetness.' This was the man Evangelia had married against her own father's wishes. He, Evangelia's father, Maria's grandfather, was 'a gay, laughing man who loved to dance and gamble and sing,' whom Evangelia adored, but he would wash his hands of her if she married the bee-like Giorgos. He died before it came to the proof.

Maria found her father in America and shared a house with him briefly as she continued to work and extend her reputation.

And then, in the *New York Times* obituary from September 1977, I read Maria Callas quoted saying, 'I know my mother wrote a book about me, but I never read it.'

Her mother wrote a book about her!

I google it at once. It is called *My Daughter – Maria Callas*, by Evangelia Callas, and was published in 1960. I can't wait to read it.

Memoirs by daughters about their mothers are two a penny,

St John's Wood

I reflect, as I make the short journey on the Victoria Line from Seven Sisters station to Kings Cross and the British Library where, a mere seventy minutes after I have ordered it online, the book is delivered into my hands. But how many mothers have written about their famous daughters? Aurelia Schober Plath edited a collection of letters by her daughter, Sylvia Plath, but that isn't quite the same. And here is Evangelia Callas, *My Daughter – Maria Callas*. There are two copies for me to read, the American edition and a later English one with an afterword – or 'Afterglow' – by the author's 'collaborator', Lawrence G. Blochman.

Although the story they tell is very different, *My Daughter – Maria Callas* seemed to me not unlike *I Was a Greek War Bride* by Irene Clarke. Or perhaps it was simply that sentences and whole paragraphs clearly owed more to Lawrence G. Blochman than Evangelia Callas. The surface tone of the narrative is polite, almost bland, but the attentive reader (or the reader who brings to the text some experience of growing up in a household with a Greek mother) can feel savagery barely reined in.

Evangelia's fury at her daughter is like a vibration. It would surely have been different if Maria had been a boy, or if she had not been a genius.

Maria wanted nothing to do with her mother and sister after she became famous and it was not, according to her mother, their fault. Or, she wanted nothing to do with her mother and sister after she married a millionaire Italian thirty years older than herself, a man her mother never met. 'He is very rich and he loves me,' Maria had explained to the press, before going off as per her schedule to Mexico City and Buenos Aires, leaving him behind. Evangelia wondered what sort of love that could be when a newly married wife would leave her husband

Not Speaking

the moment after they were married. She concludes that her daughter loved the money not the man. She doesn't conclude that Maria Callas was fulfilling professional commitments, let alone realising her divine gifts.

And money, after all, turns out to be the problem. Evangelia has no money. The contrast between Maria's money and fame and Evangelia's no-money and no-fame is intolerable. It is intolerable to be a mother, and spurned. It is unnatural.

Or love is the problem. (Maria loved Onassis.)

Maria's sister wrote a book about Maria too, some years after Evangelia's book was published, but my appetite is sated. I don't need to know how Maria Callas's sister dealt with her feelings about Maria Callas's genius and her fame. I have no interest in the sister, and I definitely don't want to read again that to be an artist and have love in your life is impossible for a woman.

Rena made a few changes to the new apartment. She had some extra shelves put up. She worked out how to store her mop and buckets. She decided that the sofas were too crowded in the living room and that the table would be better in the kitchen. She asked Nicky to move the table for her.

It was a simple request. She didn't understand why he made such a fuss about it. But he did it. Afterwards, it was possible to sit comfortably in the sitting room. The kitchen, where we had to eat, was impossible.

'Think of it as Madron Street,' Linda said, being philosophical and stoical, squashed under a shelf of saucepans stacked one inside the other. In front of her on the table was a bowl of haricot bean soup, piled to right and left were heavy-framed photographs, the second freezer whirred at her ear, and there was no room to put the bread basket without moving the olives, feta salad, taramosalata, tzatziki, rice and leeks, and stuffed courgettes, let alone find a place for the leg of lamb that was looming. Michael's eldest girls, Angelica and Christiana, slim and not too tall, were squeezed in alongside.

One by one the boxes and suitcases had been emptied. (Some of the empty suitcases, about fifteen, went for storage in my garden shed.) Little by little the possessions were sorted. Rena settled. She liked the flat. She agreed that the other place had been too large. Resilient and resourceful, she was tired by her efforts but, anxious to please Nicky, she didn't complain. She knew he needed help. She was worried about him. She noted that his anger had, if anything, increased rather than abated as the months went by. He continued to pick her up on Sundays and take her to church, sent his assistant, Lucie, round with plates of ready cut choice fruit, or cough linctus, or skin cream, or flowers, collected and took his mother to his house for dinner, and very occasionally came with Kelly for dinner at hers but only if he was assured that neither Michael nor Tina were expected. He was his usual self so long as she didn't mention Michael or Tina, but of course she always did mention them.

It was a deliberate policy, weaving old threads and keeping up the sense of connection. When she was with Michael she spoke often of Nicky, and when she was with Nicky she told him all about Michael's twins, and the property Michael had bought next door to the salon, and the one he was hoping to buy, and his plans to knock through and into the basement to make a granny flat, and more storage space, and a larger office.

Nicky said bitterly, 'He can afford to buy property in W1 and he can't afford to help pay his mother's rent.'

She told him that Tina's daughter Tishian was working for Michael now as one of his managers and desk staff, and camping temporarily in the new property while Michael waited for planning permission. Tina had bought Tishian a bed and was looking to buy her a flat in North London.

'And she won't pay four hundred pounds a month towards her mother's rent,' Nicky growled.

Rena assured me later, 'I didn't say anything. I didn't want to upset him.'

She tells me again her theory that Nicky is jealous of Michael and of Tina. Tina's rented apartment in LA is a particular bugbear. 'It makes him mad. It's ridiculous. He's not going to talk to her for two hundred years because she's got a house in America and a long tongue?'

She was worried, but not deeply worried. Things were as they were and as they always had been. The not speaking was an episode in a long history. Even longer when she recalled her father and his brother: Nicky was like her father, Michael was like her uncle, the good businessman; her father didn't speak to his brother after they quarrelled. Nobody was not speaking to her, and for as long as the boys went on not speaking to each other, she would have plenty to speak about.

'I want to see them friends again before I die,' she said. And, not for the first time, reminded me, 'I want a proper Greek Orthodox funeral.'

'Yes.'

'And I don't want to be burned up.'

'No.'

'What will happen to your father's bones if Tina sells the house?'

'She isn't going to sell the house.'

Tina was appalled at the prices of flats in London. She had looked at some squalid rat-holes in Finsbury Park and come away chastened.

In November the lease on the St John's Wood apartment came up for renewal. The rent was increased by a very small amount and Nicky absorbed the extra into his contribution. Rena had refused to have a direct debit set up that would take money out of her account and put it into what she persisted in calling Nicky's, relying instead on her memory and going to the bank on a certain day each month to make the transfer. In January she was late and the account went into the red.

Over Christmas, when we gathered at Michael's or met to see a film or have dinner at Côte in Devonshire Street, our new regular haunt, we discussed the problem of housing – whispering, speaking out of the corners of our mouths.

In 1995 London house prices were 2.7 times higher than earnings. By the end of 2015 they were 10.1 times higher and going up by £500 per day. Michael watched the figures rising. The sum his brokers had to raise if he was to buy the second property next door went up to 1.3 million.

'I should never have left the Elephant and Castle,' Rena said. 'I should have stayed where I was.' She was bitter about the bank charging for the overdraft.

'You didn't have any choice. You were one of the lucky ones.'

I opened my laptop and showed her a documentary about the Heygate Estate, *Home Sweet Home*, made by Enrica Colusso. Colusso had followed the proceedings as Southwark Council decanted the residents after 2008. Off and on for four or five years Colusso had taken her camera and walked the estate, registering decay. She filmed Council meetings, allowed the venal to convict themselves out of their own mouths, interviewed locals, and gave plenty of air time to the original architect, Tim Tinker, whose vision had been so traduced.

'The Council would have given us another house.'

'Probably.'

Colusso tracked the progress of several residents who held out as long as they could, resenting changes that had been imposed and expressing bewilderment and the sense of loss many felt as they were caught up in one of the biggest urban regeneration projects in Europe. Council leader Nick Stanton and his deputy Kim Humphreys explained that Southwark, situated so close to the booming City, had the opportunity to throw off its long history of being poor and miserable. The Elephant and Castle could be a new Piccadilly Circus south of the river. But not if the poor and miserable stayed.

It was a far cry from Maud Pember Reeves. Colusso included a clip from 1964 of Harold Wilson, Labour Prime Minister, speaking about the importance of housing provision for the nation, seen as a family. That everybody should have a roof over their heads was a core Labour value. In 1997 Tony Blair chose the Aylesbury Estate, next door to the Heygate, to deliver his first major speech as Prime Minister. He said we needed to build a new Britain, one in which the poorest and most needy were not forgotten. Wealth was essential if we were to go on remembering the poor. Wealth at the top would trickle down. New Labour took up the Thatcherite creed: popular capitalism, a property owning democracy, private investment as a way of funding public care on the way to independent living. The poor and miserable in Southwark were regarded by the Council – or so it appeared from Colusso's film – as social failures.

I recalled Thatcher's infamous and astonishingly ignorant remark: a man who, beyond the age of twenty-six, found himself on a bus could count himself a failure. By that yardstick most people were failures: half of them weren't men, most didn't make much money, many were unfit or old. The notion that you constructed your society around an idealised vision of energetic, combative, testosterone-fuelled young men was hardly forward-thinking. It was back to the *Iliad*.

Tony Blair soon forgot the Aylesbury, and in 2002 Gordon

St John's Wood

Brown declared that markets were in the public interest. Southwark Council wrapped their comments in philanthropic concern and ludicrous pieties about 'mixing' communities, those who had money with those who didn't, so that they would 'understand each other'. But the financial crash of 2008 undid their projections, and promises to build new units for social renting as per the glossy brochures were not kept. 'They lied,' said Helen O'Brien, one of the last to move out.

Secure tenants were rehoused. Temporary tenants – the sort who had rented our parents' flat after they sold it – had no protection. Tim Tinker, the architect, mourned the ending of the post-war consensus, that the public sector and social housing best served the nation's needs. Thatcher, Blair and Brown deployed the new rhetoric: popular capitalism was a crusade to return power to the people. Colusso showed the people on the Heygate forced to leave homes they had lived in for over thirty years.

In 2011 the estate was demolished.

'Anyway,' I said, 'the Council wouldn't have rehoused you because you weren't any longer a tenant. They would have had to purchase the property back from you.'

'I could have stayed.'

'It wouldn't have been much fun. After you left in 2006 it was miserable.'

'I could have bought somewhere near the Elephant and Castle.'

'You wouldn't have had enough money.'

'I would have, if I did it then, if I didn't listen to all of you.'

That was possibly true, but would it have been desirable?

'Is that what you wanted? Is that what you wish you'd done?'

'Now? Yes, of course.'

'Well it's too late now,' I said, and changed the subject.

'She could have bought a flat for two hundred and fifty

thousand in 2006,' Michael said. 'Only not in St John's Wood. Mind you,' he suddenly remembered, 'the Maida Vale flat that Nicky and Lesley bought, Cropthorne Court, was under £300k, but that's because it had a short lease, and they should have extended the lease when they bought it. It would have cost them £175k. They didn't do it. Now, of course, it's cost them millions. That's why they couldn't afford to let Mum stay there. The property had to pay its way.'

Marylebone

At the end of January I turned on the radio to find that Nicky was the headline guest on Radio 4's Saturday morning chat show. He was telling listeners about his idyllic childhood.

Linda texted me. 'Did you hear Nicky?'

Some friends said to me later, 'We heard your brother on the radio this morning.' He came across very well, they said: modest, amusing, warm.

Nicky recalled the shop back gardens over the wall at Madron Street and the gym they had made there with Dad's help. He talked about being born into the working class but not being held back by it: he had got on and risen through the ranks. He was evidence of the fluidity of British social life, a testament to social mobility. So, it appeared, was I: 'My sister is a professor.' Hmm. If I had been on the programme I would have talked about the Beveridge Report and the welfare state, the 1944 Education Act, the introduction in 1948 of the National Health Service, and the post-war consensus that the public sector was best placed to provide for the nation's housing needs.

My own vehemence surprised me. I liked being a working-class success story, too, but it wouldn't have happened, I

Not Speaking

wouldn't have had my story, without the political and social changes of the twentieth century.

Those changes included the expansion of university education and building of six new universities in the 1960s, at one of which, Lancaster, I was given a place because they had a policy of reaching out to working-class children. (Getting a place at a university in the 1960s was competitive.) Like state schools, universities were publicly funded. Their mission was to develop the nation's talent, a project of benefit to the nation as a whole. Few students paid fees; most had maintenance grants that were not loans but gifts.

And it wasn't only socialists (now I was arguing with Nicky in my head) who had seen the need for reform. Octavia Hill, the Victorian pioneer of housing improvement for the urban poor who started her work on slums in Marylebone (I was arguing with Michael, too) was fiercely opposed to municipal socialism. She was anti-suffrage, anti-social services, and against the Old-Age Pensions Act of 1908. Her creed was self-reliance. She began in 1865 by managing three cottages in Paradise Place (now Garbutt Place, a stone's throw from Michael's salon in Beaumont Street) bought for £750 by the art critic John Ruskin, 'in a dreadful state of dirt and neglect'. Low-income tenants were put in once the cottages had been improved and the rents were collected on a weekly basis by Hill's team of volunteer middle-class women. Hill laid stress on the personal touch: supportive but stern, friendly but also intrusive. No back-sliding, no excuses; 'extreme punctuality' in the payment of the rent was a requirement tenants were made to understand. The small profits that accrued were used for repairs, as were the profits from another five cottages in Freshwater Place off Homer Street, a little further west.

Self-reliance under benevolent paternalism was probably my father's ideal. He would have taken pride in being a model

Marylebone

tenant under Octavia Hill. It had pained him that the back gardens of the shops on Old Kent Road were wasted space, when his boys had only a tiny yard, and it was because they began to play over the wall, running about amongst weeds that hid all manner of horrors – splintered wood, rusty nails, broken glass – that he began to clear it. What Nicky remembered with such nostalgia could have been an early version of Occupy, I thought, or an assumption of squatters' rights, or a mini mass trespass like the mass trespass on Kinder Scout in the Peak District in 1932 when walkers protested at being denied access to areas of open country and the Ramblers' Association was born. Access was all Dad wanted, not ownership. He climbed politely over the wall and set to work. The shop manager was agreeable so long as the boys confined themselves to gymnastics or badminton and didn't play football. It was an informal arrangement that survived many years, ending only with the move to the Heygate estate. But had circumstances changed, had the shop been sold, had sheds or houses been built on the land, the idyll would have been over.

Nicky's loving recollections were imbued with our father's political quiescence overlaid by Thatcherite opportunism. I had been formed and given my opportunities by the politics of post-war socialism; Nicky was a product of 1980s Thatcherism.

It was some months since I'd seen Nicky. Christmas had been and gone. Our only exchanges were about the St John's Wood apartment and the payment of the rent.

Linda said, 'It's really sad. I miss him.' But when she went through her emails from Christmas 2014 it made her angry. 'He said such horrible things.'

'Horrible things were said to him.'

'It makes me feel sick when I look at it.'

'Why don't you delete them?'

No, she didn't want to delete them.

Not Speaking

We were gathered round the long table at Michael's and we were looking at the architect's preliminary plans for the property next door. Linda had been downstairs in the salon having her hair done, and I had been in the salon having my hair done, and Tina had been to the dentist and then in the salon having her hair done, and so we'd all gone upstairs to see the twins. Mum was already there, as she was most days, having made her way by bus and tube, the Freedom Pass in her pocket proof, she liked to declare, that no country treated its people as well as England. (The Older Person's Freedom Pass was introduced in 1973 by the GLC.) She was sanguine about the complicated journey: bus to Warwick Avenue tube, steps, Bakerloo line to Regent's Park station, steps and a steep ramp out and more steps, bus for one stop, walk down Marylebone High Street, left into Beaumont Street, across Devonshire Street (no pedestrian crossing – cars just had to be patient) and on to Michael's front door, rain or shine, ready to climb his stairs ('Michael's bloody stairs') and be uplifted by the joyful shouts of recognition that issued from the throats of the twins.

'Those twins,' Tina said. 'They've rejuvenated her. Look at her, bouncing and skipping. Every time I phone she tells me, and tells me again, how clever they are, how much they like her.'

'They know me,' Mum still says, as if it's surprising that at aged six months, eight months, a year, and now almost a year and a half, the children should recognise a grandmother who visited four or five times a week.

It was no longer 'my Michael' or 'my Nicky' but 'those twins', 'those boys', 'they're so lovely'. There was no longer debate about who was number one.

She would never want to live under anybody else's roof, but now as we pored over Michael's plans and he assured us the square footage of the apartment he envisaged would be very little less than where she was now, and better designed – 'It will have higher ceilings, we'll lower the floor level, and if I can manage to get the flat above we can work between the two, the space will be better distributed and there'll be fitted units all through. She won't need all those tallboys' – (Linda, Tina and I thought, as one, 'How are you going to persuade her of that, then?') – I noticed Mum smiling quietly, sphinx-like, seated at the far end in her usual upright chair, pausing after kicking a soft ball about, not trying to understand the details, only reminding us at intervals that she wanted her own front door.

'There'll be a hall connecting to us, at the bottom of the stairs,' Michael said.

'And a door?' She didn't want any Tom, Dick and Harry walking in and out whenever they felt like it. 'Not like here. I'm not like you. I don't want everybody in and out all the time.'

'And a door.'

'A front door?'

'Two doors. You'll have this door and a front door on Weymouth Street as well.'

She nods. I can't tell if she thinks it is a serious proposition or not. Is she really prepared to go through the whole performance of moving house again? Does she understand the immediate and long-term implications? Tallboys, to take one example. How many tallboys has she got? How many drawers crammed to bursting with how many sets of treasured cottons and linens? Looking at Michael's designs I can see how the sofas and armchair might be arranged, I'm sure he's thought about the television, but I'm not sure about the glass cabinets – where will they go? – and I definitely don't see where the table and all the velvet plush dining chairs are going to be put.

Not Speaking

'She won't need a huge table,' Michael says. 'We cook up here. I'll get a bigger table here.'

'What's going to happen to her table?'

'She won't need it,' Michael says firmly.

And what about transport? From St John's Wood she can get a bus. There isn't a bus in Beaumont Street or Weymouth Street. In fact, there isn't a bus at all in easy reach. This part of Marylebone is a bus desert.

'She doesn't need a bus,' Michael says impatiently. 'We order taxis for her all the time as it is.'

But she does need a bus, as she needs her table and her own front door.

And what about Nicky?

Michael says he wants to 'draw a line under' the quarrel with Nicky. To 'draw a line under' means bring to an end. We all want that. Nicky has used the same image: he wants to draw a line under it too. Is Michael's plan the route to reconciliation? Perhaps. I hope it is. It is a plan that his sisters, gathered around his table and scrutinising the architect's drawings while Michael assembles a large salad in a huge bowl, have welcomed without hesitation except to check that he has considered the matter from all angles.

We are thinking this will make our lives easier.

Gaby is upstairs, putting the twins to bed. Rena decides to go up and join in. (More steps to climb. For how much longer will she be able to climb them?) Tina goes too.

If this is the future, I think – and sheer force of numbers (so many growing children) as well as the fact that Michael and Gaby, no less than Nicky and Kelly, are open-handed and hospitable, suggest it is – it looks promising. But it's hard to imagine that it will work. Can it? It asks a lot of everybody – by which I mean Michael and Gaby. Michael has already expressed mild surprise that his mother isn't more appreciative.

Marylebone

And what about Nicky? Michael's plan, if it went ahead, would engineer a shift that would take Mum out of Nicky's orbit. In Maida Vale and St John's Wood, where she has lived for ten years, she has been 'round the corner' from Nicky. Moving to Marylebone would be moving into Michael's household, under Michael's roof, into Michael's care.

Of course Nicky would be free to come and go through her front door as she chose. But he would no longer be the son responsible for her on a daily basis (if that is what he has been; opinions differ). There would be liberation for him from some niggling demands as well as freedom from blame, and entry into the luxury of blaming others when little things went wrong. The advantages were clear. He would gain in exoticism; he would be more like a courtier. On the other hand, he might consider that Michael's actions were a territorial gambit, a raid, a bold and bodily seizing of the object of desire, an assault on the enemy's ground. No military tactician could have devised a better strategy. Engrossing his mother thus, setting her up in his own camp, the younger son took possession. She became in effect, or might be seen as having become, depending how you viewed the matter and through what lens you understood it, his prize, his spear-captive. The twins, meanwhile, were the Trojan horse.

In 2015 Peter Green, a classicist almost as old as our mother, published a new translation of the *Iliad*. He began it when he was ninety; he had dreamed of doing it since childhood but a 'mass of other work got in the way'. The preface and introduction are full of Green's delight at his accomplishment: the improbable had been realised. He explained that he began his *Iliad* 'in a curiously relaxed mood', feeling no pressure, only excitement. The challenge was to translate not just an ancient language but alien concepts, preserving the strangeness while producing a text that would hold the attention of a modern, Greekless audience.

I read Peter Green alongside Pope's *Iliad*, carrying the two hefty books around with me for weeks – Green a solid hardback from University of California Press, Pope a stubby Penguin paperback – and had the happiness of inhabiting many worlds wherever I was, in cafés, on the underground, waiting to meet a friend, at work, at home, in bed.

Sometimes when for the sake of the rhyme Pope's compression made his meaning opaque, Green provided clarity. Green's breezy colloquialism was refreshing: 'You clotheshorse for shamelessness, mind obsessed with profit', Achilles says to Agamemnon when Agamemnon resists the priest's demand that his prize, Chryseis, be returned to her father. Agamemnon insults Achilles; he accuses him of being a man who loves quarrels. Achilles accuses Agamemnon of being a coward: 'You wine-sodden wretch, dog-faced, deer-hearted, not once / have you dared to arm yourself for battle with your troops.' And so the stand-off begins. Achilles refuses to play any more part in the grand cooperative venture, the war against Troy that had begun when Paris took Helen and lasted ten years.

Nestor tries to arbitrate between them, advising Agamemnon not to take Achilles' prize, and Achilles not to oppose the authority of his leader. Agamemnon insists Achilles needed to know who was boss. Agamemnon was lord; Agamemnon must give the orders, not Achilles who wants to be 'above all others, / He wants to dominate all, be lord over all, give orders / to all.' Agamemnon sends his envoys to take Briseis, and Achilles, furious, weeping, dishonoured, appeals to his mother to put things right.

Pope's translation is in the high heroic manner – Milton's

manner, in the English tradition – because Homer was 'elevated'. For the scene of the mother's arrival, Pope pictures Briseis being led silently away 'in soft sorrows and pensive thought', and Achilles, 'stedfast in his hate', going down to the sea shore, hanging 'O'er the wild margin of the deep', 'bathed in tears of anger and disdain' and 'loud lament[ing] to the stormy main'. His mother comes:

> Far in the deep recesses of the main,
> Where aged Ocean holds his wat'ry reign,
> The goddess-mother heard. The waves divide;
> And like a mist she rose above the tide—
> Beheld him mourning on the naked shores,
> And thus the sorrows of his soul explores:
> 'Why grieves my son? Thy anguish let me share;
> Reveal the cause, and trust a parent's care.'

It is a lovely moment, rare in literature I think, in which a mother invites a grown son to speak freely about his anguish and asks him to trust her as a parent. In Green's translation Thetis strokes Achilles as he weeps, addressing him by name, and telling him it was better to speak his grief. She will do what a mother's love can do.

Thetis goes to petition Zeus. Thetis, a mother sharing her son's anguish, serving a son who trusts he is all in all to her, asks Zeus to do the following: she asks him to allow the Greeks under Agamemnon to be defeated and the Trojans to triumph, so that Agamemnon will beg Achilles to rescue them and thus Achilles will restore his honour. Zeus tells Thetis that his wife wouldn't like him to do that, especially as Thetis has reinforced her arguments by physical caresses. Pope is politely vague here, Green more vivid. In Green, Zeus says:

> 'This is a nasty business—you'll bring me into conflict
> with Hērē, make her provoke me with reproachful words.

Not Speaking

As it is, she constantly nags me before the immortal gods,
says that I give my support to the Trojans in the fighting.
You go back home now, lest Hērē notice you; I
shall figure a way to get this matter accomplished.

It is indeed a nasty business. Zeus's main concern is what his wife will say. As soon as Thetis is gone, Hērē, or Hera, appears and 'with mocking words' shows she knows exactly what's been going on. Zeus, the leader, the great power on Olympus, shrinks into a puny, shifty, cowardly man.

The moral question – is it right to arrange so much suffering, so many deaths of Greeks and Trojans, to avenge one man's sense of dishonour, or wounded pride? – gets lost as the gods quarrel amongst themselves. A deeper moral question – does what a mother wants for her son trump everything? – is not asked.

It is Hephaistos, or Vulcan, 'famed craftsman' in Green, 'the Architect divine' in Pope, the son of Hera who, with 'Peace at his heart, and pleasure his design' reconciles the gods – for the moment at least. He hands round goblets of nectar. He tells his mother to be patient and endure. They feast until the sun goes down. Apollo plays his lyre and the Muses sing in sweet voices 'responding one to another'.

I'm glad to have Green, but in the end I keep faith with Pope's rendering of the grand poetry of Homer's 'wild paradise', the fire and rapture. While reading Homer, Pope writes, 'the reader is hurry'd out of himself by the Force of the Poet's Imagination', 'every thing moves, every thing lives, and is put in action.'

The translation of Homer made Pope's fortune. He never married, and lived with his mother, 'the most dutiful son I have ever known,' according to Jonathan Swift. Pope's mother, a devout Catholic, didn't have much understanding of her

Marylebone

son's literary life, especially with regard to his translations of Homer, imitations of Horace and mock-epics like *The Rape of the Lock,* because she had no classical learning. She read prayers. Pope had an elder sister, Magdalen, who was very much not dazzled by her brother's celebrity, and bequeathed to posterity some anecdotes about him. 'For you know, to speak plain to you,' she told Pope's loving admirer Joseph Spence, 'my brother has a maddish way with him.' Part of that maddishness was his passion for books: 'He did nothing but read and write.'

We're in Côte in Devonshire Street to celebrate Devan's Duke of Edinburgh award, gold medal. Tina went with him to St James's Palace where the Duke of Edinburgh himself shook Devan's hand.

Mum asks Devan if he knows Prince Philip is Greek.

Michael, wanting to mark the tenth anniversary of Dad's death, has acquired a huge picture frame in which to mount a display of Dad's treasures: the British Empire Medal at the top, a number of carefully selected photographs, his service pay book, the letters from Major General Geake and Major General Sir Leslie Hamlyn Williams, and his campaign medals. He intends to hang the picture in the hall that will be made when he knocks through from his downstairs entrance to the new apartment. He now wonders whether we might be able to get the family together for a lunch somewhere, a party to celebrate Mum's ninety-third birthday in April. His memorial to Dad – a sort of shrine or icon – could be unveiled and what would also be nice, he thinks, would be to take a formal photo with everybody in it, twins at the front with Mum, the rest according to size beside and behind.

Everybody?

Meanwhile, the amount his brokers needed to raise to secure

the second property next door has risen from 1.77 million to 1.85 million.

'It's becoming a joke,' Tina said. She has been lying awake at night worrying about Michael overextending himself.

There were new conditions. Matching money had to be in Michael's accounts for a minimum of three months in advance of signing. He was a few hundred thousand pounds short. The deadline was the end of March.

'Mum,' Michael said, a few days later when they were discussing her finances and she was complaining that she had no money because the whole of her pension went to pay the rent in St John's Wood, 'you know that interest rates are very low these days, and the money you've got in the bank isn't growing.'

It had been growing, but not by much.

'My money is for all of you,' she said.

'Yes,' Michael said, 'but that's far in the future.' (Death was never going to happen.) 'I'm thinking what's best to do about it now.'

'Why do we have to do anything?'

'We don't have to. I'm thinking what's best, what we might do.'

Michael consulted me, Linda and Tina. We agreed that property, especially in London, especially in W1, was the safest place to park money.

'To begin with, she needs to rationalise her accounts,' Michael said. 'There are too many of them and they're all over the place. Then we need to work out what's the right amount to keep as savings, bearing in mind that once she's living here she won't be spending her pension on rent, she'll have a monthly disposable income again, and she won't be paying bills.'

'Greek television?' Tina asked. The annual payment for the

Marylebone

Greek television signal was a particular bugbear, for reasons none of us could understand.

'I'll get the Greek television, don't worry about that. If she invests a certain sum in the property that sum will still be part of her estate, it will still be divided according to her wishes, afterwards, when the time comes, but, depending when that is, I might need a bit of leeway to realise the cash, a couple of years possibly.'

The end of March is only a few weeks away.

'She needs to know that you all agree. She needs to know I'm not stealing her money but putting it into the property. It's best if you can all be there when I get her to agree.'

Mum says quite cheerfully, 'Michael's always been the same, ever since he was a boy.'

She knows what she's doing, but she doesn't quite understand how she can give Michael £300k to spend on a house, and for the money to somehow not be spent. 'How can it still be there?' she asks. 'Are you sure it's a good idea?'

'It is still there,' I say, 'but it's not twenty-pound notes any more. It's a building.'

I want to explain about money and property prices in England, especially in London. Instead I start a conversation about money in banks in Cyprus and Greece, about how unsafe it turned out to be, about 'haircuts' on people's savings. Soon the air is peppered with the word 'thiefs'. In place of cheerfulness is a glinting anxiety.

'My money is for all of you.'

'Yes.'

'Don't tell Nicky.'

'No.'

'Don't upset him.'

'No.'

I've seen Nicky. Barbara and I spent a pleasant evening at his house, hoping to persuade him and Kelly to join us all at Mum's ninety-third birthday lunch for which they had received an invitation from Michael. That mission ended in failure. We discussed the terms of the St John's Wood rental, however, in the light of a potential move, and Nicky said he would check how much notice to leave would be required. It was clear that he knew something of the plan, but not the full extent.

'Surely it must be a relief to him,' Barbara said afterwards. 'Surely he must want this. He must be glad to think he can shift the burden.'

Linda and I mention Michael's plan to Jason, Linda's eldest son, finance director of a law firm in the City. Jason has bought himself a two-bedroom apartment in a warehouse conversion near London Bridge where he stays for three nights midweek, returning to the family home in Cookham on Thursdays. We arrive early to view it. Along the expanse of naked brick, amongst the exposed beams of the large, open-plan sitting-and-dining area, are lovely black and white photographs of old London.

Later, Mum, Michael, Gaby, Lee (who is filming nearby), Geoff, Sarah, Sarah's husband Xavier, and Xavier's daughter's boyfriend will join us.

Jason orders dinner in.

Borough Market, a step or two outside his gated entrance, where his grandfather ran as a child, is now a foodie heaven. 'This area is the heartland of family history,' I say, recalling Jason's love of history as a boy.

'One side,' he says, reminding me his father's family came from Yorkshire. 'Are you ever going to finish that book of yours about the family?'

'I hope so.'

'Is it going to upset people?'

'I hope not.'

'Am I in it?'

'You have a walk-on part.'

Jason notes that the scheme we have sanctioned does allow Michael to grow his property portfolio; it is advantageous for him in that respect. Nicky might well look askance. On the other hand, Michael is taking over direct care of his elderly mother. Jason says to Linda, 'Has Michael thought it through, do you think?'

Shortly after Pope was born in 1688, the Bank of England was established and a financial revolution began. Stocks, lotteries and other kinds of speculative investment emerged, along with systems of paper credit. Most people didn't understand the new financial instruments, nor the way markets could rise and fall, but those who had capital rushed to invest. Pope had a broker who advised him; he didn't want his money 'lying dead'. The South Sea Company offered dizzying returns. Pope wrote:

> I daily hear such reports of advantages to be gaind by one project or other in the Stocks, that my Spirit is Up with double Zeal, in the desires of our trying to enrich ourselves ... I hear the S. Sea fell since, & should be glad we were in: I also hear there is considerably to be got by Subscribing to the new African Stock, Pray let us do something or other ... tis Ignominious (in this Age of Hope and Golden Mountains) not to Venture.

The South Sea was a bubble and it burst in 1720, ruining many investors. Pope had sold most of his stock at a profit a few months earlier. (African stock was in the slave trade.)

Pope's fortune was made by Homer – '(thanks to Homer) since I live and thrive, / Indebted to no Prince or Peer alive' – although not only by Homer: Pope's canny business sense in marketing his poetry was a factor, too. He became the

Not Speaking

wealthiest poet of his day. In his poetry he excoriated those who wrote for commercial gain, and all the while, in the age of hope and golden mountains, he was busily investing and spending large sums renovating the villa with gardens running down to the Thames at Twickenham where he lived with his mother.

The year of Pope's birth, 1688, used to feel like a very long time ago to me. It no longer does. That may be an effect of familiarity and repeated reading. It must also be because now has come to be like then in ways that were unthinkable when I first became a student of the era. Between post-war, welfare state Britain and Pope's early eighteenth century there had seemed to be an absolute historical distance.

In the eighteenth century wealth was aligned with virtue. To be poor in Southwark in 1714, the year Pope put his name to the five-canto version of *The Rape of the Lock* and sold, so he boasted, 3,000 copies in four days, was to be regarded as little better than vermin. It was 'ignominious' not to strive to be as rich as you possibly could be. Rich and poor were like separate species. In the nineteenth century, once agitation for reform had begun, Benjamin Disraeli called them 'two nations'.

In the general course of things, the nations did not speak to each other: they occupied distinct territories and were immediately recognised by clothes, manners, speech, gestures. The rich encountered the poor as servants, beggars, mobs, thieves (and the less poor as tradesmen and women) but didn't imagine they shared a common humanity. They might participate in charitable initiatives and efforts to relieve suffering, but were not asked to subscribe to a vision of an inclusive society. Only the rich entered politics – a route to more riches: in Pope's day, the opportunism of politicians, the wholesale corruption and enrichment of the ruling classes, was

Marylebone

taken as read. Vast sums of money were siphoned off into private accounts.

Since money – however acquired – was virtuous, there was no taboo about mentioning it in the eighteenth century. Jane Austen tells us exactly how much her characters are worth. It was the reforming Victorians who decided it was impolite to talk about money, making eighteenth-century frankness, naked greed and the pursuit of self-interest seem strange.

The twentieth-century welfare state was the triumphant apotheosis of Victorian philanthropy and reforming zeal. The impetus came from all sides of the political spectrum, from the Conservative Prime Minister Disraeli to Karl Marx himself, on whose grave in Highgate cemetery are written the words: 'The philosophers have only interpreted the world, in various ways. The point, however, is to change it.' The two nations were to be viewed as one family. The old and the sick were to be cared for, nobody was to die of starvation, all would have access to education. In the new meritocracy the brightest and best would rise.

When Britain turned its back on the welfare state in the 1980s, under the leadership of Margaret Thatcher, it ushered in a new age of hope and golden mountains for some. Once again there was virtue in wealth. Not everybody had wealth but all could recognise it as a good, including, one presumes, the unemployed workers in depressed Hartlepool where Peter Mandelson was MP. Mandelson, one of the architects of New Labour, was the grandson of Lambeth-born Herbert Morrison, deputy Prime Minister in the post-war Labour government. In 1998, Peter Mandelson was quoted as saying that he was 'intensely relaxed about people getting filthy rich', a statement that followed him around thereafter (without the qualification 'so long as they pay their taxes', and along with a story of going into a fish and chip shop and ordering guacamole with his cod

– he was looking at a bowl of mushy peas on the counter.) Mandelson himself was not filthy rich in 1998 but he became so by way of advisory roles to banks and through property investments that enabled him to buy a house in north London for £8 million in 2011.

The bubble had already burst by then. The banking crisis of 2008 ushered in a period of austerity. Curiously, it was the poor who were seen to be at fault rather than the rich who had caused the crisis. Across this gap of understanding and interpretation it did not seem possible to build a bridge. The two nations were again not speaking and in that sense the eighteenth century came closer.

A few weeks after Rena's ninety-third birthday, after the cheerful lunch party for fifty or so guests hosted by Michael in the upstairs room at 34 Mayfair – which Nicky didn't come to (Nicky: 'I would have come if it had been something we all organised together') – my mother and I met for dinner at Côte in Devonshire Street.

She was already there when I arrived. I handed over, unwrapped, a small present I'd failed to give her earlier: a half bottle of Samos, a Greek sweet wine she particularly liked, and a CD. She put them in her bag without looking.

She was a difficult person to buy presents for. Trying to get it right (trying to please, trying to score points) was a mug's game I'd given up long ago.

I explained about the CD. She had an old CD player which she didn't know how to use. I was going to show her how, even though I knew she wouldn't remember, because at Michael's there would always be somebody on hand to explain which button to press. I thought it would be good for her to have some music in her life.

'You'll recognise these songs,' I said. 'They're by Sofia Vempo, the Vera Lynn of Greece.'

Vera Lynn puzzled her but she knew at once who Sofia Vempo was. Her eyes lit up. She sang a few bars of a love song.

'Yes,' I said. 'Yes, yes.'

I had played the CD and it was like being a child again and my mother singing in the kitchen.

'The Greeks loved Sofia Vempo,' she said.

'She was a national treasure.'

Sofia Vempo was arrested in Athens when the Germans first arrived. She had been singing marching songs and urging the people to resist. There was such popular clamour that she was released, and then ordered to appear on stage to demonstrate that the Germans were nice and meant well to the Greeks. From then on she specialised in songs with double meanings. The Germans thought she was trying to reconcile Greeks to the new world order under Germany; Greeks understood her message: the war would end and life would have meaning once more. When that message became more specific and incited sabotage she had to escape to Cairo where she continued singing for the Resistance. Vempo was a less equivocal figure for Greeks than Callas; there was less ambiguity about her relation to the Nazis. (She had her nose broken by a fascist who didn't appreciate a song satirising Mussolini.) It was Vempo's songs in her rich contralto that reached the hearts and were on the lips of Greek soldiers. She toured America after the war and told a journalist for the *New York Post* that she'd been influenced by George Sand, and that Chopin and Schubert were among her favourite composers.

'Shall we have some wine?'

We got a couple of glasses of rosé, drank a toast to Dionysus, and I sent up a prayer of thanks to a God I didn't believe in for my mother's life and good health. She looked so well in a

Not Speaking

dark blouse that suited her, hair done, face and nails expertly attended to (no make-up, only a tinting of brows). It's true her ankles were swollen, but she was out and about all day ('Why should I stay at home doing nothing?'), covering distance and relishing small encounters.

'People are so kind to me. You wouldn't believe how people come up to help me.'

'Is that when you've got six bags of groceries and you're trying to get on the bus?'

Her appetite and love of food were undiminished. It was true, too, that her uncompromising individualism could be a trial, and if one thought too much about the past it could be toxic (Paul: 'You're all so nice to her, after all she's done, I don't get it'), but there was much to be grateful for.

I ordered a chicken and walnut salad.

'I had that yesterday,' she said. 'I came here on my own last night.'

'Did you?' That surprised me.

'I was at Michael's. I left when they put the babies to bed and then I thought I couldn't be bothered to cook anything when I got home, so I came here and I had what you're having.'

'Was it nice?'

'Yes. I sat over there.' She pointed to a table by the window. 'I thought, why shouldn't I? I've got money in my purse, I can do what I like. I don't have to wait for somebody to give me permission.'

When did you ever do that? I started to say, and stopped.

I thanked God for her vitality, the capacity to keep going and changing. I knew perfectly well it was a two-edged sword. But still. There was something to celebrate in this show of female autonomy.

We talked about Paul. Paul had made the journey up from Hastings to be at the birthday lunch. He travelled the day before, intending to stay overnight with his mother at St John's Wood. It was a major expedition for him, made worse by train cancellations. He arrived four or five hours later than expected, carrying a number of plastic bags that he sorted through in the lobby while the porter on the desk rang up. Rena didn't like what she saw when she came down in the lift. Paul, entering the apartment, not having been there before, made some slighting remarks.

Mother and son had a brief, emphatic quarrel.

Paul said he wished he'd stayed at home.

Rena said nobody was stopping him if he wanted to leave. She opened the door.

Paul left.

'Was I right or was I wrong?' she demanded. 'He said he wanted to go home.'

She knew she was wrong, which is why she kept returning to the subject. She knew she would have to sort it out with God. Her conscience was troubled. It wasn't right to be showing her son the door. On the other hand, it had been an immediate relief when he walked out of it.

Except that he didn't go quietly. 'Fucking this and fucking that. It wasn't very nice.'

She didn't want the neighbours to hear.

'I phoned him afterwards.'

'What did he say?'

'Nothing. He put the phone down. He's not speaking to me.'

'I expect he's upset.'

'I'm upset. I'll wait a week and then I'll phone him again.'

'He made a big effort,' I said feebly, knowing it was pointless. There were so many ways in which she was wrong and would go on being wrong where Paul was concerned.

It was easier to talk about Nicky who, whatever his griefs, whatever his resentments, had ways of speaking to his mother

Not Speaking

that gave him what he wanted. Nicky had taken her out for a birthday dinner the evening after Michael's lunch party.

'Where did you go?'

'I don't know. Somewhere expensive.'

'Because he hasn't got any money.'

'Because he hasn't got any money.'

'Was it nice?'

'It was OK.'

Nicky then went to Majorca (Mum: 'Because he hasn't got any money') but was back now. 'Did he take you to church?'

Yes, he took her to church.

'How is he?'

'He looks very well.'

'Is he taking you to Majorca in August?'

'I hope so. He hasn't mentioned anything yet. Will you come?'

'I'll try. If you stay in his apartment like you did last summer – and that worked out very well – I'll get a room in the hotel.'

'Why don't you stay with us in Nicky's apartment?'

'He's only got one spare room.'

'We can share it. I know it's a double bed but we can manage.'

'I'll stay at the hotel.'

'Suit yourself.'

She looked at me as if she was remembering what an enigma her second daughter had always been to her.

'Does Nicky know you're going to move into Michael's? Have you mentioned it to him?'

'Me?'

'Yes, you. Have you had a conversation with him about moving out of the St John's Wood apartment and into Michael's place?'

'I don't want to upset Nicky.'

Marylebone

'There's no reason for him to be upset. He knows it's happening, he knows Michael's got the property, he knows you've put your savings into it, he knows you spend most of your time at Michael's anyway...'

'Those twins are so lovely.'

'He probably doesn't know the details.'

'He doesn't need to know the details.'

'I just wondered if you've had a conversation with him about it.'

'I don't need to have a conversation.'

It was ten by the time we left. We walked, wincingly slowly in the fresh evening air, to Regent's Park tube, Rena insisting all the way that she didn't need to be accompanied but admitting that it was nice to have the company for as long as my route home was the same as hers, which it wasn't.

She asked me, 'You're taking the train as well?'

Yes, I was taking the train as well, though I would be just as happy to put her in a cab.

'I don't need to get a cab. It's nice to walk. Where does your train go?'

'My train goes to Seven Sisters station.'

'And you can get your train from the same station that I get my train?'

Yes.

'But it goes in the other direction?'

That depends.

'I don't need you to take me home.'

'I know.'

It's almost 10:30 p.m. She's ninety-three. I should stop all this and hail a cab.

We're at the steps leading down to Regent's Park tube. She lets go of my arm, puts her stick in her left hand and taking hold of the rail begins to descend.

'So long as you're not telling me a pack of lies.'

As if.

We're at the platform. She looks at me suspiciously. 'So which way is your train going?'

'The same way as yours.'

We get on.

'I don't understand. What station are you getting off?'

'Well, I'm going with you to Warwick Avenue. Then I'll get the bus with you to Hall Road, then I'll loop back and take the Bakerloo Line to Oxford Circus and then the Victoria Line to Seven Sisters.'

She can't hear me above the noise of the train.

'That's not how you usually go home from here.'

'It's more or less the same.'

'Lies,' she says. 'All lies.'

'Once we get you settled at Michael's,' I say, as we walk to the bus stop in Clifton Road, 'meeting for dinner at Côte will be easier.'

Even so, I'm pleased we took the long route home and already feel something like nostalgia for good times gone. Buses and tube lines and the streets of London are this warrior's battleground. If she is a spear-captive, I have been cup-bearer, shield-carrier, scribe. I may be called other names when the story – my story, our story, my version of my family story, whatever 'my' or 'I' or 'our' may be said to mean once it is on the page – goes out. I feel a sense of an ending that is no ending. The unravelling and unrolling of events since the selling of Cropthorne Court have brought us to a new stage but so far as the main protagonists are concerned there has been little movement. Nicky and Michael are still encamped across a no-speaking zone. Does it matter? Each in his own life moves freely; individually neither gives cause for concern, they are not trapped in the wreckage. Linda says it matters

Marylebone

for the younger generation of the family, her grandchildren, our nieces and nephews, great-nieces and great-nephews. She wants the story to have a happy ending, and who could argue with such a wish? Perhaps Paul should tell his story, perhaps some good might come of that.

We get off the bus in Hall Road, opposite the entrance to the old flat in Cropthorne Court.

'Has Nicky sold it?' I ask her.

She doesn't know. She doesn't care.

We take our time climbing up Hall Road.

I bid her goodnight at the entrance to her apartment block. She says, 'Now I have to worry about you going home on your own.'

'Nothing to worry about.'

'Watch where you're going.'

'I will.'

I walk away.

'Be careful.'

The night porter opens the door. She stands on the top step and waves me goodbye with her stick.

Epilogue

By November 2016, Rena, aged ninety-three and seven months, was on the move again. Michael had transformed the ground floor flat next door to his salon into a comfortable one-bed apartment with open-plan kitchen-cum-living room. Rena packed boxes at St John's Wood. She was sad to go; she had made friends with the neighbours. And at the same time she was glad to go. The advantages of being near Michael and his family and staff were obvious. She would see the twins on a regular basis without having to negotiate journeys on the underground; she could have her hair and nails done as often as she liked; she wouldn't be paying out all her pension in rent.

Once again, battle was joined about things: cupboards, tallboys, tables, armchairs, mats, towels, bed linens, tablecloths, coats, shoes, saucepans, stuffed toys, dolls. There was far too much to fit into the new apartment, even after substantial, secret sifting: one large doll, thrown down the rubbish chute, wailed and cried all the way down, reducing me and Tina, her killers, to hysterical guilty laughter. (The porters weren't thrilled either: there were rules about how and what was thrown down the chute.)

Not Speaking

When everything was in the new place there was barely room to move.

Rena was adamant that was how it had to be. It wasn't her fault the flat was so small. She was ashamed that she lived, as she put it, in the kitchen. 'When I think of what my life has become,' she said tragically. 'Look at me. I live in the kitchen.'

'In W1,' Tina said, but the postcode meant nothing to Rena.

In general her mood was not tragic. She enjoyed exploring the neighbourhood, walking up and down the back streets, sometimes venturing as far as Marks & Spencer on Oxford Street. She appreciated that Waitrose in Marylebone High Street was only minutes away. Michael urged new practices with regard to shopping. 'We don't store lots of food,' he said, having taken care to throw away most of what she tried to put into the new freezer. 'We go out and buy it when we need it. And anyway, you'll be eating with us quite often, and you can eat in the salon. This fridge doesn't need to be full.'

Michael, worrying about hobs being unattended, would have preferred her not to cook at all.

There was always company in the salon and Michael's staff were like extended family. They admired her spirit; and some of the disinhibition she displayed was amusing for those who understood her cryptic comments.

With her monthly disposable income, and a renewed gaiety about female independence, she ate most days at Côte in Devonshire Street. The staff there welcomed her, and one waiter in particular, Matteo, from Italy, became her special friend. She tried to time her custom to fit in with his shifts. Matteo's attention was a tonic.

At about the time Rena moved out of St John's Wood, Kelly discovered that she was pregnant. The following summer little Nico was born (oddly enough, on his uncle Michael's birthday). Nicky was happy to be a father again and Kelly was

Epilogue

keen that Nico should know the cousins nearest to him in age, the twins, and she started bringing him to Marylebone. Gaby and Kelly between them quietly normalised relations. Without making speeches they fixed what was broken, at least to the extent that the warring men put aside their weapons. Tina, who had gone back to America, sent congratulations and good wishes to Nicky and Kelly. When Kelly put up pictures of Nico on Facebook, Tina liked them.

It was after Rena's ninety-fifth birthday that she began saying her mind was 'not what it was' (she still wouldn't agree that she was becoming deaf). Her mental decline has been gradual but is now unignorable. There had always been difficulty in being understood when you spoke to her; and as the range of her ability to follow what was being said has narrowed, and our habit of simplifying our expression become more pronounced, we mostly are reduced to ritualised, repetitive exchanges. But she can still spring surprises.

'My mother didn't love me,' she told me one afternoon, after saying how much she hated living alone. 'But I loved her. And if she was here now I would make her come and live with me even if she didn't want to.'

The reproachful hint was unmistakeable. I chose to disregard it, picking up instead on what I knew was a false reading of her mother's behaviour.

'Why do you think your mother didn't love you?'

'I don't think, I know. I'll tell you. Listen. When Toni said she wanted to go and work in Germany, Mother fainted clean away. But when I said yes to your father and said I was going to England, she said good, go.'

'She wanted what was best for you.'

'She didn't love me. She loved Toni.'

Not Speaking

We were in her flat. She was sitting on the uncomfortable sofa that she won't let us replace for something smaller and better, dolls and stuffed animals piled on one half of it. At her feet was a bag of brightly coloured balls of wool. These she was in the habit of winding and unwinding, declaring her intention to make scarves for everybody and asking us to pick our colours. She would knit an inch or two, then undo it.

'You're like Penelope,' I said.

She smiled.

Bit by bit she has given up shopping and cooking. She retains her imperious approach to life, but without those core activities she struggles to think what to do with her day except go to Côte or to the salon or upstairs where she might find the twins, if they aren't at tennis, or football or swimming. In company she is still animated. Alone, she no longer reads, and finds it difficult to follow the dramas on Greek TV.

Sometimes she forgets that she's been to Côte already and goes again. She has occasionally gone into the salon in her nightdress.

We have settled into a new routine. A carer comes for an hour each morning to help her bath and choose her clothes. Linda spends one or two half days a week with her and I likewise; Nicky takes her for dinner one evening a week and continues transporting her to and from church on Sundays. Tina makes herself available when she's in England. Paul sometimes phones. We all liaise with Michael and Gaby.

Michael and Gaby are front-line, and Gaby coordinates the care services and local GP, for which we are all grateful. There have been a few falls and a couple of visits to A&E but all tests returned the same results: bruising apart, she remains in astonishing physical shape.

This Rena attributes to God. But God has fallen short in another respect. 'I pray to God to send me a man,' she began

Epilogue

saying recently. 'There's so much you can do with a man. He hasn't sent me one yet.'

And then, with a sly look, 'Don't you think that sometimes? It's good to have a man about.'

She still plans to travel. 'What's the point of having money if I don't go anywhere?'

She tells me it's no fun going on your own. She doesn't say – what is a simple truth – that she can't manage alone because that would be to acknowledge weakness. For the same reason she appears not to notice how much effort and organisation is involved in the family project of caring for her.

When, at the end of a long day, after she has had lunch, had her hair done, gossiped in the salon, seen the twins, walked about a little leaning on my arm, or Linda's, or Michael's, or Nicky's, and sat and rested, talking, winding wool, knitting, dozing, she might sigh and say, 'It's a pity I don't have one sister, not one sister left to keep me company.'

If she had a sister left she would go to Greece. She suggested I should go to Greece with her and 'spend a few weeks in the islands, why not? I'll pay for you.'

It seems harsh to deny her a last look at her own land, a last visit to Greece, but any such trip would require heroic levels of organisation and back-up support. It would need a huge amount of joint planning. Perhaps next summer, I find myself thinking. Perhaps Nicky and Michael, now they are talking, might put their heads together (or, more accurately, Kelly and Gaby) and organise a large house party in Greece. We could all pitch in. Perhaps. Perhaps it would be worth speaking to them about it and seeing what they have to say.

Select Bibliography

Aeschylus, *Oresteia*, Penguin Classics, 1977.
Aristotle, *Poetics*, Penguin Classics, 1996.
Baker, Deborah, *In Extremis: The Life of Laura Riding*, Hamish Hamilton, 1993.
de Beauvoir, Simone, *The Second Sex*, Bantam Books, 1964.
Booth, Charles, *Life and Labour of the People in London* (Booth.lse.ac.uk)
Callas, Evangelia, with Lawrence G. Blochman, *My Daughter – Maria Callas*, Fleet Publishing, 1960.
Clarke, Irene, *I Was a Greek War Bride*, Life-Book Ltd, 2014.
Cleland, John, *Fanny Hill, or, Memoirs of a Woman of Pleasure*, Penguin, 1986.
Cooper, Artemis, *Patrick Leigh Fermor: An Adventure*, John Murray, 2012.
Davies, Philip, *Panoramas of Lost London*, Transatlantic Press, 2011.
Erikson, Erik, *Childhood and Society*, W. W. Norton & Co. 1950.
Euripides, *The Trojan Women*, OUP, 2008.
— *Medea and Other Plays*, Penguin Classics, 2003.

Gage, Nicholas, *Eleni*, Panther, 1997.
Graves, Robert, *Goodbye to All That*, Penguin Modern Classics, 2000.
— *Majorca Observed*, Littlehampton, 1965.
— *The White Goddess*, Faber, 1948.
Graves, William, *Wild Olives: Life in Majorca with Robert Graves*, Pimlico, Random House, 2001.
Harlan, Elizabeth, *George Sand*, Yale University Press, 2004.
Hesiod, *Works and Days, Theogony and The Shield of Heracles*, Dover Publications, 2006.
Homer, *The Iliad*, translated by Alexander Pope, Penguin Classics, 1996.
Homer, *The Iliad*, translated by Peter Green, University of California Press, 2015.
Leigh Fermor, Patrick, *Roumeli: Travels in Northern Greece*, John Murray, 1966.
March, Jenny, *Cassell Dictionary of Classical Mythology*, Cassell, 1998.
Maule, Henry, *Scobie, Hero of Greece: The British Campaign, 1944-45*, Arthur Barker Limited, 1975.
Maurois, Andre, *Lélia: The Life of George Sand*, Jonathan Cape, 1953.
Mazower, Mark, *Inside Hitler's Greece: The Experience of Occupation, 1941-44*, Yale University Press, 1993.
Mearns, Andrew, *The Bitter Cry of Outcast London*, James Clarke & Co., 1883.
Miller, Henry, *The Colossus of Maroussi*, New Directions, 1975.
Pember Reeves, Maud, *Round About a Pound a Week*, Virago, 1979.
Phillips, Teresa Constantia, *Apology for her Conduct*, London, 1748.

Pope, Alexander, 'The Rape of the Lock' in *The Poems of Alexander Pope*, ed. J. Butt, Methuen, 1968.

Riviere, Joan, 'Womanliness as a Masquerade', *International Journal of Psychoanalysis*, 10, 1929.

Rogers, Pat (ed.), *The Cambridge Companion to Alexander Pope*, CUP, 2007.

Sand, George, *A Winter in Majorca*, Edicions Cort, Palma, 1998.

— *Lelia*, Indiana University Press, 1978.

Seymour, Miranda, *Robert Graves: Life on the Edge*, Doubleday, 1997.

Shakespeare, William, *The Two Noble Kinsmen*, Riverside Shakespeare, 1997.

Suetonius, *The Twelve Caesars*, Penguin Classics, 2007.

Tolstoy, Leo, *Anna Karenina*, Penguin Classics, 2003.

Trelawny, Edward, *Records of Shelley, Byron, and the Author*, Penguin, 1973.

Tressell, Robert, *The Ragged-Trousered Philanthropists*, Penguin Modern Classics, 2004.

Tsiolkas, Christos, *Dead Europe*, Penguin, 2011.

— *The Slap*, Allen & Unwin, 2008.

Wolf, Naomi, *The Beauty Myth*, Vintage, 1991.

Vickers, Hugo, *Alice, Princess Andrew of Greece*, Hamish Hamilton, 2000.

Acknowledgements

This book would not have been possible without the cooperation of family and I thank all those who trusted me as I told the story my way. I've tried to be accurate about facts, and have listened where interpretations differed; errors and misinterpretations that remain are my own. I'm grateful to all those who gave up time to talk to me and those who read early versions of the manuscript. Special thanks to Piers Torday who directed, filmed and edited the videos for the book on the Unbound site. Publishing with Unbound has been a revelation and a pleasure. Thanks to the in-house editorial and design teams who have done such a marvellous job, and to those who keep up the good work online. Thanks also to every one of the subscribers listed: your support has been truly uplifting.

Unbound is the world's first crowdfunding publisher, established in 2011.

We believe that wonderful things can happen when you clear a path for people who share a passion. That's why we've built a platform that brings together readers and authors to crowdfund books they believe in – and give fresh ideas that don't fit the traditional mould the chance they deserve.

This book is in your hands because readers made it possible. Everyone who pledged their support is listed at the front of the book and below. Join them by visiting unbound.com and supporting a book today.

Chris Abbott
Chris Adams
Mark Belcher
David Bellwood
Fran Bennett
Rossella Black
Lucy Bland
Mónica Bolufer
Catherine Bott
Nicky Browne
Iain Bruce
Michael Caines
Lesley Caldwell
Brycchan Carey
Brian Cathcart
Judith Clark
Cheryl Clarke
Nicky Clarke
Jane Clarkson

Judi Coburn
Andrew Collier
Ivan Collister
Claire Connolly
Ros Coward
Marc d'Abbadie
Camilla de Quetteville
Lindsay Duguid
Lou Edwards
Markman Ellis
Inanch Emir
Barbara Evans
Andrew Fallaize
Ilaria Favretto
Lucie Gledhill
Sue Goddard
Linda Gordon
Bonnie Grahame-Betts
Michael Griffin

Mary Grover
Eric Guibert
Marybeth Hamilton
Robbie Hand
Moyra Haslett
Sarah Hayes Mooney
Liz Heron
Rachel Hewitt
Katharine Hodgkin
Sally Hoyle
Kathryn Hughes
Barbara Kalirai
Anne Karpf
Carol Knott
Sylvia Lahav
Samir Lee
John Lesirge
Tanya Levine
Gael Lindenfield
lizzieroper lizzieroper
Stephen Maddison
Michael J. Maguire
Robert Mahony
David Male
Josephine McDonagh
Andrew McDowell
Aisling McKeown
Gemma Miller
Kate Murray-Browne
Richard Murray-Bruce
Carlo Navato
Clíona Ó Gallchoir
Susie O'Dwyer
Matthew Oldham

Ursula Owen
Tony Page
Kate Pasvol
Diana Paton
Ruthie Petrie
Sam Plumb
Nicole Pohl
Linda Powell
Wells Powell
Andrew Prescott
Sarah Pullen
Dinny Ravet
Nina Romancikova
Tricia Scouller
Poppy Sebag-Montefiore
Rebecca Servadio
Alexandra Shepard
Paul Shuter
Kate Soper
Carol Stegmann
Tiffany Stern
Sela Still
Charlie Talbot
Dylan Townley
Gail Trimble
Jeni Walwin
Sophie Watson
Ann Whitehead
Miranda Whiting
Margaret Williamson
Jane Willingale
Tristan Wood
Alex Woolnough